ROUTLEDGE LIBRARY EDITIONS:
ACCOUNTING HISTORY

Volume 33

THE NEW YORK STATE SOCIETY OF CERTIFIED PUBLIC ACCOUNTANTS

THE NEW YORK STATE SOCIETY OF CERTIFIED PUBLIC ACCOUNTANTS

Foundation for a Profession

Edited by
JULIA GRANT

LONDON AND NEW YORK

First published in 1995 by Garland Publishing, Inc.
Introductory material copyright

This edition first published in 2021
by Routledge
2 Park Square, Milton Park, Abingdon, Oxon OX14 4RN

and by Routledge
52 Vanderbilt Avenue, New York, NY 10017

Routledge is an imprint of the Taylor & Francis Group, an informa business

British Library Cataloguing in Publication Data
A catalogue record for this book is available from the British Library

ISBN: 978-0-367-33564-9 (Set)
ISBN: 978-1-00-304636-3 (Set) (ebk)
ISBN: 978-0-367-49592-3 (Volume 33) (hbk)
ISBN: 978-1-00-304678-3 (Volume 33) (ebk)

Publisher's Note
The publisher has gone to great lengths to ensure the quality of this reprint but points out that some imperfections in the original copies may be apparent.

Disclaimer
The publisher has made every effort to trace copyright holders and would welcome correspondence from those they have been unable to trace.

The New York State Society of Certified Public Accountants

Foundation for a Profession

Edited by
Julia Grant

Garland Publishing, Inc.
New York and London 1995

Library of Congress Cataloging-in-Publication Data

The New York State Society of Certified Public Accountants : foundation for a profession / edited by Julia Grant.
p. cm.— (New works in accounting history)
Includes bibliographical references and index.
ISBN 0-8153-2238-0
1. Accounting—United States—History. 2. New York State Society of Certified Public Accountants—History. 3. Accountants—United States—Biography. I. Title. II. Series.
HF5616.U5G7 1995 95–32129
657'.61'060747—dc20 CIP

All volumes printed on acid-free, 250-year-life paper.
Manufactured in the United States of America.

Design by Marisel Tavarez

TABLE OF CONTENTS

FOREWORD

For the past two decades, there has been an increased interest in the development of Accountancy's institutions as evidenced by formal academic and professional interest in events such as the centennial anniversary of the initial CPA law passed in New York State in 1896. The Garland Press's sponsorship of Professor Julia Grant's collection and commentary on the writings of the NYSSCPA's history committee is a welcome form of contribution to the celebration of this centennial. The accountancy profession, represented in professional circles initially and principally by the CPA community, will benefit from the development of this convenient resource which contains a cross-section of education issues, topics, and biographies, identified with the acceptance and development of Certified Public Accountancy in New York State—and the entire nation. This collection of papers and essays covers almost a quarter century, beginning in 1949.

It is an important sign of the maturity of our discipline that the effort of scholars, such as Professor Grant and, also, Professor Brief, the series editor, continue to find acceptance in the commercial marketplace on a regular basis, and in this case on a timely basis too, so as to renew and honor the New York State Society's tradition of contributing to the historical literature of our profession.

Gary John Previts
Professor of Accountancy
Weatherhead School of Management

PREFACE

This volume presents a compilation of the historical articles published between 1949 and 1972 in the *New York Certified Public Accountant*. These articles contain institutional, educational and personal histories, all of which provide insight into the professional history of accountancy in the United States. These pieces have been categorized according to the general topic areas of professional history, educational history, history of the New York State Society of Certified Public Accountants, and individual biographies. Nevertheless, most present some intersection of the personal and institutional histories that combined to create the profession. Thus, the articles on the early educational and professional institutions summarize outcomes of the activities and achievements of the people described in the biographies.

A bibliography of the articles reproduced herein is presented in an appendix, listed in order of publication date. The author listed on the published article was frequently The Committee on History; however, the appendix includes the names of the individuals to whom each article was attributed, according to available records. The article copies available were inadequate for publication as exact facsimiles. The goal in this compilation has been to present the articles in a manner similar to the original publication to retain the sense of the language and usage. Although the original two-column newspaper format has not been retained, the text has been reproduced as faithfully as possible. All punctuation and spacing are reproduced as appeared in the *New York Certified Public Accountant*, even though it frequently does not conform to modern rules and customs. To avoid interference with the text, editor's notations are used only infrequently with obvious misspellings or other irregularities. These notations appear italicized, in square brackets, for example, [*sic*]. (The notation '(sic)' appears in the original text.)

The accepted format for presenting direct quotations has varied over time; each article uses the original published format to the extent possible. Titles, authors' names, and marginal notes have been reproduced in an attempt to provide the same emphasis as in the original text. Because footnotes were used in some of the articles, they are reproduced in the same manner herein. Tabular material has been replicated to the extent possible within the format limitations of this volume.

Many different types of historical research could be conducted using data such as that contained in this volume. Those readers who wish to explore this material in detail may want to know that the text of this book is available for research in electronic format.

Julia Grant
Weatherhead School of Management
Case Western Reserve University

INTRODUCTION

The distinct identity of a profession develops for many reasons. Among these are educational needs, restriction of entry, economies of scale, and efficacy of competition. Another, perhaps the most important feature of a profession is the establishment of a reputation for unique ability and quality in the provision of a service. To achieve a group reputation requires motivated individuals to act in the interest of the larger group. A professional association provides the structure within which the establishment and maintenance of a professional reputation can occur. The development of the accounting profession reflects an implicit understanding of this requirement by its first leaders. The collected articles in this volume portray the early efforts of accountants to establish a professional identity.

The profession of accountancy in the United States was influenced by men with European training, who brought their abilities and preparation primarily from England and Scotland. As long as accounting services were individually provided by a small number of readily-identified people, their services could be evaluated directly by the users. In these articles, the earliest examples of advertising (1861) described in detail the personal character and idiosyncratic skills of the men offering the services later identified with accountants. As the numbers of accountants grew and their potential duties increased, it would have become more difficult for each seeker of accounting services to measure the potential value of these services because of uncertainty over the individual's qualifications and motivation. Fortunately for the development of the profession, some of the early accountants in the state of New York recognized the need for the identification of accountants as distinct and uniquely qualified professionals. These articles present numerous examples of efforts to create a professional identity for accountancy.

Two obvious types of group identities emerged. First, there was the creation of firms or partnerships to provide support and assistance, and for competitive advantage. There are many examples of such groupings evident in these articles. Numerous partnerships arose and dissolved with the business needs of the early members of the profession. However, the existence of these relationships did not fill the need for a broader professional identity. To achieve this second level of group identity required a focus on accountants as professionals first, uniquely qualified and motivated to perform a specialized set of services. It was this distinction that provided the requisite professional reputation for common principles and educational achievement. Thus, by 1900, an advertisement still focused on the accountant's ability to examine "disputed handwriting," with his status as a Certified Public Accountant listed second. But this ad included, in smaller letters at the very bottom, the accountant's association with both national and state C.P.A. societies.

The legal establishment of the profession was accomplished by the enactment of the C.P.A. law by the New York State Legislature in 1896. As related in several of these articles, its passage was attributable at least in part to the efforts of several prominent accountants of the time. Following this enactment, John Hourigan wrote an open letter to his colleagues in early 1897, pointing out the importance of establishing a voluntary professional association of certified public accountants. By March of the same year the accountants of New York State had achieved this level of organization, creating the New York State Society of Certified Public Accountants.

Simultaneously, other members of the profession were preparing the groundwork for accounting education. The New York School of Accounts, under the leadership of Theodore Koehler, began successful operation in 1897, following an earlier failed attempt by others under the same name prior to the passage of the C.P.A. legislation. Others offered individual training for the work of the accountant and for preparation for the C.P.A. examination. Koehler's school educated several of the profession's early leaders; and by 1900, members of the profession had convinced the Regents of the State of New York to support the establishment of the School of Commerce, Accounts and Finance of New York University.

As the education for the profession became more formalized, and as individuals created various accounting associations, both at the state and national levels, the contributions of the profession could be valued more confidently by those requiring accounting services. The new profession could point to its group reputation for both ability and trustworthiness, thus creating enhanced opportunities for future participation within the economic structure. The articles reproduced in this volume convey vividly this early evolution of the accountancy profession in the United States. These articles portray the founders and historical leaders of the New York State Society of Certified Public Accountants as they contributed the essential elements to the establishment of the profession.

ACKNOWLEDGMENTS

The CPA Journal has generously granted permission to make these articles available to the larger audience interested in the early days of the accountancy profession in the United States. Thanks to Mr. James Craig and Mr. Michael Rosencrantz for their assistance in obtaining this permission.

Anyone who uses this compilation of articles should realize that the determination of Professor Gary John Previts has led to their availability. Without his assistance, this project would not have been possible. Finally, many thanks to Marcia Strachan for her excellent work on this manuscript.

The New York State Society of Certified Public Accountants

CHAPTER 1

HISTORY OF THE PROFESSION

Early Development of Accountancy in New York State

By THE COMMITTEE ON HISTORY

Accountancy in New York State had its genesis long before the passage of the first C.P.A. legislation in 1896. Richard Brown of Edinburgh in his "History of Accounting and Accountants" written in 1905, said on page 271: "The history of the profession in the United States may be said to have commenced only about twenty years ago." In 1925 James Thornley Anyon in his "Recollections of the Early Days of American Acocuntancy" [*sic*] began with: "Public Accounting in this country as a profession, I have reason to believe, had its birth some time between the year 1880 and 1883."

It is believed that Richard Brown relied upon information furnished at his request by the American Association of Public Accountants and the New York State Society of Certified Public Accountants. Mr. Anyon, who came from England late in 1886 to head the New York office of his firm, Barrow, Wade, Guthrie & Co., organized in 1883, wrote from memory and quite possibly had never seen the existing records of earlier practice.

As the public practice of accountancy is directly related to business, it would seem that the date business began in this state and the establishment of the profession is of interest.

The earliest European to visit this locality was the Florentine, Verrazano, in 1524, but there is no record of any business transacted and no one of his party remained here. After an interval of 85 years, Henry Hudson, an Englishman sailing for Dutch adventurers, found this harbor and the river which bears his name in 1609. Then business began, for the records show that there were "handsome profits" from that expedition and from others which followed in 1613 and 1621. That

---

This is the first of a series of articles on the History of Accountancy in the State of New York. It was prepared by the Society's Committee on History.

The source material for the portion hereof dealing with the founding of New York University is to be found largely in the book, "Charles Waldo Haskins, an American Pioneer in Accountancy."

business was largely in peltries acquired from the Indians by barter. Five years later, in 1626, a real estate transaction was completed when Peter Minuit bought Manhattan Island from the Indians and named it New Amsterdam. Two decades later, in 1647, the colorful Peter Stuyvesant became Governor and it seems that trade had increased because in April, 1651, the Dutch Directors engaged Johannes Dyckman as "bookkeeper in New Netherland." A year later the Directors of Amsterdam wrote that since they were "not properly informed of prizes captured, ships sold, etc.," they had sent over another man. There seems to be no record of his name so it is not possible to decide whether this second man was a public accounant [*sic*] or an internal auditor. Perhaps three centuries ago they did not make such a distinction.

Bookkeeping here probably started prior to 1651 but it was surely in use at that date. That there was a growing appreciation of the need for it is indicated by the newspaper announcements by those who stated that they were prepared to teach the art, some of whom also offered to pen or close books of accounts.

In July and August, 1729, an anonymous advertiser stated that by inquiry at the Post Office or Coffee House: "Any merchant, or others, that wants a Bookkeeper, or their accounts started after the best methods, either in private trade or company, may hear of a Person Qualified." And teachers of bookkeeping announced themselves as follows:

> George Brownell, "Merchants Accounts" and other subjects June 21, 1731.
> Michael Christian Knoll, "Merchantile [*sic*] Accounts, Italian Fashion" 1750.
> James Gilliland, "School for Merchants Accounts" 1772.
> "Mercantile and Mathematic School" in Broad Street 1775.

Fifty years later, teachers of bookkeeping offered their services to design systems, adjust and explain accounts, which was tantamount to the public practice of accountancy. Whether all of these earlier teachers also sought and accepted such engagements is not known but seems probable; it is doubtful, however, that these persons gave all their time to such practice.

The first *Directory of Edinburgh, 1773*, listed seven accountants; that for 1774 contained fourteen names. The first *Directory of Glasgow, 1783*, listed six accountants; in 1790 the *British Universal Directory* contained the names of five accountants in London, and *Liverpool Directory* also listed five.

The first *New York Directory* was published here in 1786, when the population was stated by Noah Webster to be 23,614. It did not contain a classified section but three names are of interest:

"Franks, D., Conveyancer &c, 66 Broadway, Page 28.
Parker, Daniel, Auctioneer, 23 Wall St., Page 42.
Tap, William, Accountant, George St." page 48.

Newspapers of that year carried items about these as follows:

"William Tapp [*sic*] has opened an office at 66 King Street for settling copartnership accounts" May 24.
"David Franks & Co. have opened a conveyancing and accountants office at No. 24 Water Street" August 1.
"Daniel Parker has opened at 16 Princess Street a scriveners and accountants office" August 7.

This first *New York Directory* was compiled by Franks and the other partner of David Franks & Co. was almost surely his son, Moses Franks, who had arrived in New York from Bristol only a day before, July 31, 1786.

David Franks' father was an attorney in Dublin with whom the son had served his apprenticeship and later acted for another lawyer, Counsellor Franklin. Where he had received his training in accountancy has not been ascertained. His son Moses came to America from Bristol, where he might have served an apprenticeship since Thomas Jones was then a public accountant in that city.

With only two or three exceptions New York Directories were issued annually from 1786, and in some years there were two issues by different compilers. Every issue contains names of accountants.

The 1890's witnessed the beginning of a rapid development of corporate consolidations designed to effect economies through large-scale operations. The attendant complexities of the financial and accounting problems resulting therefrom were alone sufficient to bring into existence a specialized profession competent to offer sound advice on how to deal with them. Moreover, the investment banking business, organized to provide industry with large amounts of new capital required for additions and improvements had assumed large proportions, and underwriters, as well as a growing body of investors, felt the need of having reports by independent auditors. Thus, it was no coincidence that rapid development of the profession of public accountancy began at a climactic point in the period of growth and consolidation of our economy.

While accountants in Philadelphia and Chicago also benefited from the results of "big business," New York, being the center of financial activities, attracted many accountants from Great Britain as well as from other cities in the United States. Early in 1896, the Legislature of the State of New York, at the request of certain practicing accountants of the state and for their protection, passed an act "to regulate the profession of public accountants." This act provided for a class of public accountants to be known as "certified public accountants" who were to have the exclusive right to use the designation "C.P.A." after their names; and it authorized the Regents of the University of the State of New York (State Education Department) to establish examinations and to issue certificates of recognition to those who proved themselves capable and expert and fulfilled other requisites. Prominent among those who fostered this legislation were Frank Broaker, William Sanders Davies, Henry R. M. Cook, Rodney S. Dennis, Francis Gottsberger and John Hourigan. Mr. Davies stated he worked for the bill only in New York City, but that Frank Broaker spent nearly all his time in Albany and without Broaker's efforts the bill would not have passed in 1896.

Shortly after the passage of the act, Elijah Watt Sells made a trip to Albany to discuss certain details of the working of the new law with Dr. Melvil Dewey, Secretary of the Board of Regents. In the interview that followed, mention was made of a Board of Examiners and Mr. Sells urged that Mr. Haskins be made a member of the Board. Dr. Dewey said the matter would be decided at a meeting of the Board of Regents of the day following, when three examiners would be appointed. At this meeting, Mr. Haskins was appointed by the Regents, as were Frank Broaker and Charles Ezra Sprague. Mr. Broaker's election was doubtless a reward for his effort toward the passage of the C.P.A. law; Colonel Sprague's the result of a long standing friendship with Dr. Dewey, who knew of his scholarly attainments. At the first meeting of the examiners, Mr. Haskins was made President. The first examination under the new law was held in December 15-16, 1896. In the year 1896-97, one hundred and twelve certificates were awarded, one hundred and eight under waiver and four the result of passing examinations.

On March 30, 1897, the New York State Society of Certified Public Accountants was organized and Mr. Haskins became its first president. The first annual meeting was held May 10, 1897. About this time, there came suggestions for the founding of a school of accounting. The Board of Regents felt the need of it; the New York State Society discussed it freely; Mr. Haskins made many plans for transforming the idea of a school into a living actuality; and other members of the profession were in close sympathy with the movement.

At the November, 1899, meeting of the State Society, Henry R. M. Cook introduced a motion requesting the President to confer with the Trustees of New York University for the purpose of arranging for the establishment of a technical course of study in the science of accounts, finance, economics, business practice, commercial law, etc. In December, 1899, Mr. Haskins, President of the Society, wrote to Chancellor Henry M. MacCracken, requesting a conference for the purpose of establishing the desired technical course of study.

The story of one part of the struggle for an educational institution of accountancy can best be told by quoting Mr. Haskins*:

> "A history of the origin of this school would be the history of accountancy, especially in America, and of the movement in behalf of higher commercial education whose wave is now washing the shores of the United States. Most of you are familiar with the laws regulating the profession of accountancy, and with the efforts of the better class of accountants to secure a solid educational and social basis for the profession, as well as with the rise and growth of what is coming to be known as the profession of administration —represented by men of marked executive ability, whose bent of mind is toward the comprehensive and detailed control of affairs. From these sources has come the two-fold demand which has been recognized by the New York University in the establishment of the new school. The more immediate story, however, of its origin is too good to be lost.
>
> "Chancellor MacCracken, in his last annual report, reminded the Council that the seventieth anniversary of the University would occur in October, 1900, and suggested the celebration of this septuagesimal in some way which might at the same time signalize the advent of the twentieth century of our era. Consciously or unconsciously, this suggestion was a preintimation of the establishment of the eighth teaching institution under the University. Shortly after the appearance of the Chancellor's report, a committee representing a large number of leading professional accountants of the State of New York

---

*From a biographical sketch by William G. Jordan in "*Charles Waldo Haskins--An American Pioneer in Accountancy*," Prentice-Hall, Inc., New York; Copyright, 1923, by Haskins and Sells; pages 65-66.

laid before him an outline of a plan for a school or college of accountancy, emphasizing also the desirability of University control of such a school, with a view to placing the profession upon a proper educational and moral basis of efficiency and reliability.

"The matter was presented to the Council of the University, and was duly considered by a special committee consisting of Dr. MacCracken, Messrs. William F. Havemeyer, William S. Opdyke, William M. Kingsley and James G. Cannon. Consultation led to further suggestion; the movement for higher commercial education received due consideration; to accountancy was added commerce, and to these finance; the practical every-day applications of the broad science of economics were canvassed as only men of large economic thought and experience are able to cope with the subject; and on July 28 the petitioners were officially notified of the decision legalizing the foundation of the new college, to be known as the New York University School of Commerce, Accounts and Finance.

"Thus in the morning watch of the dawning century, comes into existence an institution of professional learning fitly characteristic of the age and memorial of an epoch in the life of a great administrative corporation."

On October 1, 1900, the new school—the first of its kind in the world—began its pioneer work in the University building in Washington Square, New York. Speeches were delivered by Chancellor MacCracken, Colonel Sprague, and other members of the faculty. The Dean of the School, Mr. Haskins, after a few general remarks, gave his first lecture as Professor of the History of Accountancy. There were about fifty matriculants in attendance at this opening session.

What may be termed the intellectual and ethical platform of the School can be expressed in Mr. Haskins' own words:

"No attempt will be made in the school to foster the notion that commerce or accountancy is a royal road to wealth, or to leisure, or to unmerited social position; but in addition to the intellectual qualifications of talent for observation, power of perception, patience of investigation, presence of mind, judgment, reflection, order and method, aptitude for calculation, abstraction, memory, mental activity and steadiness, which it is hoped the student will possess in some fair degree, the moral virtues of honesty, candor, firmness, prudence, truth, justice, economy, temperance, liberality, politeness, good temper, self control and perseverance will be inculcated as necessary to his own personal welfare and the stability of the business world."*

The first professors and instructors, who were nearly all certified public accountants, gave their time and abilities almost gratis and at a

---

**Ibid.*, page 68.

real personal sacrifice. It was with them largely a labor of love and a fine spirit of devotion and helpfulness to their profession. The sessions of the School, contrary to all accepted traditions, were held in the late afternoons and in the evenings. The majority of the students were employed for the greater part of the day in some line of business activity.

Despite all the hardships, struggles, discouragements, and obstacles, the new venture conquered and flourished and within a few years this, the youngest School in the University, had the largest enrollment of students. It not only performed fine, loyal, direct service to the profession in the number of young men it trained to take their places with splendid equipment and high ideals in the ranks of certified public accountants, but the School itself became an exemplar and an inspiration to other schools, more or less similar, started in other parts of the country.

Some of the early struggles are set forth by Leon Brummer, who had been a devoted ally in the movement to get the School organized, and was a teacher in the beginning:

> "The students were permitted to enter certain classes of the Law School, and other than the teachers of those Law School classes, there were but six teachers of accountancy, one teacher of economics, and one other instructor. I know that, judging from my own class, the accounting knowledge of the students was so ungraded; the knowledge of the teacher and his ability to teach was so uncertain; and the confidence of the scholars, who were continually asking for instruction in higher accountancy, was so wanting, that nothing but the persistent efforts and the personal encouragement and glorious example of Charles Waldo Haskins kept the school from following in the footpaths of those schools which had gone before. As I look upon this scene and upon the inexperience of the early teachers, the absolute absence of guiding precedents, the want of literature, the eagerness of all those students of more than average intelligence for instruction in accounting, it is not at all surprising that the older and unschooled accountants of today fear to undertake the duties of a teacher in this school, but leave this task mostly for the men who have been graduated from the school."*

Another outstanding pioneer for the right kind of education, if the profession were to occupy that position in economic life to which it was

---

*"*The Inception and Foundation of the School of Commerce, Accounts and Finance*," by Leon Brummer. The Journal of Accountancy, Vol. XI, No. 4, February 1911; pages 254-255. (Reprinted in "*Charles Waldo Haskins*," *supra*, pages 68-69.)

entitled, was Charles Ezra Sprague. Then president of the Union Dime Savings Bank, he became a member of the faculty of New York University, teaching classes at night until his death. His teachings were of subjects for which there were no texts or allied readings; it was new in every respect, demanding the devising of methods and preparation of materials, both of which consumed untold hours outside the classroom.

The late Joseph French Johnson, when dean of the School, described Colonel Sprague's connection with it in a part of the introductory material of the fifth edition of the Colonel's *Philosophy of Accounts*:

> "Very few realize what an important part Colonel Sprague played in the organization and development of the School of Commerce, Accounts and Finance of New York University. * * * He realized the necessity of the right kind of education if the profession was to occupy that position in economic life to which it was entitled. When the New York State Society of Certified Public Accountants appointed a committee to consider the question of professional education, Colonel Sprague made himself an unofficial member of that committee. Their labors resulted in a report presented to the Society in December, 1900, in which the members of the Society were advised that New York University had agreed to establish a school for the purpose of training men for business. The progress made in twenty years is strikingly shown by comparing the curriculum of today with the outline of courses incorporated in that report.
>
> "University administrators are conservative by nature and the organization of a frankly professional school of business was an innovation. Not only was it looked at askance within the University itself, but the so-called practical men of business as well as administrators of other colleges opposed the movement. It was not to be expected that Chancellor MacCracken of New York University would view the matter differently from most college presidents. He was a man of vision and the process of conversion was more easily undertaken on that account, but he knew that the proposed school would have no endowment and he clearly saw that he could not safely add to the financial burdens under which his institution was laboring.
>
> "When things appeared darkest and when it seemed as though the project was likely to fail, Colonel Sprague decided to adopt unusual measures as an unofficial committee of one. He rented the house of one of the University professors for the summer vacation. In this way he was bound to meet the Chancellor on the campus, and during frequent walks together, they discussed the project that was nearest to the Colonel's heart. We cannot measure the extent of the influence which Colonel Sprague brought to bear upon Chancellor MacCracken through this unusual step. He made his own opportunity; the method was novel; the Colonel's quiet and modest manner was effective and he communicated something of his own conviction to the

Chancellor. Although no endowment was provided, the Chancellor was assured that no deficit would result. Whatever may have been the effect, we know that the Chancellor finally gave his approval. The Colonel was a member of the original faculty and served the University until his death.

"Colonel Sprague was the first member of the faculty of New York University School of Commerce whom I heard speak from a lecture platform. It was in the winter of 1900-1901. I was then connected with the University of Pennsylvania and was spending a few days in New York in attendance on some convention. I had heard of New York University's new School of Commerce and, under the escort of Dean Charles Waldo Haskins, two of my colleagues and I paid it a visit. Colonel Sprague was lecturing on the philosophy of accounts to a class of forty men ranging in age from twenty to fifty who knew little about accountancy, but I was greatly impressed by the clearness of the lecturer's ideas, by the grace of his manner of speech, and by his most courteous responses to the questions asked now and then by some of the students. I remember that I was somewhat surprised when I was told after the lecture that Sprague was not by profession a teacher or writer, but was president of a savings bank and lectured without compensation because he loved his subject and had great faith in the future of the new school.

"His students all loved him. On the platform he was intensely in earnest, always serious. I never heard of any student willingly cutting one of his lectures. He usually came to his lecture room in evening dress. If any of his colleagues had done the same there would have been comment and undoubtedly some chuckles among the students, but there was an instinctive feeling that Colonel Sprague came in full dress, not because of pride of appearance, but because he had a deep respect for his evening's task and wanted to do it as nearly right as possible. He was a most modest man, unassuming and without pretense of any sort.

"After I came to the School in 1901 I had many delightful talks with Colonel Sprague in my office before and after his lectures. We never talked about accountancy, perhaps because he knew that I didn't know much about it. He liked to talk about the books that both of us had read, and about our college days and studies, and about what had to be done to make accounting a real profession. I remember being greatly impressed by his enthusiastic devotion to the welfare of his Alma Mater and by his almost boyish love of his old college fraternity. In fact, Colonel Sprague was one of the most human men I have ever met."*

Limitation of space precludes narrating in detail the splendid efforts of other pioneers in furthering the profession among whom were: Arthur W. Teele, Farquhar J. MacRae, F. W. Lafrentz, John R. Loomis, Anson O. Kittredge, Leonard H. Conant, John R. Sparrow, Theodore Koehler.

---

*From Dean Johnson's Introduction (pages v-vii) to "*The Philosophy of Accounts*," (Fifth Edition) by Charles E. Sprague; The Ronald Press Company, New York, 1923.

The late eminent jurist, Oliver Wendell Holmes, Jr., speaking of the legal profession said:

> "However much we may codify the law into a series of seemingly self-sufficient propositions, those propositions will be but a phase in a continuous growth. To understand their scope fully, to know how they will be dealt with by judges trained in the past which the law embodies, we must ourselves know something of that past. The history of what the law has been is necessary to the knowledge of what the law is."

Recently an injunction was granted by Justice Samuel Null of the New York State Supreme Court staying the hands of the wreckers of Castle Clinton, better known to the present generation as the Aquarium. In his opinion granting the injunction Justice Null said, *inter alia*:

> "A people indifferent to the landmarks and monuments of its past will not long retain its capacity to achieve an honored future."

Certain it is that the pioneers of accountancy in New York had the vision, the courage and other attributes so essential for the present day success of the profession of accountancy and left a debt most difficult for the present generation to discharge. Such a heritage should be jealously guarded, to the end that the public be served in a manner which reflects credit upon the individual members and the profession as a whole.

Is Accounting History Important?

By THE COMMITTEE ON HISTORY

As an answer to this question here are some quotations, and references to some actions, by accountants and educators. While probably there were other such items which might have been included, those here given are all that were noted.

A general answer to the question was stated in the report of Clem W. Collins at the end of his service as president of the American Institute of Accountants in October, 1939. He said:

> "The accounting profession in this country has had a rich experience since its beginning over a half century ago. The records of the early years are still retained in the minds of a few who were privileged to participate in building the foundations. Written records undoubtedly also exist, but each year makes their discovery more difficult, and each year takes from us some member who could make a valuable contribution to the history of our profession. The present generation has an important duty to perform in gathering historical data, and it is my hope that my successor will complete the organization necessary to carry on that work. The colleges and universities may be counted upon to assist in this important undertaking. Through the cooperation of practising accountants, teachers, and students a proper history of the profession in this country may be compiled. Without it there is an unfortunate gap in accounting literature. (AIA Year Book 1939, p. 74-75)

Most of the answers were not put into words as was done in the report here quoted, but they were indicated by actions, and some of the early ones were by accountants in practice as follows:

In 1898, Thomas Cullen Roberts, secretary of the American Association of Public Accountants contributed to "New York, the Second City of the World" (a publication celebrating the consolidation of the greater city) a chapter on the history of the American Association with sketches of many of its members, perhaps the only available source material for facts as to some of them.

In September, 1903, George Wilkinson contributed to *Business World* (v. 23, p. 414) a story on "The CPA Movement." The next

---

This is the thirteenth in a series of articles on the History of Accounting in the State of New York. It was prepared by the Society's Committee on History.

year, at the request of the committee which planned the first Congress of Accountants held in St. Louis in October, he expanded that story which was published in the Official Record of the Congress at page 91. And much later he extended the story for the American Society of Certified Public Accountants by which it was published in *The Certified Public Accountant* (1928, v. 8. p. 264).

On April 15, 1907, at the Tenth Anniversary of the New York State Society of CPA's its secretary, Leon Brummer, presented a short history of that society during its first ten years.

In March, 1908, the Pennsylvania State Board of Examiners of Public Accountants issued a manual with its Rules in force from January 1, 1907, which on pages 11-12, under Preliminary Examination, stated:

> "Candidates should also be prepared to pass a satisfactory examination in the following subjects:
> "History of Accountancy—This will include the history of bookkeeping with reference to its form and use in ancient times; origin of double entry bookkeeping, and its gradual development down to the present time. The rise of accountancy, its growth and history in Scotland, England, United States and other countries, with special reference to professional legislation.
> Students should study Brown's "History of Accounting and Accountants," the "Proceedings of the Congress of Accountants" and other current books and papers bearing upon this subject."

As no records of these Preliminary Examinations have been found, it is not possible to state how fully this rule was enforced.

Many educators who were the authors of textbooks upon specific principles or procedures introduced their subjects with histories of the earlier literature thereon. But some educators were the authors of articles which were largely or wholly histories or arguments as to the value of a knowledge of the history of accountancy.

In 1923, Henry Rand Hatfield of the University of California read a paper on "An Historical Defense of Bookkeeping" at the Eighth Annual Meeting of the American Association of University Instructors in Accounting which was published in its *Proceedings* (v. 8, p. 65). The numerous references to this article indicate that it has been considered a classic on its subject.

Beginning in 1927, and for some years thereafter, A. Charles Littleton of the University of Illinois contributed to various periodicals articles upon the development of accounting principles and procedures some of which told much of the persons who had parts in those developments. For that reason, probably, some of the articles carried the word "Pioneer" as a part of their titles. Then, in 1933, the American Institute Publishing Co. issued his Accounting Evolution to 1900 in which some of the facts in his earlier articles were incorporated. Primarily, as the title indicated, it was a history of the technical features of the subject of accountancy, but it included much about its persons.

In 1931, Joseph C. Myer of St. Johns College in Brooklyn furnished to the *Accounting Review* (v. 6, p. 47) an article upon Teaching the Accountant the History and Ethics of His Profession, in which he said:

> "My experience has impressed me with the lack of knowledge that many accountants have of their profession. * * * not only a lack of knowledge but also a lack of desire to gain such knowledge."

And in March, 1939, Hugh S. O'Reilly of Fordham University published in the *Accounting Forum* (v. 10, p. 15) of the School of Business and Civic Administration of The City College, New York, an article of five pages with the same title as this story. The author's affirmative answer to the question appears in almost every paragraph. They are too numerous and too long for quotation but they are briefly indicated in the heading of one section—"Accounting History in Neglect."

Some educational institutions considered accounting history important and provided for instruction in it for their students. Quite understandably these were institutions which had or secured for their faculties men who were not only informed on the subject but were also convinced of its importance to the students.

Perhaps the first such instance was that of the School of Commerce, Accounts and Finance of New York University, organized in 1900. Its first dean, Charles Waldo Haskins, was appointed Professor of the History of Accounting as well as of Auditing. His first lecture at the opening of the School on October 2, 1900, was an introduction to the History of Accountancy. Earlier that year on January 25, he had addressed the New York Chapter of the Institute of Accounts, his subject being Accountancy: Its Past and Its Present. During the three years before his death in January, 1903, he addressed many organizations—the societies of accountants in New York,

Massachusetts and Pennsylvania; the Institute of Bank Clerks; the American Economic Association; the National Municipal League; the Eastern Commercial Teachers Association and others. Some of his papers were largely historical, but even when they were mainly as to the situation then present or a forecast of the future he illustrated his statements by historical reference. No record of a successor to his professorship of accounting history has been found, perhaps because no other was equally informed and enthusiastic.

At various times during the last ten or fifteen years teachers of accounting have complained of the dearth of accountancy history. One was the late Hugh S. O'Reilly of Fordham whose article has been mentioned. He secured all he could find for his students and asked at least one accountant to talk to them on history.

Perhaps the earliest organized effort for the study of the history of accountancy was at the University of Illinois where, in 1922, graduate instruction in accounting was begun, and a part of the program was a year's course in theory. Soon this developed to where some time was given to certain aspects of history. About a decade later, theory material filled all the time and history became a separate semester course. Some students selected history topics for their Master's theses. And after another period of nearly ten years several Ph.D. candidates wrote their dissertations on phases of history and this has continued to the present time.

The most highly developed effort for education in the subject may have been that organized in 1928 in the School of Accounting, Commerce and Finance of St. John's College in Brooklyn (now the School of Commerce of St. John's University). That School was organized in May, 1927, and began operation that Fall. Its organizers were three professors of whom one, Joseph C. Meyer, was its first Dean and continued in that office until his death on April 5, 1934. He was of the class of 1918 in the Amos Tuck School of Dartmouth College, but withdrew and joined the Army as a 2d Lieutenant in 1918. He entered business in 1919 in New York; taught accounting evenings at Pace Institute; and became a CPA of New Jersey in 1925 and of New York in 1930.

Because of his experience, as stated in the quotation already noted, he included in the curriculum for freshmen a one-hour course on History and Survey of Accountancy which, as stated in his article in the *Accounting Review* (v. 6, p. 47), "comprised sixteen class lectures on the following topics: History of accounting and bookkeeping, accountancy legislation, education and societies and the very important subject of accountancy ethics," besides "incidental topics such as how to apply for a position in public accounting." To conduct this course the School had Wilmer L. Green, who had about ten years experience in handling the employment of staff men for a nationally organized firm of accountants, and who about three years later brought out a text book on the subject.

The course was continued only one year after Myer's death as the faculty "did not believe at the time it was necessary for students majoring in Accounting to have such a History as was in the book used at that time."

Some years ago A. C. Littleton, whose authorship has been noted herein, lectured on accounting to his students and procured for them all the literature on history he could find, which was largely that in periodicals or brief pamphlets. During the second semester of the year 1952-1953, he delivered a course of lectures to graduate students at Denver University. It was proposed that this should be a course in history and while he was preparing for this part of the required course for these students he wrote about it concluding his letter with the following quotations:

> "Whoever wishes to delve deeply into a subject must also come to know its history." *Jager*
>
> "If you would understand anything observe its beginnings and its development." *Aristotle*

Perhaps there may be some who will have read this story and who may be convinced that they would like to read accounting history. There is much source material in old and later books on bookkeeping and accounting and a mass of it in pamphlets and periodicals—too much to list here. Societies have issued year books and several have published histories of their activities and of the profession of accountancy in their areas. But exclusive of a few biographies, the published books are as follows:

British:

Professional Accountants

by Beresford Worthington. Gee & Co., London, 1895

History of Accounting and Accountants
by Richard Brown. T. & E. C. Jack, Edinburgh, 1905
Short History of Accountants and Accountancy
by Arthur H. Woolf. Gee & Co., London, 1912
Chapters in the History of Bookkeeping, Accountancy and Commercial Arithmetic
by David Murray. Jackson, Wylie & Co., Glasgow, 1930

American:

Recollections of the Early Days of American Accountancy
by James T. Anyon. Privately Printed, New York, 1925
History and Survey of Accountancy
by Wilmer L. Green. Standard Text Press, Brooklyn, 1930
Accounting Evolution to 1900
by A. C. Littleton. American Inst. Pub. Co., New York, 1933

Public Accountants Practicing In Syracuse, New York, Before 1900

By THE COMMITTEE ON HISTORY

Two Syracuse newspapers, *The Courier* and the *Syracuse Journal*, and the classified business section of early Syracuse directories rewarded the search for information about early practitioners of public accounting in Syracuse.

The earliest record found is an item which appeared in the July 31, 1861, issue of *The Courier*. It is quoted here in full:

> "COLLECTING AND POSTING ACCOUNTS.
> —Persons in need of the services of a good collecting firm will find their wants supplied by calling on Messrs. Z. H. Wright, or Wm. L. Palmer, who have opened a business office in the room formerly occupied as the *Courier* Counting Room. They will devote their attention to the posting of books, collecting of accounts, and all other business in their line. Zed Wright is well known for his abilities as a collector, having been many years in the business, and as a "thief catcher," he has no equal hereabouts—be he horse thief or burglar. Mr. Palmer is a good accountant, and will be chiefly engaged indoors, while Mr. Wright will attend to matters that require outside attention. His duty will include the purchase of horses, carriages, buggies, and other articles, to be sold on commission. He has now several fine horses, well matched and gentle, fit for the saddle or buggy, together with buggy wagons and family carriages. The new collecting firm promise satisfaction in every department, and we are certain that the promise will be redeemed."

While the division of duties between Mr. Wright and Mr. Palmer is not entirely clear, since the firm is twice described as a "collecting firm," it seems likely that Mr. Palmer may have participated in this activity as well as handling the "posting of accounts."

An item dated nineteen years later, published in the same newspaper on January 7, 1880, discloses a closer concentration on books and records. It, too, emphasizes the subject's qualifications as a handwriting expert and plays up the detection of fraud. It reports the removal of Mr. William Stevens' office and describes him as an

---

This is the seventeenth in a series of articles on the History of Accounting in the State of New York. It was prepared by the Society's Committee on History.

"expert accountant, public auditor, and detective of forged handwriting":

"EXPERT BUSINESS.

Removal of William Stevens' General Accounting and Auditing Office.

We desire to inform the readers of the COURIER that Mr. William Stevens, general and expert accountant, public auditor and detective of forged hand writing, recently of the firm of Hinman & Stevens, has removed his office from the Bastable block to apartments directly over Kent & Miller's, No. 20 South Salina street, where he will now be pleased to welcome any who choose to honor him with a call.

Mr. Stevens is not only well-known in this city as an expert at solving accounts, detecting forged hand writing, and in straightening out complicated book accounts generally, but his reputation for reliability and honest judgment in all matters pertaining to his peculiar line of business, has extended many miles over the state where his services have been called into requisition. Mr. Stevens is ready at any time to investigate the affairs of corporations and firms, detect frauds and errors, adjust partnership accounts, open or close books, and properly look into assignments. He can always show the highest references from persons for whom important work has been done. His long experience is a guarantee that he is fully able to unravel any knotty business affairs, and he therefore invites any, desirous of his services, to give him a call in his new rooms, No. 20 South Salina street."

After a lapse of sixteen years we find an even greater emphasis on accounting matters, as well as a mention of the preparation of financial statements, although identification of handwriting is mentioned twice in this item published November 14, 1896, in the *Syracuse Journal*:

"ACCOUNTANT.

Laurence W. Myers.

The profession of the expert accountant is well represented in Syracuse by Laurence W. Myers, whose office is in the Onondaga County Savings Bank building. Mr. Myers is a native of the city, and has had a practical experience of thirty years, and sixteen years ago established a [*sic*] independent business as an expert and consulting accountant, and he renders efficient service in behalf of corporations, railways, banks, private firms, etc., in the examination of accounts, the preparation of statements and all kinds of expert accountants' work, also in investigation in connection with work for the courts and is constantly employed as an expert witness in regard to penmanship as well as accounts, and identified with prominent cases. One of the foremost of these with which he has been identified was the Wilkinson bank case in 1884 and 1885 in which $500,000 was involved. He is constantly employed in cases involving the questions of accounting and penmanship in local courts and also throughout New York and other States."

There was no apparent reason for the publication of this item. It may have been a news item or perhaps a paid advertisement.

The earliest Syracuse directory in which accountants were listed in the classified business section is that for the year 1875. The persons mentioned in this directory and subsequent ones through 1900 are as follows:

Times Listed	Name	Years
3	Barker, Frederick W.	1877, 1878, 1879.
3	Barker, Henry M.	1892, 1893, 1894.
24	Gardner, George J.	1875; 1878 to 1900.
2	Hinman, James H.	1879, 1880.
20	Mann, R. DeWitt (later a CPA)	1877 to 1881; 1886 to 1900.
1	Markell, John S.	1880.
19	Myers, Laurence W.	1882 to 1900.
3	Stevens, Williams [*sic*]	1878, 1879, 1880.

Three of these men stand out as being permanently in public accounting practice. Of the others, Frederick W. Barker was prominent later in local banking for many years as president of the Syracuse Savings Bank. One of the newspaper articles previously quoted was about William Stevens and was dated early in 1880, but his name did not appear as an accountant in the classified section of any of the later directories. Mr. Gardner was listed in the earliest city directory on file in the Syracuse Public Library, that of 1851, as a teller at the Onondaga County Bank.

George J. Gardner was an accountant whose interests took him into many fields and made him an outstanding person in his community. He apparently practiced public accounting continuously from 1875 to 1896, at which time his listing in the classified section was discontinued. His name appears afterward, as an accountant, in the general section of the directories until his death, July 17, 1902, at the age of eighty-four. Mr. Gardner was born in Boston, Massachusetts, in 1818. In 1826, his family moved to New York City, where he attended Public School No. 2 on Henry Street. This was the only mention of his schooling. In 1829 he moved to Syracuse. His business activities from that time were so numerous that they are presented in the form of a list:

1829-31	Learned business of printer; printers "devil" on first paper in Syracuse; delivered papers once a week on horseback.
1831-41	Clerk in bookstore.
1841-43	Owner of same bookstore.
1843	Bookkeeper in Onondaga County Bank.
1843-60	In banking.
1848	Appointed Notary Public.
1861-66	Assistant Postmaster.
1866-72	Secretary, New York Life Insurance Company.
1872-1902	Public Accountant.

He married Phoebe A. Teall in August 1843 and they adopted three daughters. That he was as active in the life of his community as he was in business is demonstrated by the following list of achievements:

Volunteer fireman
Lieutenant in old 149th Regiment
Twice Supervisor
Three times Alderman
Member of Board of Health
Twice Member of Board of Education
Member of first literary society organized in Syracuse
One of founders of Franklin Institute in 1850, President in 1856
One of "corporators" of Genesee and Water Street Railroad Company in 1865
One of "corporators" of Trust and Deposit Company of Onondaga
Treasurer of Episcopal Diocese of Central New York for many years
Member of Odd Fellows for sixty years; Grand Master of Grand Lodge of New York State
Member of Masonic organizations for forty-six years; Thirty-third degree Mason
Collector of curios

At the time of his death, a six-inch two-column picture and three full columns describing his life and activities appeared in the *Evening Herald*, followed next day by an editorial. Obviously Mr. Gardner was an early exponent of the idea that an accountant should enter fully into community service.

R. DeWitt Mann is the only one of those listed who was found to have become a CPA. He is listed in the Ten-Year Book of the New York State Society of CPA's as holding certificate No 77, and as having been admitted to the Society in March, 1898. His name appears as an accountant continuously in the classified section of the directories from 1877 to 1917. From 1918 to 1920, he is listed in the general section of the directories as an accountant. He died January 29, 1920, at the age of eighty. Mr. Mann was probably born in Poughkeepsie, New York, in July, 1839, and is believed to have received a high school education there. He moved to Farmer Village (later Interlaken), New York, where he owned and operated a general store. In 1871, he came to Syracuse with the newly organized Syracuse and Northern Railroad Company. In the 1875 directory he is listed as cashier and general passenger agent of this company. Mr. Mann was secretary of the Masonic Relief Association of Central New York for several years. During the period when he was in public accounting he either audited or kept books of the City of Syracuse for many years.

Much of this information was obtained from his son, Henry D. Mann, who in 1955, at the age of eighty-nine, was still doing some public accounting work. Henry Mann did not immediately follow in his father's footsteps, but started his own practice in 1920.

The following quarter-page advertisement for R. DeWitt Mann appeared in the city directory for the year 1900:

R. DEWITT MANN,

Examiner of Disputed Hand Writings,

Certified Public Accountant,

328 Kirk Building, : : SYRACUSE, N. Y.

Member of National and State Societies Certified Public Accountants

TELEPHONE

Apparently he regarded his ability as a handwriting expert as more important than possession of the CPA certificate.

Of *Laurence W. Myers* very little has been found, other than that he was continuously in public practice from 1882 until his death on May 16, 1901, at the age of sixty. The next day the following editorial appeared in the "Syracuse Journal":

> "*Laurence W. Myers* who died yesterday was widely known by the business men of Syracuse. As an expert accountant there was none better in this country."

From these articles and biographical sketches it appears that public accounting in Syracuse before 1900 included such things as collecting accounts, posting books, and examining disputed handwritings, which seem to have little to do with an expression of opinion on financial statements or preparation of income tax returns. The development of the profession from those years to 1955 has been remarkable.

Attention is called to the fact that of the three outstanding public accountants, only one was active in community affairs. It is especially significant that biographical material concerning this one is almost unlimited, while as to the others it is very sparse.

Early Accounting Firms in New York City

By THE COMMITTEE ON HISTORY

To determine the scope of this narrative it was necessary to fix upon the year to which it should be carried. It seemed that the final year should be when relatively few firms had been organized, and before the general adoption of the partnership form by practitioners. In this as in other matters the pioneers would be few, the followers many. Two principal sources were used to decide upon that terminal year.

The first was the list of "The Public Accountants of New York City" in the June, 1896, issue of *Business*. It named 24 firms and 97 persons, a few of whom are recognized as partners in some of the named firms. The ratio of firms to individuals—more than 1 to 4—indicated that the period of the formation of partnerships had begun before 1896.

The other source was the "Directory of Early American Public Accountants," compiled by A. C. Littleton and published in 1942. It was prepared from the New York Directories from 1850 to 1899. It listed the 24 firms shown in the earlier list and 24 others as well. This was additional evidence that the change from sole practice to that by firms had begun before 1896.

Examination of the 48 listings of firms in this second source and a few facts found elsewhere showed that most of the listings were in the decade from 1887 to 1896. And since the first national society—American Association of Public Accountants—was organized late in 1886, it was decided to classify as early firms only those formed before 1887. However, those organized during the next 10 years to 1896 include many firms which persisted for many years—some to the present; therefore they are here scheduled with the year of their earliest listing in the Directory.

This is the eighteenth in a series of articles on the History of Accounting in the State of New York. It was prepared by the Society's Committee on History.

In *Business* and the Directory

1891— Deloitte, Dever, Griffiths & Co.
Harney, Henry & Co.
Hart Bros., Tibbetts & Co.
1892— Broaker & Chapman
Brummer & Co.
Smith, Reckitt, Clarke & Co.
Waud, Edmonds & Co.
Whitehead, Clerihew & Co.
1893— Patterson & Corwin
Teele & Dennis
1894— Abrahams, John W. & Co.
Duggett & Ryan
Good & Fellows
MacRae & Cowan
1895— Jones, Caesar & Co.
Kavanagh & Sullivan
N. Y. Acct'g. & Adjustment Co.
Sherton & Chalmers
Waltermire & Co.
1896— Ellis, George S. & Son

In the Directory, only
1887— McKean & Hall
1888— Bureau of Audit
Hartt & Brown
Smith & Inston
Turton, G. L. & Co.
1889— Kerr & Campbell
Townsend, Charles E. & Son
1890— Kane & Peebles
Smith & Moller
1891— Gane, Jackson, Jeffreys & Kenworthy
North, Charles F. & Co.
Price, Waterhouse & Co.
1892— Bergtheil, Horley & Co.
Dixon, Hiram R. & Co.
Safeguard Account Co.

1893— Conant & Crook
Lescher, Herman & Co.
Reid, W. Norton & Co.
1894— American Acct'g. Co.
Byers & Reid
Donnelly & Fisher
1895— Lindsay, Reid & Co.
1896— American Acct'g. & Bkpg. Co.
Haskins & Sells

The New York Directories for the 20 years, 1820 to 1840, have not been examined. But in the other 80 years of the century from 1786 to 1886 the names of 15 accounting firms were found. Of these much has been learned about 5 firms. The other 10 are here named, with the year of the listing and a few facts about 4 of them:

1841	Treadwell & Clark
1868-1869	Bigood & Company
1872-1876	Collins & Co., followed by Jas. R. Collins to 1881
1874	Frederick Ogden & Co.
1876	Butler & Bacon
1878	Dean, Parsons & Buchanan, possibly John Dean, 1878
1878-1882	Cowdrey & Franklin; DeWitt C. Cowdrey followed in 1884
1880-1883	Harding & Burnap; William A. Harding followed to 1898
1881	Campbell & Gifford
1883	Alfred Luttman & Co.

Of these, 3 were listed in 4 or 5 years, 1 in 2 years and 6 in 1 year.

Forty-four firms organized during 1887 to 1896 as outlined in the scope of this study having been listed, as well as 10 firms formed during 1841 to 1883 of whom little more is known, there remain 5 firms of whom something has been learned regarding their practice and more about their partners.

David Franks & Co.

David Franks & Co., 1786, was, so far as learned, the earliest firm of public accountants in New York—possibly in the United States.

All that has been learned of the firm and of the partners was found in "The New York Directory" for 1786, compiled by David Franks, and in quotations in "Annals of New York City for 1786 from Newspapers of the Day," both republished by Trow City Directory Company in 1886. They are here given:

> "Franks, D., Conveyancer &c., 66 Broadway"
>
> Directory, p. 28

> "NB: Mr. Franks has ready for Publication, a Treatise of BOOKKEEPING, digested for the inland and foreign Trade of America"
>
> Directory, p. 81

> "DAVID FRANKS, Conveyancer and Accountant, No. 66 Broadway
> (Thanks for past favors and
> quotations for 4 documents)
> "Mr. Franks having served a regular apprenticeship to his father, a very eminent attorney in Dublin, and having, besides, transacted business, for some years, for Counsellor Franklin of said city,
>
> . . . .
>
> Mr. Franks has lately engaged a young man from Dublin of unexceptionable abilities."
>
> Directory, p. 82

> "The New York Directory is this day published and to be sold by S. Kollock at his bookstore, opposite the Coffee House; and by Francis Childs, No. 189 Water Street."
>
> Annals, Feb. 11, p. 102

> "To be let, 132 lots in the Out Ward; inquire of David C. Franks No. 93 Broadway"
>
> Annals, July 26, p. 161

> "David Franks & Co. have opened a conveyancing and accountants office at No. 24 Water Street"
>
> Annals, Aug. 1, p. 162

> "On Monday (31st. ult.) after a short passage of 46 days the ship Harbinger, Capt. Wardell, from Bristol, in which came. . . Moses Franks, second son of David Franks. . . ."
>
> Annals, Aug. 1, p. 163

The second New York Directory was compiled by David Carroll Franks.

At that time, 1786, Bristol was an active port with much foreign trade and was the address of at least one public accountant and probably more.

The foregoing quotations do not tell anything of the practice of the firm of David Franks & Co. But as to its personnel they disclose some facts and suggest others about David Franks and his two sons. David Franks had been in New York prior to 1786, long enough to have had some engagements as a conveyancer for which he expressed thanks. About the first of that year, or earlier, he wished to be known as a public accountant prepared to accept conveyancing and accounting engagements. David Carroll Franks, probably the older son, was located at 73 Broadway, while his father was nearby at 66 Broadway, both residence locations. His offering real estate for rental suggests that he acted as an agent and that these functions were related to activities with his father as a conveyancer. Moses Franks came from Bristol, where there was opportunity for training in accountancy, but that he had such training is not known. However, the fact that the father, who had previously announced himself as an accountant, should have publicized that occupation in a newspaper on August 1, 1786, suggests that it was because of the second son's arrival. Considering the facts shown by contemporary records and the surmises which, though not demonstrated, seem reasonable, it appears that in 1786 David Franks continued to serve as a conveyancer and, with his son David Carroll Franks, kept up directory work; while with his second son, Moses Franks, he opened an office at 24 Water Street for the practice of public accounting, which previously he had conducted from his house at 66 Broadway. Until records of another firm are found it seems proper to assume that David Franks & Co. was the earliest public accounting firm in New York.

While nothing is known of the practice of the Franks firm and too little of its personnel, and while even less has been learned about the 10 firms listed herein as organized between 1841 and 1883, much has been found regarding the practice and partners of 4 firms formed between 1873 and 1883.

The Veysey Firms

This practice was begun by William H. Veysey in 1866. It was conducted by Veysey & Fabian from 1873 to 1876, by Veysey alone from 1876 to 1885, by Veysey & Veysey to 1896, and by James N.

Kelley from 1896 to 1904. In March, 1892, an item in *The Office* stated: "This firm was established in 1866 and made many friends by close attention to business, promptness and efficiency of services". That reputation may have caused The Mutual Life Insurance Company of New York to engage the firm early in 1886 to design, install, and supervise the operation of a system of bookkeeping and records for its foreign business. The engagement, which lasted 6 years to March 1, 1892, was carried on by the younger Veysey, who then went with the client. Brief sketches of the 4 partners are here given.

William Henry Veysey was born in Exeter, England, February 10, 1826. Family traditions are that he was educated in a private school, received accountancy training in England, and had a quarrel with an older brother as a result of which he came to America. However no record has been found of any facts or dates relating to his first 31 years. The Jersey City Directory of 1857 showed his residence address as 178 Harrison Street and his employment as accountant at 123 Broad Street, New York. But probably his employment was not in public practice because he was listed as a bookkeeper in 1863, and as with a dry goods house in 1864. In 1866 he was listed as a clerk, the English term for an accountant's assistant. New York Directories of 1869-1872 showed him as in insurance, possibly a side line, and in 1873 as public accountant. But his card in *The Bookkeeper*, October 26, 1886, stated: "Professional Accountant, No. 150 Broadway. Established 1866." He was in practice 30 years: alone from 1866 to 1872 and from 1877 to 1885; in Veysey & Fabian from 1873 to 1876; and in Veysey & Veysey from 1886 to 1896. He was a charter member of the Institute of Accounts and of the American Association of Public Accountants and at once became an officer in each. He read papers before the Institute and wrote articles for *The Bookkeeper* and *The Office*. On his statement as Treasurer of AAPA he used the now outmoded "E&OE." But he could look ahead as in his letter in *The Banking Law Journal* of December 15, 1895:

> "I was the only correspondent who suggested that it should be made illegal for an accountant not to give proper information for investors whose stocks or bonds were offered for sale. I suggested it being made illegal as to accountants only, not as to vendors or promoters, because I wished to see the highest possible standard of honor taken by accountants in the exercise of their obligations."

He died in Brooklyn on July 14, 1896.

Robert Letchworth Fabian was born in England in 1821, a younger son in a prominent family. He went to sea as a cabin boy and became an officer. By 1849 he had come to Cincinnati, and to 1852 was listed as bookkeeper and in 1853 as of Kidder & Fabian, commission merchants. Probably he served in the Civil War. Later, he married Emily S. Johnston. He removed to New York in 1871. From 1873 to 1876 he was a partner in Veysey & Fabian and practiced alone thereafter to 1887. No facts regarding his ability as an accountant are known but it may be implied from his association with Veysey. His standing in this profession is indicated by his election to the committee which formed the AAPA, by his election as its first President, and by the fact that his name is first on the list of incorporators, though he did not live to attend their first meeting. He died in New York on November 16, 1887, and was taken to Spring Grove Cemetery, Cincinnati, for burial.

Walter Hugh Peyton Veysey was born in Jersey City on May 16, 1862, and was the older son of William H. Veysey. He was employed for some time—probably several years—to 1885, when he became a partner in Veysey & Veysey. The next year he took on for the firm the Mutual Life Insurance Company engagement. On March 1, 1892, he became an employee of that company and his status in the firm became that of a special partner. On February 15, 1907, he became Deputy Superintendent of the Foreign Department of the insurance company, retiring October 1, 1919. Like his father he was a charter member of the Institute of Accounts and of the AAPA. He was an incorporator of the latter. He became CPA No. 192 of New York in 1901 and joined the State Society in 1904 and the Accountants' Roundtable in 1910. After his retirement in 1919 he removed to Glendale, California, where he died October 14, 1930.

James Nicholas Kelley was born in County Galway, Ireland, in 1850. When he was 18 he was employed by a London bank and in that and a similar institution spent the 16 years to 1884. Then he came to New York and was on the staff of Veysey & Veysey to 1892, when he was made a partner in the firm in succession to Walter H. P. Veysey, who then became a special partner. He became New York CPA No. 49 in 1896, a member of the State Society in 1897, and its Treasurer from 1898 to 1903. receiving a loving cup at the end of his service. After the death of William H. Veysey in July, 1896, Kelley liquidated the affairs of Veysey & Veysey and succeeded to and carried on the practice under his own name. He became ill and retired in 1904, and died on January 20, 1905.

The Yalden Firms

This practice was begun by James Yalden in 1876. It became Yalden, Brooks & Donnelly in 1889; Yalden, Brooks and Yalden in 1893; Yalden, Brooks & Walker later in 1893; Yalden, Walker & Co. in 1896; Yalden, Walker & Weiss in 1900; and James Yalden & Co. again in 1902.

A few items indicating the scope and volume of the practice are here given. In December, 1892, when the AAPA was seeking a charter for the New York School of Accounts, Henry R. M. Cook told the Regents about the firm and its senior partner as follows:

> "Mr. James Yalden is the senior partner of the firm of Yalden, Brooks & Donnelly, probably the largest and best known firm of public accountants in the United States. He has been connected with some large matters in accountancy, for instance the celebrated gas investigation in which he was employed by the State, and many others too numerous to mention. His firm has recently completed a long investigation of the whole of the municipal accounts of the City of Detroit."

The gas investigation which Cook mentioned was made for a Special Committee of the State Senate and covered the accounts of several public service corporations. The report, signed "J. Yalden, Public Accountant and Auditor," was included in the Committee Report and covered 24 pages, from 635 to 658. The Detroit engagement was for an audit of the city accounts for the 3 years ended June 30, 1891, which Yalden, Brooks & Donnelly began January 2, 1892, and on which they submitted their report dated July 22, 1892. *Business* of January, 1892, carried the firm's report dated June 9, 1891, on its examination of the accounts of a wholesale grocery for the 10 years ended January 31, 1890. And an industrial client was the United States Milling Company.

Besides the six partners whose names appeared in one or more of the firm titles there were at least three others who were partners. Nothing has been found as to partners, if any, in the first title of J. Yalden & Co., 1876 to 1889. Sketches of 9 partners are here given.

James Yalden was born in Bentworth, England, March 26, 1842. Nothing is known of his education and training but he was in practice as J. Yalden & Co. at 70 Cheapside, London, in 1866. In 1875 and also in 1876 he was a trustee of insolvent estates and had made other investigations. He came to New York in 1876, was a charter member of the AAPA and its President after the death of Robert L. Fabian, held offices in it continuously during 18 years, was guarantor of expenses and trustee of the New York School of Accounts, where he taught government accounts, became CPA No. 138 in 1898, and joined the State Society in 1903. His portrait suggests that he was large and dignified, his speeches indicate that he was thoughtful and optimistic, and AAPA minutes show that he was courteous to those less prominent.

William Henry Brook was born in London in 1851, was graduated from Kings College, Oxford, and became a Fellow of the Institute of Chartered Accountants. He had come to New York by 1886, when he became a charter member of the AAPA and was elected to its council. He resigned in April, 1888, and went to Detroit. There he was with an insurance company for several years and later was Treasurer of Banner Cigar Company. Between these positions he was associated with John H. Clegg on the audit of Wayne County and later was a partner in N. A. Hawkins & Co., while at times he practiced in W. H. Brook Audit Co. He was a founder of the National Association of Accountants and Bookkeepers in 1896, and later was a member of the Incorp. Assn. of Public Accountants of Michigan. He was graduated from Detroit College of Law in 1900, attended the first Congress of Accountants held in St. Louis in 1904, became CPA No. 17 of Michigan in 1906, joined the Michigan Association in 1905, and was its President in 1908. About 1920 he moved to Cleveland, where he taught in Spencerian College and founded the Brook School of Commerce, Accounts and Finance. In 1927 he returned to Detroit, where he died June 23, 1930. It is not certain that he was of the Yalden firm. Some of the items found may refer to him or to William M. Brooks, whose career is covered in the next paragraph.

William M. Brooks was born in England—place and date not learned. He had come to New York and been employed by the Yalden firm to 1889, when he became a partner in Yalden, Brooks & Donnelly and later in its two successors. He became an Associate of the AAPA in 1888, a Fellow in 1892. He was a guarantor of expenses of the New York School of Accounts, in which he taught insurance accounting. January 16, 1895, was his busy day. The previous day he had submitted his report for the Yalden firm on the accounts of the Detroit

Fire Commission. On the 16th the *Free Press* said the report "charged many irregularities and shortcomings." That afternoon the *News* stated that the Secretary of the Fire Commission had made an affidavit for the arrest of Brooks, "charging that he had damaged his character and claiming that the report was false, libelous and malicious." That morning a Deputy Sheriff arrested Brooks. But within a few hours Mayor Pingree and Alderman Berk provided bail and he was released. The affair seems to have been a fight by the Mayor and at least one Alderman against the majority of the Council. Brooks remained at liberty. He returned to England in 1896.

George W. Donnelly probably was born in England, since all other partners were Englishmen except Walker, who was next door, a Canadian. He had been with the Yalden firm for several years when, in 1889, he became a partner and remained as such for about 4 years. He had become an Associate of the AAPA on March 6, 1888, and was advanced to Fellow on January 26, 1892. After he left the Yalden firm he was of Donnelly & Fisher in 1894, and was listed as in practice alone from 1895 to 1897. Nothing more has been found; perhaps he returned to England.

Louis Yalden, brother of James, was born in Medsted, England, on March 30, 1861. He had been in New York and probably in the employ of the Yalden firm several years before 1888. He may have been a partner in Yalden, Brooks & Donnelly, and he surely was a partner in Yalden, Brooks &Yalden from 1892. He was one of the first Associates of the AAPA (March 6, 1888) and became a Fellow on January 26, 1892. Immediately thereafter, on February 6, 1892, he was elected a Trustee. He attended the meeting with the Regents on June 18, 1892, when the Association asked for a charter for a College of Accounts. He was a guarantor of the expenses of the New York School of Accounts, in which he had agreed to teach the theory and practice of bookkeeping, but was prevented from doing so by his death on September 19, 1893. As to his ability as an accountant the *Banking Law Journal* of October 1, 1893, quoted a "most eminent financier" as having said of him: "the most promising accountant—the most brilliant man of the future—has passed away."

Alfred Percy Walker was born in Canada about 1862 or 1863. He was a brother of Sir Edmund Walker, who for many years was the head of the Canadian Bank of Commerce. He was employed by the Yalden firm from 1885 to 1893, became a partner in Yalden, Brooks

& Walker in 1895, and continued in the succeeding firms to 1903. Then for a short time he was a partner in Walker & Kenworthy, but in 1903 went with Standard Milling Company, of which he was President from 1914 to 1929. He became a Fellow of AAPA in 1893 and attended the Joint Legislative Meeting on March 13, 1895, the purpose of which was to obtain statutory recognition of the profession. He became New York CPA No. 74 in 1896, a Governor of the National Society of CPAs in 1897, and a member of the State Society in 1903. He died in Pelham Manor about 1932.

Richard Neville Hutchinson, of whom no biography has been found, was born in England. He became CPA No. 46 in 1896. This indicates that he had been in public accounting since 1891, either here or in England. After some time with the Yalden firm he was a partner in Yalden, Walker & Co. from 1896 to 1900. Then he practiced alone in New York all or part of 13 years. From 1914 he was listed as practicing alone in Hartford, Connecticut, and in 1915 as of Rothwell, Hutchinson & Co. By 1920 he was shown as having branches, perhaps only correspondents, in New York and Washington. He had become an Associate of AAPA in 1896 and a Fellow in 1897, when also he joined the National Society of CPAs. He returned to England in 1921.

William Frederick Weiss was born in Germany in 1860 and in 1880 came to New York, where he worked for Armour & Company for several years. In 1894, after a brief period in practice, he became president of New York Steam Company. During 1897 and 1898 he was in practice as Weiss & Johnson, and for a little over two years, 1900 to 1902, he was a partner in Yalden, Walker & Weiss. From 1903 he was the head of his own firm except for a period in 1913 when he was the New York partner in Macpherson, Weiss & Co. He became New York CPA No. 141 in 1898, a Fellow of AAPA in 1899, a member of the State Society in 1902, and its President in 1912. He died April 16, 1939.

Percy A. Yalden, son of James, was born in Brixton, England, on November 4, 1873. After employment by Yalden, Walker & Co., he became a partner in that firm in 1903 and afterward in its successor, J. Yalden & Co. After the death of his father, in 1905, he continued the practice under the same firm name, but probably alone. He became an Associate of AAPA in 1896. He died in New York late in the summer of 1936.

The Martin Firm

The Martin firm was not mentioned in the "Recollections" by James T. Anyon, as were the Veysey and Yalden firms. This account is based upon stories in the *Financial Record* of May 9, 1894, and January 9, 1895, the *Pace Student* of October, 1932, the New York Directories, and correspondence with the founder's grandson.

The practice was begun by Andrew B. Martin in 1863, continued by the firm of Andrew B. & Clarence A. Martin from 1880 to 1911 (although the firm was listed in the 1882 Directory as Martin Brothers), and then by Clarence A. Martin alone from 1911 to 1928. While information to segregate the engagements by these periods is not available, there are records which indicate that the practice included engagements on commercial, fiduciary, and utility accounts, with perhaps an exceptional number on municipal accounts. Sketches of two partners and of a possible third are given here.

Andrew B. Martin was born in Monoghan, Ireland, on February 7, 1830. His schooling ended when he was only 11. When 19 he came to Montreal, where he was employed on a newspaper. Later he spent 4 years in the west, but by 1863 was living in Brooklyn and had an office in New York. He served on the Brooklyn Board of Education and, in 1883, became Commissioner of Accounts of New York.

Clarence A. Martin, son of Andrew B. Martin, was born in New York on January 7, 1859. He attended Brooklyn public schools. In 1878 he began work for his father and in 1880 became a partner.

Father and son became CPA's Nos. 24 and 25 in 1896; both were members of AAPA 1896-1898; both joined the National Society of CPA's in August, 1897, and the New York State Society of CPA's in November, 1897. Andrew B. Martin died July 18, 1911, and Clarence A. Martin died October 22, 1928.

Henry Marshall Tate was associated with Andrew B. Martin or the firm on an examination which covered nearly a century of the accounts of the Chamberlain of New York. This may have been a special partnership for that one job.

The Barrow Wade Guthrie Firm

The only account of the organization of this firm in 1883 is that contained in the "Recollections" of James T. Anyon, published in 1925. But the author, who came here in October, 1886, stated that he wrote it on trains. His story must have been written from memory of what he had been told. He wrote that "the firm was of sudden and somewhat spontaneous creation." But Edwin Guthrie and his partners in Manchester, England, probably knew that Quilter, Ball & Co. and Turquand, Youngs & Co. had been here in 1870 in connection with the accounts of the Erie Railroad and that Price, Waterhouse & Co. of London had sent accountants here on several occasions. And they may have thought that a branch office or correspondent in New York might lead to their being engaged for such overseas work. Also, it is unlikely that Guthrie would have put Wade into an American firm unless that idea had been considered before he came here from Manchester, England.

In the "Recollections" the author stated that upon arrival Guthrie's "first thought was to find a good accounting firm to assist him in his investigations." Perhaps also he sought a firm to become a branch office. As shown herein, the Yalden firm was the largest in America and the Veysey and Martin firms were well established. Thomas Bagot, William Calhoun, James Cox, Robert L. Fabian, Ebenezer Irons, Henry M. Tate, and others had been in practice for 5 to 10 years or longer. Probably some would have been willing to become correspondents but were not disposed to forego their independence and to become branch offices. However Guthrie found one individual with whom he could accomplish both purposes. The "Recollections" stated that the partnership was formed in October, 1883.

The earliest mention of the firm was that in *The Accountant* of London on January 5, 1884, as follows:

> "Messrs. Thomas, Wade, Guthrie & Co., chartered accountants, of 32 Brown Street, Manchester, announce that they have made arrangements with Mr. J. W. Barrow, of New York, by which Mr. Wade and Mr. Guthrie become members of the firm of Barrow, Wade, Guthrie & Co., public accountants, in that city, Mr. Barrow (who has been a resident there for 30 years) taking the personal management of the New York office and staff. Mr. Thomas (in view of his early retirement) has not joined in the American arrangement, but retains his usual conduct of business; Mr. Wade and Mr. Guthrie continuing theirs, and residing at Manchester as hitherto."

The firm continued the practice previously conducted by Barrow, which was described in the "Recollections" in two sentences:

> "His main business was in connection with certain British fire insurance companies, being employed by them to check the vouchers and certify to the clerical accuracy of the monthly statements prepared by the Branches here

> before being sent to the home offices abroad. This work constituted his only practice."

The story also stated that Barrow was an actuary. After his death and the retirement of his successor, who had been Barrow's assistant, an actuary came from England in 1886, and in 1887 became a partner at the same time as Anyon. Therefore it seems that the Barrow practice was not only that of checking vouchers and the clerical accuracy of statements but was also at least actuarial work upon the transactions which preceded the vouchers and statements. And research to learn more about Barrow and the assistant who became a partner after Barrow died has developed facts which show that before 1883 Barrow had indicated his availability as auditor and for other public accounting services. Sketches of eight accountants who became partners before or by 1904 are given here.

John Wylie Barrow was born in London on June 18, 1828. His parents' names have not been learned, but his father's sister, Elizabeth Barrow, married John Dickens and was the mother of Charles Dickens. This relationship, his father's help in financing his education, and his appointments in the British diplomatic service while in his early twenties suggest that the family, though not rich, was that of the middle-class Englishman.

His early education was acquired at Calcutta House and St. Peters School. When eight years old he won a first-class prize in Greek and later won others. In 1842, when 14 years of age, he left school and spent two years in an office, using his first earnings to buy a copy of Clarke's *Homer*. At 16, with his father's permission, he left that work and entered a school at Frankfort-on-Main and prepared for admission to the University of Heidelberg. But he remained at the University only a few months because, it was stated, of a want of means, but possibly also because he was appointed Secretary of Legation at Rome, where he made valuable acquaintances and was allowed privileges for study at the Vatican. A special privilege there was that of taking casts of all the sculptures in the Vatican.

Afterward, before he was 22, he filled a similar position in Vienna. During this service he made a short visit to England, where, on February 14, 1850, The Freedom of the City of London was conferred on him.

In the summer of 1851, following his experience in the British diplomatic service—probably because of it—the Italian and Austrian

Governments appointed him one of their Commissioners to the London Exhibition. For that service he received a bronze medal from Prince Albert, and from the Emperor of Austria a copy of the Lord's Prayer in 608 languages.

Then, in 1853, when he was 25, he served as commissioner to the Crystal Palace in New York, where he had charge of the works of art of German and Italian artists. Before taking up his business and professional life in New York it seems appropriate to continue the story of his linguistic and other attainments and their recognition.

Prior to his appointments as legation secretary in Rome and Vienna he was speaking fluently all modern languages of Europe. Earlier, when only eight, he read the New Testament in Greek and was proficient also in Latin. But he was preeminent in the Hebrew and Chaldean languages. And with a dream of entering the East India service he mastered the rudiments of Arabic and Hindustani and made much progress in Chinese. Yale College conferred on him the honorary degree of M.A. The scope and depth of his learning are indicated by his memberships. The Semitic Club of New York was organized in his residence. The Greek Club of New York welcomed him—he corresponded in Greek. The American Oriental Society admitted him October 14, 1868, made him a life member in October, 1869, and elected him a director on May 21, 1879. His paper "On a Hebrew MS of the Penteteuch, from the Jewish Congregation at Kai-fung-fu in China" was read before the Society on May 19, 1869.

Besides his proficiency in languages, Barrow was a mathematician and was interested in electricity, chemistry, and other sciences. He collected much apparatus for scientific purposes which was used by the Franklin Scientific Association, of which he was the founder and first president. After his death the collection was placed at Yale University.

In 1853, after the close of the Crystal Palace, he decided to remain here. While not an important fact it is a matter of interest that his great-great-grandfather, Gualterius DuBois, had been an early minister of the Dutch church here.

Despite Barrow's learning and diplomatic experience he entered upon a long period in the mercantile business. From 1853 to 1874 he was associated with J. R. Jaffray & Co., which apparently specialized in laces and other imports. Prior to 1861 he was listed as a clerk. It is uncertain whether that meant a salesman as the word is used in the United States or a bookkeeper, etc., as used in England. But from 1861 to 1874 he was a partner in the New York and London houses of the

Jaffray firm, whose address was 350 Broadway. The 1875 Directory did not show his occupation but in the 1876 and 1877 issues he was listed as a merchant at 31 Broad Street, where also he had been listed in 1875. Perhaps the 1875-1877 issues should have listed him as auditor or public accountant, as did the later issues, 1878-1884.

When, where, or how he had learned bookkeeping is not known. Perhaps it was during the two years from 1842 to 1844, when he was employed in an office, or during the periods when he was in the diplomatic or exposition services, or while he was with the Jaffray firm. With his disposition to study, he may have taken it up without any expectation that he would ever use it.

In 1883 Barrow accepted Edwin Guthrie's suggestion that he become the American representative of the Manchester firm of Thomas, Wade, Guthrie & Co. But that his name should lead in the title of the new firm may not have been because of his family connections, or of his literary and scientific attainments, or even of his ability as an actuary. More probably it was because Guthrie had learned of Barrow's practice as a public accountant since 1878 or 1875 and considered that Barrow's acquaintances during thirty years would look at the new firm as an expansion of Barrow's practice.

All that is known of this practice is that it included work from four British insurance companies. That gave him some standing in England. And his business life of thirty years in New York gave him a standing of which Guthrie's attorneys knew. His listing as a public accountant must be accepted as correct unless clearly disproved. Probably Barrow knew of the early firms and sole practitioners. And possibly he had been engaged for some work other than that for the British insurance companies.

But his management of the new firm was brief, not over eighteen months, at the most, from October, 1883, for he died April 25, 1885. His funeral service was held on April 28 at St. Bartholomew's Church.

Charles Henry Wade and *Edwin Guthrie* of the Manchester firm of Thomas, Wade, Guthrie & Co. were mentioned in *The Accountant* of December 21, 1878, as present at a meeting on December 16 attended by many Manchester accountants and by representatives from 7 or more nearby cities. It had been called for the purpose of forming an association. Wade was chosen as chairman and he made and Guthrie seconded a resolution by which the "meeting resolves itself into the Accountants Incorporation Association." Later both were elected to a committee of 9 to draft its rules and by-laws. No later mention of this Association appeared in that periodical but an earlier Society of Accountants established in 1871 at Manchester was one of those which secured the Charter for the Institute of Chartered Accountants in England and Wales on May 11, 1880. The Charter named Wade and Guthrie as among the 45 who were the first members of the Council. Wade served thereon until his resignation was accepted on October 3, 1906, Guthrie until his death on August 21, 1904. Both were present at many of its meetings and one or the other was present at most of the other sessions.

While Barrow, Wade, Guthrie & Co. was not a branch of the Manchester firm, they were closely associated, and events in Manchester were reflected in New York. Mr. Thomas, whose retirement was forecast in the January, 1884, item, withdrew from the Manchester firm December 31, 1892, and Henry Simmons became a partner. In September, 1895, that firm was dissolved. Then C. H. Wade & Co. continued the Wade practice in Manchester and London, and Guthrie and Simmons (John Jackson and F. T. Wooley from January 1, 1896) retained the firm's offices in both cities and practiced as Edwin Guthrie & Co. At that time, September, 1895, or earlier, Wade and Guthrie retired from the New York firm and the Guthrie firm became its correspondent in England. There is no record that Wade ever came to New York or that Guthrie was here after his visits in 1883 and 1886. On his last visit he had assisted in the organization in 1886 of the American Association of Public Accountants, and both he and Wade were invited to become members of it but neither did so.

Nothing has been learned regarding the place and dates of Wade's other activities or of his birth or death. But Guthrie's obituaries state that Guthrie was born in London in 1841 and went to Manchester at an early age. Although the notices do not tell anything of his education or training as an accountant, one states that in 1875, when he was 35, he was made a partner in Thomas, Wade, Guthrie & Co. and that he was active in many civic and philanthropic movements.

Oscar E. Morton was listed in the New York Directories of 1886 to 1906 and in the list of New York CPA's as well as in the "Recollections." While no record of his birth, education, or training has been found, it is probable that he had been with Barrow for some time—perhaps several years prior to the fall of 1883—and understood not only the accounting work but also that of an actuarial nature. That he was experienced in these fields seems clear because he carried on the work for 18 months after Barrow's death, and promptly after he was displaced late in 1886 an actuary was brought from England. The "Recollections" state that he notified the English partners by cable of Barrow's death and that he was conducting the business of the firm. Thereupon he was made a partner, practically taking the place and interest of Barrow. The Directory therefore listed him in 1886 as at 45 William Street, to which Barrow had removed the firm's office about 1884. Morton applied for a CPA certificate by waiver and became New York CPA No. 78 not long after Anyon became CPA No. 31, both in 1896. Morton continued in practice for 13 years or more, being listed until 1899. Nothing later has been learned.

James Thornley Anyon was born in Preston, England, October 3, 1851. He was educated as an engineer at the Normal College in Manchester. But in 1874 he began an apprenticeship with Charles Tattersoll & Co., accountants, and became an ACA, later FCA. After a period with Thomas, Wade, Guthrie & Co., FCA, of Manchester, he came to New York with Edwin Guthrie on October 25, 1886, and became manager of Barrow, Wade, Guthrie & Co. and a partner in that firm in October, 1887. On or before September 30, 1895, when Wade and Guthrie dissolved the Manchester firm and withdrew from Barrow, Wade, Guthrie & Co., he, perhaps with his New York partners, acquired the interests of the foreign partners. Thereafter he was the head of the firm and during that period it began its nation-wide expansion. During World War I he was Treasurer of Eddystone Ammunition Corporation, acting for the British government.

Very soon after he came here in 1886, Edwin Guthrie told him of his conference with John Heins and John W. Francis in Philadelphia. Anyon then called a meeting of accountants in New York which resulted in the formation of the American Association of Public Accountants, whose name was proposed by him and which he served as Secretary and as a member of the Council. He became CPA No. 31 in 1896, and in 1897 joined the National Society of CPA's and the New York State Society of CPA's. He served about one year, 1897-1898, on the New York Board of Examiners. He contributed articles to various journals and in 1925 published his "Recollections," which, because based only on his memory, is not always accurate as history but is very useful in its mention of persons and incidents. He died February 7, 1929.

While the story of this early firm might be considered as complete at this point, sketches of three other early partners are given because they have not appeared elsewhere.

Edward Henry Sewell was a native of England, place and date not learned. He was trained as an actuary and perhaps was employed in that capacity prior to 1887, when he came to New York to take over the insurance work previously handled by Barrow and Morton. He was made a partner in 1887, at the same time as Anyon. He was a Fellow of AAPA in 1887 and its Vice President in 1889. He returned to England in 1891.

Samuel Hardman Lever was born in Liverpool, England, on April 18, 1869. He came to New York in 1890, was employed by Barrow, Wade, Guthrie & Co., became CPA No. 40 in 1896, and was made a partner in 1898. *The Accountant* of July 16, 1904, stated that he, James T. Anyon, and A. Pyott Spence had formed the firm of Lever, Anyon & Spence with an office at 18 St. Swithin's Lane, London, which had been the location of C. H. Wade & Co. However, he remained in New York until the outbreak of World War I, when the British Government requested his services and he returned to England. For this service he was made a baronet and thereafter was known as Sir Hardman Lever. He retired from the firm in 1922 and died in 1947.

Alexander Pyott Spence was born in Dundee, Scotland, in 1872. He was trained in the office of David Myles, C.A., and became a Scottish C.A. He came to New York in 1899, was employed by Barrow, Wade, Guthrie & Co., and was made a partner in 1904. In 1903 he became Illinois CPA No. 34, joined the Illinois Society of CPA's in 1905, and came into the AAPA through that society. After the death of Mr. Anyon in 1929 he was the senior partner in Barrow, Wade, Guthrie & Co., but ill health caused him to retire. He died April 27, 1931.

CHAPTER 2

HISTORY OF EDUCATION FOR THE PROFESSION

The New York School of Accounts

By THE COMMITTEE ON HISTORY

Prior to the establishment of the School of Commerce, Accounts and Finance of New York University, which opened its doors on October 1, 1900, a much needed facility for the training of recruits for the rapidly growing profession of accountancy was the New York School of Accounts, an enterprise personally conducted by Theodore Koehler, a Certified Public Accountant who had an office in the St. James Building at Broadway and 26th Street, New York City. There had been an earlier school with the same name, which was chartered by the Regents in 1892, and financed and operated by the American Association of Public Accountants in 1893-94. This institution, however, was short-lived and was dormant at the time of the passage of the C.P.A. law in 1896. In *Accountants Directory* and *Who's Who*, 1925, page 540, Mr. Koehler's biographical sketch stated that he "organized and incorporated the New York School of Accounts immediately after enactment of the C.P.A. law, the first school in the United States devoted to the preparation of students for the C.P.A. degree." His booklet, *A New Departure*, 1909, described the school as, "Established, 1897. Incorporated, 1905."

Theodore Koehler was the holder of Certified Public Accountant Certificate No. 76, issued under the New York State law that became effective with the signature of Governor Levi P. Morton on April 17, 1896. He was a member of the State Senate when the C.P.A. bill was introduced and actively advocated its passage. He sensed the need for specialized training in preparation for the new certificate and shortly after the enactment of the law he started a school which offered

---

This is the third of a series of articles on the History of Accountancy in the State of New York, prepared by the Society's Committee on history. The first two articles, published in the March and May, 1949, issues of *The New York Certified Public Accountant* dealt, respectively, with the early development of accountancy in New York State and the genesis of The New York State Society of Certified Public Accountants. The organization and early history of the School of Commerce, Accounts and Finance of New York University were discussed briefly in the first article.

instruction in bookkeeping, accounting theory and practice, auditing and commercial law, on a level high enough to meet the requirements of the new law (which was the first of its kind in the United States).

The school was housed in a room adjoining Mr. Koehler's office and was equipped with high bookkeepers' desks and other appropriate furnishings. Mr. Koehler planned and personally directed the course of study. He was assisted in teaching by his small office staff and by the student-teachers as they progressed in the course. The reading of treatises on accounting and auditing was encouraged. Lectures on commercial law and technical subjects were given by experienced public accountants. Sessions were held in the late afternoon and evening hours. There were no organized classes; instruction was individual and students were permitted to complete the course according to the time and skill which each could devote to it.

The enterprise was a success from the start. Besides Theodore Koehler, the instructors included former students, some of whom were:

Theodora Daub, a student in 1904.
Benedict F. Buhle, a student in 1903 or 1904.
Frederick Haberstroh, a student in 1904.

As lecturers were:

Frank Broaker
Joseph Hardcastle
Arthur W. Smith

Among the students enrolled were the following:

Diedrick P. Bierman
Herbert G. Collier
William D. Cranstoun
Theodore Daub (Koehler)
William Henry Dennis
James J. Driscoll
Edward J. Enthoven
A. S. Fedde
John Fraser
William Fraser
John Gordon
Charles C. Goldsborough
Harold Dudley Greeley
Frederick Haberstroh
Henry Abbott Horne
Orrin R. Judd
Samuel D. Leidesdorf
Harriet B. Lowenstein (Goldstein)
John H. May
Homer S. Pace
William Sheperdson
Alfred J. Stern
Ernest N. Wood

"A New Departure", issued by the School in 1909, shows the following:

Officers:	
President	Theodore Koehler
Vice President	Albert Bierck
Treasurer	Richard M. Chapman
Secretary	Duncan MacInnes

Trustees:

Henry R. M. Cook, CPA	Duncan MacInnes, CPA
Richard M. Chapman, CPA	W. F. Weiss, CPA
Albert B. Bierck, CPA	Theodore Koehler, CPA
Charles H. Stocking, CPA	Franklin Allen, CPA
	William Raimond Baird, LLB

Many of these names will be recognized as certified public accountants who in later years achieved distinction in public accounting and business.

A booklet, issued about 1910, listed 67 students of the School who had already passed the C.P.A. examination. Mr. Koehler was offered an opportunity to join the faculty of the New York University School of Commerce, Accounts and Finance, but preferred to continue his independent teaching.

Theodore Koehler had a colorful career. He was born in the duchy of Schleswig-Holstein, then a part of Denmark, on June 30, 1856, and was educated in the schools of that country. In 1876, as a young man of twenty, he came to the United States, landing in Philadelphia. He was disappointed in not finding the employment which he had reason to expect and undertook such work as he could find. This included representation of an English firm on an exploring expedition to South America and as an exhibitor at the New Orleans Cotton Exposition of 1884.

In 1885, he became head bookkeeper and auditor for the East River Gas Company at Long Island City, New York, a position which he held for about ten years. At about the same time he was employed by a number of business firms to adjust their accounts and later was engaged by the municipal authorities of Long Island City to make an examination of the books of the City Departments covering a period of years. Largely as a result of the reputation he made in these assignments and his contact with local politics, he was nominated and elected in 1893 to represent the City on the Queens County Board of Supervisors and served with distinction for two terms. His name was particularly associated with measures for highway improvement and the construction of a tunnel under Newtown Creek. In 1896 he was elected to the State Senate, serving until 1898. He was a member of the Committees on Finance, Insurance, and Agriculture.

As already noted, one of his early students was Theodora Daub. Later she assisted him as an instructor in the School and also as a co-author of some of his books. Still later they were even more intimately associated when on June 24, 1920, she became Mrs. Theodore Koehler.

Mr. Koehler was a man of boundless energy, a forceful speaker and a prolific writer on accounting subjects. He published "The Accounting Mentor of Theory and Practice" in two volumes; "Manufacturing Accountants Manual" in three volumes; "Municipal Accountants Manual", and a series of thirteen volumes called "The Accounting Quiz Answerer." He died in his seventy-third year on March 27, 1929.

Pace Institute

By THE COMMITTEE ON HISTORY

Looking back over the last fifty years and reviewing the early efforts for accountancy education in New York, one notes an interesting alternation in the procession between the schools which were promoted by associations of accountants and which even at first had relatively large faculties, and the other schools which were founded and largely conducted by only one or two men. The first schools in New York, organized for the purpose of preparing their students for the public practice of accountancy, were the New York School of Accounts (I) 1893-1894, promoted by the American Association of Public Accountants and chartered by the Regents of the University of the State of New York; the New York School of Accounts (II) 1897-1929, founded and conducted by Theodore Koehler, which, though expanded and incorporated in 1905, did not ask for recognition by the Regents; the School of Commerce, Accounts and Finance 1900—promoted by the New York State Society of Certified Public Accountants, organized within New York University and thereby recognized by the Regents; and the Universal Business Institute, organized about 1904 by three accountants and one lawyer.

Prior to 1906, there had also been started at least three coaching courses with the primary object of preparing candidates for CPA examinations. Though the purpose of these courses was thus limited, they were parts of the provision for accountancy education then available and therefore deserve mention here.

The first was that of Frederick Samson Tipson, which began about 1900. He had been educated in one of the English public schools (he was often pictured in cap and gown), had practiced in London, had arrived in New York perhaps about 1890, and became New York CPA No. 84 in 1896. Another such course was that of George A. Law who became New York CPA No. 260 in 1902, and announced his course in

---

This is the fourth of a series of Articles on the History of Accounting in the State of New York, prepared by the Society's Committee on History.

The earlier articles appeared in the March, May, and December, 1949, issues of this publication.

October, 1902. Frank Broaker, New York CPA No. 1 in 1896, and Secretary of the first New York Board of CPA Examiners, may have been the third to offer to prepare students for the examinations. He had attended The College of the City of New York, had worked for John Roundey, a Scottish accountant, and had practiced on his own account from 1887. He had also been a teacher in the first New York School of Accounts during its one year, 1893-1894 and had lectured at the second school of that name, Theodore Koehler's.

The fifth institution for accountancy education in New York, now known as Pace College, like Koehler's New York School of Accounts, was and long remained a private enterprise. During its first three decades it did not seek recognition by the State and although, because of its larger student body, it had a larger faculty, yet like the earlier private school, it was developed very largely by and around one man. As in the case of the Koehler school, it seems fitting to introduce the story of Pace Institute with a brief account of the man who created it.

Homer St. Clair Pace as born in 1879 at Rehoboth, Ohio, and was the son of Prof. John F. Pace, who, it is stated, was a well-known educator in the public school system of Ohio. By 1896, the family had removed to Chase, Michigan, where in that year (when he was 17) Homer Pace was associated with his father as an editor and proprietor of the *Pere Marquette Journal*. It is understood that this activity gave him his first experience in bookkeeping as well as in journalism. Some time later he went to Chicago and held a secretarial position with A. B. Stickney, president of the Chicago Great Western Railway, and he was secretary of the Mason City & Fort Dodge Railroad from April 12, 1901, to January 5, 1907. During the latter part of this period and as early as 1904, he was located at 31 Nassau Street, New York City.

He was a student at Koehler's New York School of Accounts and after passing the Certified Public Accountant Examination in June, 1906, received certificate No. 352 on August 27, 1907, when he had acquired the necessary experience in practice. In 1908, he became a member of the New York State Society of CPA's, and of the American Association (now the American Institute of Accountants), serving as president of the former for two years, 1924-1926. He was also a member of the American Society of Certified Public Accountants.

As a practicing accountant, he was a member of the firms of Pace & Wythes, Pace & Pace, and Pace, Gore & McLaren. He was Deputy Commissioner of Internal Revenue during 1918-1919, and in charge of the Income Tax Unit in Washington. Perhaps it was due in part to his early experience in journalism that for many years he was the owner of the Plandome Press. His activities in accounting literature embraced the authorship of several textbooks on accounting and auditing and the editorship of a series of magazines which will be mentioned later in this story. His interest in history found expression in his collection of old books and maps. In accountancy education his activities extended beyond his own school, and for a time he was a lecturer at Columbia University and a long-time member of the American Association of University Instructors in Accounting, now the American Accounting Association. He died May 22, 1942.

Very shortly after the completion of his studies at the Koehler School, Homer St. Clair Pace with his older brother, Charles Ashford Pace, the two constituting the firm of Pace & Pace, began their work in accountancy education. Charles A. Pace was an attorney and a member of the bars of New York and Ohio, and though he retired from the firm in 1933, he continued to give his advice and counsel until his death on December 12, 1940. Their first enterprise, called the New York Institute of Accountancy, was conducted by them in, and it is understood under the sponsorship of, the 23rd Street Branch of the YMCA at 215 West 23rd Street, New York, beginning in 1906. About the same time the firm established another school in Manhattan which was operated entirely under the firm's auspices at its headquarters in the old Tribune Building, 154 Nassau Street. This school was variously referred to as the Pace School, the Pace Private School, the Pace & Pace School, and Pace Institute of Accountancy. In 1907, a similar school called The Accountancy Institute of Brooklyn was started in the Central Branch of the YMCA at Fulton and Bond Streets, Brooklyn. In 1909, the firm opened similar schools in three other cities, entitled the Baltimore Institute of Accountancy, Washington School of Accountancy, and The Accountancy Institute of Los Angeles.

Some of the facts here assembled were found in the following issues of three periodical publications issued by or for the schools:

Bulletin of New York and Brooklyn Institutes of Accountancy; First issue October 22, 1908, 2 pages 11" x 8", mimeographed, 500 copies.

The Accountancy Student, published for the 6 schools then in operation; First issue October, 1909, 8 pages 9½" x 6", printed.

The Pace Student, published by Pace & Pace, 30 Church Street, N.Y., Sub. $1.00; First issue, December, 1915, 16 pages 11" x 8½", illustrated.

While no one of these periodicals named the editor, probably he was Homer S. Pace, who perhaps was the author of much or all of the contents. *The Pace Student* was continued through 1926, after which *The American Accountant* was published and edited by Homer S. Pace from its first issue February, 1927, 74 pages 12" x 8½", illustrated, Sub. $4.00.

In 1906, there was a dearth of accounting literature compared with that which later became available. At the outset, therefore, the Pace brothers, like other early teachers of accountancy, found it necessary to provide their own text materials. Charles A. Pace developed a series of lectures upon different sections of Commercial Law and Homer S. Pace did the same for Theory and Practice of Accounts. From time to time some lectures were revised or expanded. By 1912 both series were published in sections but some of them were still further revised in later editions. In January, 1916, *The Pace Student* stated that 50 schools were using the Pace educational material.

Upon the establishment of the Washington School of Accountancy, a Bulletin of 63 pages (1909-1910) was issued describing the course of study and listing its faculty. Presumably similar bulletins were published for the other schools but copies are not available for this story. However, the few issues of the first two school organs, the two issues of *Accountants' Directory and Who's Who* and some miscellaneous material, furnished facts about the early faculty and students which while probably not complete have been brought together to show some of the teachers and lecturers.

Some of the early members of the accounting faculty in the Metropolitan District of New York were Philip N. Miller, BA, CPA, a former student who became an instructor in 1909; James F. Farrell, also a former student who lectured during years 1910-1917; Edward J. Enthoven, a graduate of Koehler's school, who became a CPA in 1906; Harold Dudley Greeley, LLM, of N.Y. Bar in 1903, CPA in 1912, was instructor 1911, and after two years was designated Director of Accounting Instruction in 1913. For law, Berton L. Maxfield was instructor in 1908, and Director in 1913. For instruction in English, Horatio Nelson Drury taught during 1913-1921. Frederick Martin

Schaeberle became an administrative aid in 1910, and was admitted to the co-partnership on September 1, 1913.

The schools began early to invite successful practitioners of accountancy and law and leaders in business to address the students in lectures on subjects directly related to their studies or of wider scope and with broadening influence. Two of the early lecturers were J. Pryse Goodwin, CA, CPA, on English Student Societies, October 21, 1908; Cordenio A. Severance, Esq., on Interstate and Intrastate Commerce, delivered on January 22, 1909.

While it seems probable that a majority of Pace students have gone into business, a list of those who have engaged in the public practice of accountancy would be much too long for inclusion here. Below are the names of a few who took the Pace courses and received the New York CPA certificate prior to 1915, when the first of the schools was not quite ten years old. The list does not include any who received his certificate during these years in some other State.

Name	*Pace Course*	*New York Certificate*
James F. Farrell	1908	1909
Philip N. Miller	1910	1909
Richard Fitzgerald	1911	1911
Henry E. Mendes	1911	1912
James F. Hughes	1908	1914
Leroy L. Perrine	1912	1914

In its early days, the social side of Pace Institute was primarily expressed in students' dinners. A copy of the program of the students' dinner held at the Hotel Marseilles in New York, June 6, 1914, appears on page 533 [*pp. 59 and 60*].

In 1920, it was determined to conduct day classes as well as evening classes. Since the Federal Government was then engaged in a rehabilitation program for disabled veterans of World War I, Pace Institute decided to make its day classes available first to these veterans. As opportunity presented itself, such instruction was extended to non-veteran students.

The increase in the scope of the activities and the developing need for registration by the State Education Department emphasized the inadequacy of the partnership form of organization as a permanent basis for the Institute. Accordingly, application for a corporate charter was made to the Regents of the University of the State of New York.

Under date of May 17, 1935, a provisional charter was granted to Homer S. Pace, Frederick M. Schaeberle, Charles T. Bryan, Robert S. Pace, and C. Richard Pace, creating the corporation of Pace Institute. The provisional charter was very broad. It authorized the corporation to conduct schools and classes for the instruction of students in cultural, liberal, professional, and business subjects in the fields of secondary and higher education.

Immediately after receipt of its charter, the corporation made application to the State Education Department for registration of its major courses. On October 31, 1935, the courses in Accountancy Practice were accorded registration as professional courses. This recognized the courses as qualifying students who completed them (and who were otherwise eligible) for admission to the examination for the certificate as Certified Public Accountant in the State of New York. The other major courses were recognized or approved by the Department as courses within the field of higher education.

Under date of February 28, 1947, the charter was amended whereby the corporation was converted to a non-stock basis and the corporate name changed to Pace College.

Pace College had grown to a student body of approximately 5,500 and a faculty of 150, and offered courses on the college level, but it was not able to confer degrees on its graduates because it did not meet the further requirement of the Education Law of the State of New York, that no institution may confer degrees unless it has resources of at least five hundred thousand dollars. By 1948, however, it had accumulated resources sufficient to qualify it in this respect, and on December 17, 1948, the Regents of the University of the State of New York, upon application of the Trustees, granted to Pace College the authority to confer the degree of Bachelor of Business Administration (B.B.A.), in conformity with the rules of the Regents and the regulations of the Commissioner of Education governing higher education.

MENU

TURTLE NECK CLAMS
CREAM OF TOMATOES
CELERY OLIVES
FILET OF SEA BASS SAUTERNE
PARISIENNE POTATOES
ROAST TENDERLOIN OF BEEF
MUSHROOM SAUCE
ROAST SPRING LAMB
MASHED POTATOES GREEN PEAS
SALAD IN SEASON
ICE CREAM CAKE COFFEE

PROGRAM

TOASTMASTER
HAROLD DUDLEY GREELEY, LL.M., C.P.A. (N.Y.)

SPEAKERS

CHARLES W. DIETRICH
BURTON [*sic*] L. MAXFIELD, PH.B., OF THE NEW YORK BAR
CHAS. H. SCHNEPFE, JR., C.P.A. (MD.)
CHARLES A. PACE, OF THE NEW YORK BAR
HOMER S. PACE, C.P.A. (N.Y.)
OTTO S. ESSELBORN
HORATIO N. DRURY, B.A.

GUESTS

GEORGE E. BECK, A.M.
FRANK L. BAILEY
MELSOM S. TUTTLE, B. SCI. ECON.
H. A. TOWNSEND, A.B.

Faculty of
Affiliated Schools of the Metropolitan District

Homer St. Clair Pace, C.P.A., (N.Y.), Practicing Accountant	Accounting, Auditing, Organization, and Applied Economics
Charles Ashford Pace, of the New York and Ohio Bars	Law, Finance, and Organization
Fred'k M. Schaeberle, B.A., C.P.A. (Ohio)	
Harold Dudley Greeley, LL.B., LL.M., C.P.A. (N.Y.)	Accounting
Berton L. Maxfield, Ph.B., of the New York Bar	Law
Harold B. Atkins, M.E., C.P.A. (N.Y.)	Cost Accounting
George F. Bauer, Jr., C.P.A. (N.Y.)	Accounting, Auditing
Robert H. Brown, C.P.A. (N.Y.)	Accounting
Paul G. Burroughs, LL.B. of the New York Bar	Law
Edward J. Enthoven, C.P.A. (N.Y.)	Accounting
Stanley G. H. Fitch, B.S., C.P.A. (N.Y., N.J.)	Accounting, Auditing
James D. Hines, LL.B., of the New York Bar	Accounting
H. H. Haight, C.P.A. (N.Y.)	Accounting, Auditing
Andrew M. Hauser, C.P.A. (N.Y.)	Accounting
Geo. W. Howland	Accounting
James F. Hughes, C.P.A. (N.Y.)	Accounting, Auditing
H. E. Mendes, C.P.A. (N.Y.)	
Homer L. Loomis, B.A., LL.B., of the New York Bar	
Frank C. McKinney, B.A., of the New York Bar	
Philip N. Miller, B.A., C.P.A. (N.Y.)	Accounting, Auditing
C. F. Noyes, C.P.A. (N.Y.)	Accounting, Auditing
Arthur L. Philbrick, C.P.A. (Mo.)	Accounting, Auditing
Albert Reese, B.A., Ph.D., of the New York Bar	Law
W. M. Ross, C.P.A. (N.Y.)	Accounting
C. Roy Snoke, C.P.A. (N.Y.)	Accounting, Auditing
Homer A. Stebbins, Ph.D. of the New York Bar	
H. A. Wythes, C.P.A. (N.Y.)	Accounting, Auditing
Albert F. Young, Jr., C.P.A. (N.Y.)	Accounting, Auditing

The School of Commerce, Accounts, and Finance of New York University

—Its Promotion and Organization

Prior to 1893, the only opportunities open to those who desired to prepare for service as bookkeepers or accountants were work under those who were experienced in those occupations, or the course of study and practice available in many business colleges. That both these ways were useful is evidenced by the many successful men who had acquired their training in one or both ways.

But those in the public practice of accountancy wanted something more, apparently for one or both of two reasons. Many, probably a majority, desired something which would widen and elevate the public understanding of their occupation, then not generally recognized as a profession. One or more methods for this purpose were proposed to the American Association of Public Accountants which had been organized during the winter of 1886-1887, but the methods had not been adopted or had not been successful.

Late in 1891, that Association suddenly had accessions which increased its membership nearly one-half. No explanation was published or even recorded before or while that growth took place. It can be surmised only by the outcome of that growth.

One of the new members was Henry R. M. Cook, who for some years had been with the Board of Education of New York City. At once he was elected to the Council and appointed chairman of a newly formed committee which at first was known as Special Committee. But by February 6, 1892, it was called the Committee on Charter, and its activities and aims were made known.

This disclosed the second reason why something more was wanted. Some influential practitioners wanted not only a more general recognition of the profession but also a greater supply of well-trained assistants. To supply those needs the Association sought and obtained

---

This is the eleventh in a series of articles on the History of Accounting the State of New York. It was prepared by the Society's Committee on History.

from the Regents of the State of New York a two-year charter for the New York School of Accounts.

By the fall of 1893 that School was organized with a Board of Trustees composed of about an equal number of prominent business men and public accountants; with a faculty composed exclusively of accountants in practice except that commercial law was taught by John L. N. Hunt, Esq., of the New York City Board of Education; and with the provision of rooms, furniture, etc., for its activities.

The School was conducted during only the one year, 1893-1894. Its faculty and trustees considered that it was a failure. Absence from the city of the regular teachers had made it necessary to get substitutes probably less well prepared, and only seven students had taken the whole course. While that was discouraging, the teachers could not know that of the five students whose names are known, three would enter upon public practice and two of them become CPA's and members of State Societies. An effort was made to have Columbia University take over the School but that attempt was not successful.

The next effort to provide education for accountancy was after the CPA Law was enacted in 1896. This effort was by Theodore G. C. F. Koehler as told in the December, 1949, issue of *The New York CPA* (v19, p735) who gave it the same name as the earlier one, The New York School of Accounts. But this private institution did not meet the desires of those who wanted public recognition of the importance of the profession.

Here Henry R. M. Cook, who had initiated the movement for the first New York School of Accounts, again came into the picture. At a meeting of the State Society on November 13, 1899, he offered a resolution as follows:

> "Whereas it is the sense of this Society that it is expedient and necessary to the development of the profession of Public Accountancy that the same be established upon an educational basis, as in the case of other professions; and that means should be taken to render the proposition effective, therefore
>
> Resolved, that the President be and he is hereby requested to confer with the Trustees of Columbia University or the University of the City of New York, or other collegiate body with the object of effecting an arrangement for the establishment of a class, and for a technical course of study therein, in the science of accounts, finance and economy, business practice, commercial law and such other subjects necessary to the special education of persons desiring to enter the profession and to become Certified Public Accountants.
>
> Resolved, that the President be empowered in his discretion to invite the cooperation of kindred societies in this State and of members of the profession

> interested in the future success of accountancy; to the end that strong effort be made to effectuate the objects of these Resolutions and thereby strengthen the profession."

The foregoing preamble and resolutions are here quoted from pages 21-22 of the Ten Year Book, 1897-1906, which also shows that they were adopted. While not so stated it is probable that they had been approved by the Directors.

At the next meeting of the Society on December 11, 1899, the record was:

> "The President reported that in accordance with the resolution passed at the last meeting he had conferred with the heads of the two universities.
>
> President Low of Columbia had suggested that a curriculum be prepared which would be available in the proposed special course in Finance as outlined by the Chamber of Commerce.
>
> Chancellor MacCracken of New York University had asked that the proposal be outlined more fully which had been done in a letter dated December 11."

The Society ordered that the letter be entered in full in its minutes. Later it was printed on pages 23-25 of the Ten Year Book, but too long to be quoted here.

At that meeting also the Society approved the Presidents' action and authorized a special committee of five to be known as the Conference Committee on University; and to be empowered to confer with the Universities with a view to the establishment of a School of Accounts. This committee consisted of Henry R. M. Cook, chairman, C. W. Haskins, J. R. Loomis, A. O. Kittridge and Leon Brummer.

Thereafter no mention of the matter was made in the Society minutes until October 7, 1900, when reports were received from Chairman Cook and President Haskins, both showing that the desired result had been attained. But during the intervening ten months there must have been conferences and correspondence as to the scope and details of the curriculum, the hours to be given to each subject, the selection of the faculty, the fees for tuition and many minor though important details. Almost surely records had been made of those actions. But recently no such records could be found at the office of the State Society or at the University and both Cook and Haskins were deceased. Inquiries at many places finally developed the fact that there had been such records and probably what had become of them.

It was learned that while Charles Waldo Haskins was working upon the organization of the School he had used as his secretary for that work Emory J. Banta, perhaps 45 years of age who though educated as a lawyer was not in practice. The only one who remembered him and his service with Haskins was Howard B. Cook, but he did not know what had become of Banta or what disposition had been made of his files.

But it was found that some years after Haskins' death, Banta had wished to dispose of his files on this matter and had given them to a friend, Herbert F. Vaughan, a graduate of the School in 1906. But Vaughan died in 1932 and his widow not knowing of anyone who might use them had carted away as rubbish a trunkful of Banta's papers including correspondence, memoranda, addresses, etc., of Mr. Haskins. The authority for this account of their disposal is an oral statement by Mrs. Vaughan to her brother, Henry A. Horne. Since all members of the Committee have died it is probable that the details of their actions prior to June 25, 1900, may never be learned.

But without knowing what had gone before there is a record of what had been accomplished before or by June 25, 1900, when the Committee submitted to the Trustees of New York University its proposed curriculum and other details including its pledge to provide a faculty for the course, all as shown on pages 28-33 of the Society's Ten Year Book.

The University as represented by a Committee appointed with power decided on July 28, 1900, to incorporate the proposed school. And on October 1st the School of Commerce, Accounts and Finance commenced operation with a faculty provided as follows:

<table>
<tr><td colspan="2">By the University—</td></tr>
<tr><td>Chancellor . . . .</td><td>Henry M. McCracken [sic] DD,LLD</td></tr>
<tr><td>Commercial Law . . .</td><td>Various professors of the Law School for the subjects of Trusts, Finance, Sales & Agency, Partnership, Bills & Notes, Insurance, etc.</td></tr>
<tr><td colspan="2">By the State Society—</td></tr>
<tr><td>Dean . . . .</td><td>Charles Waldo Haskins CPA</td></tr>
<tr><td>History of Accountancy</td><td>Charles Waldo Haskins CPA</td></tr>
<tr><td>Auditing . . . .</td><td>Charles Waldo Haskins CPA, and Ferdinand W. Lafrentz CPA</td></tr>
</table>

Theory of Accounts .	Charles Ezra Sprague MA, PhD, CPA, and Anson O. Kittridge CPA
Practical Accounting .	Henry R. M. Cook CPA, and Leon Brummer CPA

Although the State Society's interest in the School continued as evidenced by its gifts of funds for the School's library and by its many members who served the School as professors, instructors or lecturers, probably its greatest contribution to the School was its effort to promote and establish the School as here briefly recited.

As previously stated herein none of these details were found in the records at the University. However confirmation of the Society's initiation of the project was given in "New York University: 1832-1932" which on page 356 stated:

> "The New York State Society of Certified Public Accountants deserves the credit for conceiving the idea of the School and shaping the plan; Chancellor MacCracken deserves almost equal credit for being broad-minded and far-sighted enough to admit this new and experimental School into full fellowship with the old and successful Schools of the University. There was no endowment; he merely had the assurance of the sponsors that no deficit would result. * * *
>
> "In 1900, however, the idea of professional training for business was generally looked upon with skepticism, if not with actual derision, not only in academic but in business circles. Fortunately, the men who approached Chancellor MacCracken were men of high character and deep sincerity, whose business success was proof that they were not visionaries."

The City College of New York: A History of Beginnings

By THE COMMITTEE ON HISTORY

A mild Saturday afternoon in January, 1849, marked the celebration in Manhattan of a significant *first*. At Lexington Avenue and Twenty-third Street a new institution of learning was opening under the name of the Free Academy. Dr. S. Willis Rudy tells us in his history of The College of the City of New York that this school was "the first municipal institution for free higher education to appear on this globe."

Though for strategic reasons it was called an Academy, from the day it opened its doors it offered a full collegiate course, and from its beginning it gave free daytime instruction to all who were qualified for admission.

Genesis of the College

The City had set up a Board of Education in 1842. An early president of the Board, elected in 1846, was Townsend Harris. He was a successful crockery merchant, a self-educated man devoted to the cause of education, a linguist, a champion of popular democracy and, like another illustrious New Yorker, an enthusiastic fire buff. He had an abiding desire to sponsor the founding of a college which would be open gratuitously to persons who had been pupils in the public schools of the city and county of New York and who met standards of intellectual ability.

His determined efforts bore fruit. On May 7, 1847, Governor John Young, whose early education had been won with difficulty, signed a bill which provided for a referendum to be held a month later, in which the City's voters should decide whether or not they wanted such an Academy. On June 7, the people went to the polls and voted for the bill in the generous proportions of six to one.

This is the twenty-first in a series of articles on the History of Accounting in the State of New York. It was prepared by the Society's Committee on History.

The new building in which the opening exercises were held that January day in 1849 was designed by James Renwick, the architect who designed Grace Church and St. Patrick's Cathedral. Though necessarily simple and practical, it followed the architectural pattern of a Gothic Town Hall of the Netherlands, perhaps in tribute to the Dutch Republic which had founded New Amsterdam.

The Early Curriculum

In general, the early curriculum was that of the typical college of the period. Its particular divergence was in the greater stress laid upon practical instruction, especially mechanical, scientific, and business subjects. Among the studies available to early pupils were mathematics, history, composition and declamation, elements of moral science, the Constitution of the United States, drawing, bookkeeping and writing, phonography (shorthand), and the Latin, French, and Spanish languages. It was one of the first colleges to give the same importance to modern as to ancient languages, and to give English the greatest emphasis of all. Drawing was included "in view of its varied and practical uses." While offering its students a full opportunity to acquire a literary education, it also had a strong program in chemistry, mathematics, civil engineering, and business subjects.

To accountants it is significant that from the first year of its existence the Academy included bookkeeping among the studies offered, in accordance with its purpose, as stated by the Executive Committee, of qualifying young men for mercantile pursuits.

The first graduates received their diplomas at ceremonies in Niblo's Garden in July, 1853, and were in addition stated to be "worthy of the degree of Bachelor of Arts" and entitled to receive the degree "when the Board shall be authorized to confer it." In April of the following year the State Legislature granted this permission, thereby conferring upon the Academy the full powers and prerogatives of a college.

It was not until 1866, however, that the word *college* became part of the official title. In that year the Legislature changed the name to The College of the City of New York, a designation which it retained until 1926. By New Yorkers this designation was often shortened to City College or C.C.N.Y.

In 1871 the College made a new approach to the problem of practical business education for younger pupils who could not remain in school more than a year. It created a separate Introductory Department which provided a special one-year Commercial Course which included such subjects as modern languages, arithmetic, bookkeeping, elementary physics, composition, penmanship, phonography, geometry, and business transactions. The classicists, however, objected to the presence of these younger students and to some of the courses offered. Because of their opposition the work of the Introductory Department began to disintegrate around 1881, and finally was discontinued.

Another facet of the problem was that from the beginning many of the regularly matriculated students were unable to complete the four-year course because the need to earn a living forced them to leave after a year or two of instruction. As early as 1874, the administration broached the idea of an evening session, but the Executive Committee vetoed the proposal as an unprecedented departure.

Evening Session Degree Work

Nevertheless, in the early nineteen hundreds, the College initiated another of its *firsts*. It established what is said to be the first night college in the United States to offer a full collegiate course leading to the baccalaureate degree. At that time Columbia and New York Universities and the University of Wisconsin were conducting night courses in special subjects only. City College alone, it is believed, conferred degrees earned in the evening session.

Classes began in 1909. The enrollment at that time was 200. By 1913 it had increased to 863. Not only in numbers but in seriousness of purpose the evening students were a promising group.

In an experiment to determine whether the College might not be of even greater service to the community, the Board voted in 1912 to admit special non-matriculated students. And in 1914 it voted that city employees, even though not high school graduates, be permitted to study in the Evening Session upon their passing certain examinations.

Establishment of the School of Business and Civic Administration

In 1912, Dr. John H. Finley, then entering his tenth successful year as President of the College, broached a project which had long occupied his thoughts—the establishment of a school of Business and Civic Administration at the downtown location. Columbia had moved uptown in 1894 and New York University in 1896. In 1906, following their example, City College had moved its operations to an uptown site.

The Trustees entered upon the first steps immediately through an agreement with Mayor Gaynor, under which the College surrendered its Twenty-second Street site to the City for a new Children's Court building, receiving in return funds needed to rehabilitate the Twenty-third Street building in order that it might serve as temporary housing for the new division. At that time, Jacob H. Schiff, a member of the New York Chamber of Commerce, was pushing a project to raise a half million dollars for the purpose of establishing a College of Commerce in New York. Bernard M. Baruch, '89, then a Trustee of the College, conferred with the members of the Chamber of Commerce, and President Finley approached, not only Mr. Schiff but, among others, Andrew Carnegie, Thomas W. Lamont, and Thomas C. Platt, in the hope of inducing them to found the school at the Twenty-third Street site. However, the Trustees and the Chamber of Commerce could not agree on the terms of joint control and curricular organization, and the project fell through.

In May, 1916, Governor Whitman approved the Fertig Bill, which had been drafted by an alumnus, M. Maldwin Fertig. This Act permitted the College to award vocational diplomas and degrees, to charge fees for special courses, and to extend special privileges and educational advantages to non-matriculated students. In that year the College organized a Division of Vocational Subjects and Civic Administration and established a curriculum leading to the Diploma of Graduate in Accountancy. Professor Frederick Bertrand Robinson (who later became the fifth President of the College) was named to be its Director. This was the nucleus from which the School of Business and Civic Administration developed.

Soon it became apparent that not one faculty, but several separate faculties, would be best suited to the work of the College. On June 24, 1919, Professor Robinson was selected to be Dean of the School of Business and Civic Administration. In 1920, the school emerged as a regularly organized academic institution with full degree-granting powers. It offered courses leading to the B.B.A. and M.B.A. degrees. In January, 1926, the State Board of Regents listed its degrees as fully approved.

On December 4, 1928, Mayor Walker laid the cornerstone of a new eight-story building at Twenty-third Street for the School of Business and Civic Administration. The College had asked for a larger building, and at the ceremonies the Mayor promised to do all he could to secure funds to add the additional eight stories which were part of the original plan. Sixteen days later the Board of Estimate appropriated $875,000 for this purpose, and in due time the additional eight stories were superimposed upon the steel framework of the eight then in progress. This is the building as it stands today.

The Municipal College System

It was Dr. Robinson who prepared a bill for the Legislature, approved by Governor Smith on April 16, 1926, which set up a Board of Higher Education to administer the municipal colleges. These then included City College and Hunter College. Brooklyn College was not organized as an independent unit until 1930, and Queens College until 1937. The Act also provided that the name The College of the City of New York should now be applied to the entire corporation administered by the Board of Higher Education. In view of this provision, the Trustees of the College, which had been known by that name since 1866, voted to change the name to The City College, a change which entailed a minimum of adjustment, as it left the familiar designations of City College and C.C.N.Y. undisturbed.

The Early Accounting Faculty

In the early days, 1915 to 1927, accounting instruction at the new division was under the jurisdiction of the Department of Economics.

Dr. Lynn Mateer Saxton (B.S., Lafayette, 1897; M.S., 1900; Pd.M., New York University, 1908; Ph.D., 1909) taught the earliest classes. Although his service as an accounting teacher extended only from 1915 to 1941, he had been on the faculty since 1903. His special subjects in the accounting field were auditing and advanced accounting problems. He was the author of several monographs in his field and was writing a book on advanced accounting problems at the time of his death in 1941.

Among the other accounting teachers who served before 1917 were Edward L. Suffern, DeWitt Carl Eggleston, George K. Hinds, Paul-Joseph Esquerre, Myron A. Finke, and Oscar J. Sufrin.

Edward L. Suffern, New York CPA No. 65, joined the faculty in 1916. He was a partner in the public accounting firm of Loomis, Suffern & Fernald and was to become a President of the New York State Society of CPAs. He died April 13, 1925.

Professor DeWitt C. Eggleston became a member of the Evening Session in 1916. A New York CPA and the author of many accounting texts, he taught cost accounting, advanced cost accounting, stock and bond brokerage accounting, commodity brokerage accounting, and bank accounting.

George K. Hinds held degrees from Ohio Northern and New York Universities and was also a New York CPA (No. 388). A member of the firm of Klein, Hinds & Finke, he came in 1916 to teach judicial accounting (including wills, estates, and bankruptcy), as well as corporation accounting, and was, in 1923, to organize the school's first "Income Tax Laboratory," where students were taught to prepare individual, corporation, partnership, and fiduciary federal and New York State income tax returns.

Many accountants will remember *Paul-Joseph Esquerre* as a colorful person. He was a New York CPA and held a B-ès-L from the University of France. He came in 1917 to teach accounting theory and problems. He, too, was the author of several books. He also conducted a school in which he coached candidates for the CPA examinations.

Myron A. Finke, a C.C.N.Y. alumnus and also a CPA and a member of the public accounting firm of Klein, Hinds & Finke, taught accounting systems and, later, advanced accounting theory and problems.

Oscar J. Sufrin was a graduate of New York University, a New York CPA, and a member of the Bar. He served twenty-five years as lecturer and instructor in accountancy. He also served in World War II as commander of the overseas staging area at Fort Hamilton, with the rank of Lieutenant Colonel. His health broke down while he was in service and in 1949 he died, without having returned to the College staff.

The first separate listing of the accountancy teachers appears in the catalog of 1917-1918. As will be seen, it includes not only those named above, but an impressive number of others as well:

David Berdon, B.C.S., New York University, 1914; C.P.A. (New York), 1917

Raymond W. Bourke, C.P.A. (New York), 1912; Accountant, Department of Finance, New York City

Robert H. Brown, C.P.A. (New York), 1910; Accountant, Department of Finance, New York City

James J. Donovan, Accountant; Department of Finance, New York City

D. Carl Eggleston, M.E., Brown University, 1905; C.P.A. (New York), 1908

Paul-Joseph Esquerre, B-ès-L, University of France; C.P.A. (New York); Head of the Post-Graduate School of Accountancy

Myron A. Finke, A.B., College of the City of New York, 1906; C.P.A. (New York), 1916

H. G. Friedman, A.B., University of Cincinnati, 1904; Ph.D., Columbia, 1908; formerly Chief of Division of Accounts, Public Service Commission for the First District of New York

Lewis Gompers, Jr., C.P.A. (New York)

George Kent Hinds, B. Ped., Ohio Northern University, 1906; M.A. (Hon.), 1908; LL.B., New York University, 1905; C.P.A. (New York), 1907

Samuel C. Hyer, C.P.A. (New York); Accountant, Department of Finance, New York City

Abraham Jablow, B.S., College of the City of New York, 1904; Accountant, Committee on Education, Board of Estimate and Apportionment, New York City

Simon Loeb, B.C.S., New York University, 1908; C.P.A. (New York), 1916

Frank E. Mandel, B.S., New York University, 1911; C.E., 1915; C.P.A. (New York), 1916

Meyer Parmet, B.C.S., New York University, 1909; C.P.A. (New York), 1912; Accountant, Department of Finance, New York City

John B. Payne, C.P.A. (New York); Auditor's Department, Board of Education, New York City

Wolf Scheinberg, B.C.S., New York University, 1913, LL.B., C.P.A. (New York), 1913; Accountant, Department of Finance, New York City

Edward L. Suffern, C.P.A. (New York)

Oscar J. Sufrin, B.C.S.; C.P.A. (New York), 1917

It is interesting to note that, appropriately, several of these instructors were associated with municipal accounting, and specifically with the accounts of the City of New York. Three different courses in municipal accounting were given by *Robert H. Brown*, as well as a course in auditing. One of his courses was designated "Municipal Departmental Accounting in the City of New York."

Simon Loeb, a member of the firm of Loeb & Troper, who was also to become a President of the New York State Society of CPAs, lectured on auditing.

Meyer Parmet was an instructor in accountancy, specializing in corporation accounting and financial statement analysis.

The catalog also listed these lecturers and consultants, who, with nine assistants, conducted war emergency courses in commercial practice:

Joseph J. Klein, B.S., College of the City of New York, 1906; A.M. New York University, 1910; Ph.D., 1911; C.P.A. (New York)

Harriett B. Lowenstein, L.L.B., C.P.A. (New York)

Reuben Weinstein, B.S., College of the City of New York, 1907

The purpose of these courses was to train older men and women in clerical procedures to replace young clerks and bookkeepers then entering the armed services. Felix M. Warburg, a partner in Kuhn, Loeb & Co., became chairman. Several hundred students were enrolled. Classes met at the Twenty-third Street building and in the Assembly Hall of the Commerce and Trade Association.

Dr. Klein and Miss Lowenstein organized the courses. Dr. Klein is a former president of the New York State Society of CPAs and a partner in the firm of Klein, Hinds & Finke. From 1916 to 1918, he taught accounting, accounting systems, and auditing, and in 1919, under the sponsorship of the United States Treasury Department, offered the first course in federal income taxation to be given in any American college.

Miss Lowenstein (Now Mrs. Jonah J. Goldstein) was an attorney as well as one of the earliest women CPAs. A previous article by the Committee on History, *The First Woman C.P.A.* (Christine Ross), touched briefly on some of her achievements.

That the College was, from the beginning, mindful of the benefits to be derived from special lectures relating to fields that concern the professional auditor is evidenced by the following list, from the same catalog, of special lectures in auditing and systems:

C. J. Morgan: The Moon-Hopkins Devices
H. J. Miller: The Burroughs Adding Machine
M. E. O'Brien: The Comptometer
L. A. Wolfe: The Elliott-Fisher Devices
Myron A. Finke, A.B., C.P.A.: Accounting Systems for Advertising Agencies
Ernest Katz: Systems for Department Stores
D. Stern: Underwood Typewriter Devices
Henry B. Fernald, C.P.A.: Mining Accounting
John B. Briggs: Filing Systems
Edwin Mayer, B.C.S.: Accounting Accounting [*sic*] Systems for Bankers

The 1919-1920 catalog shows the following additions to the accounting faculty:

Lecturer on public utilities accounting:
Milton B. Ignatius, LL.B., Union University, 1911; LL.M., 1913

Instructors in accounting:
James J. Donovan, C.P.A. (New Hampshire), 1918
James E. Tallent, B.S., Cooper Union, 1913; C.P.A. (New York), 1916
A. G. Belding, B.S., New York University, 1904; C.P.A. (New York), 1902
Leonard Blakey, B.S., Beloit, 1904; Ph.D., Columbia, 1912

Special instructors in accounting:
David Miller, B.S., College of the City of New York, 1909; C.P.A. (New York), 1917
John Linker, B.S., College of the City of New York, 1900; LL.B., New York University, 1903; M.A., 1911
William H. Burns
Benjamin Freeman, A.B., College of the City of New York, 1905; C.P.A. (New York), 1908
John F. Hickey, C.P.A. (New York), 1912
Conrad J. Saphier, B.C.S., New York University, 1917; M.C.S., 1919

Tutors in accounting;
Charles R. Taylor, B.C.S., New York University, 1913
David Berk, B.S., College of the City of New York, 1918
Morris C. Troper, A.B., College of the City of New York, 1914; B.C.S., New York University, 1917; M.C.S., 1918
Benjamin L. Blau, B.S., College of the City of New York, 1918
Benjamin Harrow, B.A., New York University, 1913
Meyer J. Ostrow, C.P.A. (New York), 1916
Ulysses S. Tasch, A.B., College of the City of New York, 1907; LL.B., New York University, 1912
Louis Weinstein, B.C.S., New York University, 1915; C.P.A. (New York), 1918

Instructor in bookkeeping:
Simon J. Jason, A.B., College of the City of New York, 1906; LL.B., New York University, 1909; M.A., 1917

The same catalog lists four instructors in the Brooklyn Branch of the Evening Session:

Instructors in accounting:
John B. Payne, C.P.A. (New York)
William N. Conant

Special instructors in accounting:
Clarence E. Cowles
Leon A. Merrill, C.P.A. (New York), 1912

The Department of Accountancy

From these beginnings the school expanded rapidly and on June 2, 1927, soon after Dr. Robinson became President, the Trustees established a separate Department of Accountancy and appointed Professor George Monroe Brett as its first Chairman.

Professor Brett was a native of Maine and a graduate of Bowdoin College. From the faculty of New York University he came to City College in 1906, where he remained until his death on November 7, 1941. In the earlier years of the school, he and Dr. Saxton taught the classes in advanced accounting. In addition to his appointments as

Professor and Head of the Department of Accountancy and Curator of the College, he conducted courses in accounting and actuarial science for the Metropolitan Life Insurance Company.

At his death, Dr. Harry L. Kunzleman succeeded him as Department Chairman. Dr. E. I. Fjeld took over the post in 1947 and was succeeded in 1950 by Dr. Emanuel Saxe, who, in September, 1956, relinquished it to Dr. Stanley B. Tunick, in order to take office as Dean of the School.

Dr. Saxe is a New York CPA and a member of the New York Bar. A City College alumnus, he also holds degrees of Doctor of Jurisprudence and Ph.D., from New York University. He came to the City College faculty in 1928 and has written several books and numerous articles on accounting. For ten years to October 1956, he served as editor of *The New York Certified Public Accountant*.

In the meantime, the school had been renamed, Bernard M. Baruch, C.C.N.Y. '89, had always been a staunch supporter of City College and an advocate of democratic education. He had never missed an opportunity to express his affection for the public schools and the free public college which started him on a career that is envied by many and is spectacular by any standards. Honoring one of the most illustrious of many illustrious City College alumni, in 1953 the school adopted the name of Bernard M. Baruch School of Business and Public Administration.

Early Accounting Coaching Courses

By the late NORMAN E. WEBSTER, CPA

Soon after the enactment of the New York CPA Law in 1896 there were several efforts to provide opportunities for accounting study. Although the aim of each was to offer to students instruction in the principles and use of accounts, the programs differed in details. Some, called schools or institutes, were formally organized, with faculties for different subjects and with courses to run two or more years. This instruction was planned to be broad and was not designed primarily as preparation for the CPA examinations. Stories of three institutions of this class have been published in THE NEW YORK CERTIFIED PUBLIC ACCOUNTANT as follows: New York School of Accounts (Koehler's) (December 1949); Pace Institute (now Pace College) (September 1950); and School of Commerce, Accounts and Finance, New York University (April 1953). Later, additional schools were established, but this story is limited to early schools whose programs were known as coaching courses. They were usually centered in or even confined to one or a few instructors, were planned for shorter periods, and included only incidentally matters which a candidate might not meet in the CPA examinations. Among them were these:

Frederick Samson Tipson, or National School of Accounts. George Azro Low (apparently no other title used). Universal Business Institute, Inc. (corporate designation). Frank Broaker, or The Technique of Accountics, Inc.

Before 1900 there were few if any opportunities for instruction in any branches of accountancy except the bookkeeping courses offered by the business colleges, which, though useful, did not go far enough. They qualified all or some of their students as bookkeepers but not as auditors. They gave instruction in business customs but not in the

---

The first draft of this article was prepared by Norman E. Webster as part of the continuing program of history studies undertaken by our Society's Committee on History. Subsequent to Mr. Webster's death, the Committee on History (Henry Lieberman and Leo L. Tauritz, current and predecessor chairmen, respectively) undertook the assignment of editing the manuscript preparatory to submitting it for publication. Our readers may wish to refer to the article "Norman Edward Webster" which was prepared by the Committee and published in the April 1957 issue of this magazine.

statutory or common law provisions under which the customs had developed.

THE TIPSON COURSE OR NATIONAL SCHOOL OF ACCOUNTS

Frederick Samson Tipson probably furnished the data for the biographical sketch in FINANCIAL RECORD of November 10, 1898, which was supplemented by a recent letter from his son and by information obtained from a few other sources.

He was born in Twickenham, England, in 1858 and attended Reading Grammar School. Probably he studied elsewhere, because in 1881, when 23, he went to Georgetown, British Guiana, where he taught mathematics and Greek in a college and was organist in a Catholic cathedral. In 1885 he returned to England and after two years at Cambridge University received the degree of Bachelor of Music. Before 1891 he had received a mercantile training and had assisted as a junior on audits. In BUSINESS of November 1901, he referred to himself as "late of Cheapside, London."

He came to New York in 1891, where, his son states, he immediately started as an accountant. However, his first listing in the New York Directory was in 1897 as "Sec., 441 Pearl." But in later issues he was listed as public accountant, at 17 Park Row in 1899, 21 Park Row in 1900, 150 Nassau in 1902, 5 Beekman Street in 1906, and 227 Waverly Place—his home—in 1912. In 1896, soon after the passage of the CPA law, he became CPA No. 84, and in 1897 he was a Fellow of the American Association of Public Accountants and a Governor of an organization entitled, National Society of Certified Public Accountants in the United States. All that was learned of his practice is contained in (1) the FINANCIAL RECORD 1898 sketch—that he had "specially studied and practiced insurance work" and "built up a large practice," and (2) in his advertisements in BUSINESS, issues of December 1901, to August 1902, viz.: "Experts supplied for all branches of accounting, in or out of city." All that is known of his assistants in his practice is that, as will be shown, one of them passed the CPA examination after having studied with him.

The earliest announcement found of the Tipson Course was in BUSINESS, issue of October 1900, page 777, and was as follows:

> CPA examination candidates thoroughly prepared by correspondence or personal instruction. The only successful candidate at the last examination was coached by FRED'K S. TIPSON, Certified Public Accountant, Park Row Building.

Other items show that the successful candidate was Howard Greenman who, then and apparently for some time before, was on Tipson's accounting staff. So perhaps this success suggested to Tipson that he offer his coaching to others.

The administration of the course was apparently all handled by Tipson. This may not have been difficult, as the students were few at any one time. The instruction also seems to have been only by Tipson, whether by mail or by personal contact of the student with the teacher. For this, Tipson may have been well prepared by his experience as a student and as a teacher in the schools and colleges previously mentioned. And his methods were metaphorically suggested by his response to a question as to the meaning of the word *coach*. His answer, as given in BUSINESS WORLD of January, 1906, was: "Well, a coach, of course, is a vehicle constructed to carry people along. I do this in the preparatory work for CPA examinations."

As for the scope of the course, it was stated generally in his advertising and in the above quotation about his work as a coach. But in detail it was presented in the books he published, which apparently were prepared from the less formal notes he had used with students. These were: Theory of Accounts (1902, 124 pages; 1921, 1922 editions, 271 pages); Commercial Law (1903, 126 pages); and Auditing (1904, 149 pages).

He also published the following short articles: The Profit and Loss Account (BUSINESS, November 1901); Relation of Auditor to Bookkeeper (BUSINESS WORLD, May 1903); and Hotel Accounts (BUSINESS WORLD, July 1904).

The fees for his instruction were stated in his advertisement in the June 1903 issue of BUSINESS WORLD to be as follows:

> TERMS, $100, payable in four monthly installments of twenty-five dollars each. Any person failing to pass the first examination will be prepared for the next one without additional charge. Text book containing all questions set at previous examinations on the Theory of Accounts with full answers and explanations, $3.00. References to successful candidates in N. Y., Conn., Cal., Penn., and Md. The only successful candidate June 1900, was coached by FREDERICK S. TIPSON.

In an interview in BUSINESS WORLD of January 1906, he said of his students:

> Speaking from memory and including those candidates who have come to me for special instruction in practical accounting only, I find by my books that I have passed

upwards of fifty candidates. . . .I have at the present time, I believe, about fifteen candidates preparing for the CPA examinations by correspondence in various States.

No list of these 65 students has been found, but from magazine items, etc., the names of 27 have been learned, of whom two were nonresident students. Of the 25 resident students, 23 became New York CPAs. One of the students, Harry Clark Bentley, attended only a few sessions but later enrolled in the second class at the School of Commerce, Accounts and Finance of N.Y.U., graduated in 1903, and became Connecticut CPA No. 2 in 1908. Leon Emile Pairaudeau, a brother-in-law of Tipson, by whom he was employed before and after 1897, seems not to have taken the examination, though he had become an Associate of the American Association of Public Accountants in 1892. And of the 2 nonresident students, one Arthur L. Patrick became Ohio CPA No. 63 in 1908, while the other, Gustavus Jacobson, who said he represented the Tipson course in Chicago, never became a CPA, though he was an Associate of the AAPA in 1902 and practiced as a public accountant.

Of the 27 students, later records show that 17 had engaged in public practice (10 as partners in firms, 4 alone, 3 as staff employees) while 3 were in private employ, 4 were teachers and 3 were in occupations which were not learned.

But the 22 who became CPAs before 1906 were less than half of the 50 he said he "had passed" at that time. And the 2 nonresidents may not have been included amongst the 15 he then had as students by mail. The number of his students, although not known, was probably many more than 65. This opinion is supported by the statement of one student who wrote:

His method of teaching was sound; if he thought a student could not make the grade, he would discontinue tutoring him for he believed that he should devote his energy only to those who in his judgment would become worthwhile practitioners.

No later mention of Tipson's coaching course was found. Probably he did not continue it long after 1906, if at all. Apparently also he discontinued public practice, because a former student wrote that "a couple of years after I obtained my certificate he became a member of my staff for a short time." At some time between 1915 and 1920 the Tipson family moved to Westfield, New Jersey. He died there or in New York in 1921.

GEORGE AZRO LOW

Although George Azro Low was the second accountant to offer to prepare students for the CPA examinations, very little is known of him. The earliest mention and the only one giving his middle name was in the 1902 College Department Report, page 100, which showed that he passed the 12th examination, June 24-25, 1902, after three earlier trials. These earlier examinations may have been any of the eleven from December 16, 1896 to January 28-29, 1902.

Later items gave his name as George A. Low, but the earliest one in BUSINESS (September 1902, p. 410) showed that the *A* stood for Azro. Listings in directories and Low's advertisements in BUSINESS to and including 1911 give some facts about him.

However, a George A. Low was listed in directories of 1891 to 1894, which gave 178 West End Avenue as his home address but did not state his occupation. The 1925 Accountant's Directory and Who's Who listed George A. Low, CPA (N. Y.), at 45 Broadway, but the only earlier edition, that of 1920, did not list him, though both editions had been prepared by the same compiler. Nothing has been learned of his birth, general education before 1901, or occupation after 1911.

He advertised his practice from October 1902 to April 1903, as a public accountant and auditor, and as a CPA thereafter to February 1907. He studied with Tipson and took four examinations, becoming Junior Accountant No. 260 in 1902 and receiving a CPA certificate of the same number in May 1903, after he had the required experience, though he was then in practice alone.

In October 1902, he advertised his coaching in BUSINESS as follows:

> Students prepared for CPA Examinations, George A. Low, Public Accountant and Auditor, 130 Nassau Street, New York City.

He was then a junior accountant, probably with less than one year of experience, in the employ of a public accountant. In the subsequent May issue of BUSINESS he changed the advertisement by substituting Certified Public Accountant, his title, and by giving his address as 45 Broadway. His advertisement as thus changed was carried to November 1906.

Nothing was found regarding the number of his students or the names of any of them.

UNIVERSAL BUSINESS INSTITUTE, INC., AND THE UNIVERSAL SOCIETY OF ACCOUNTANTS

Universal Business Institute, Inc. differed from the earlier coaching courses in that it was incorporated. It had four instructors from the start, and it was planned predominantly as a correspondence course. But like the others it offered instruction in the four subjects of the CPA examinations.

Its promoter was Edward Malcolm Hyans, who had experience in instruction by mail and was a signer of its certificate of incorporation which was dated March 10, 1904. It was planned as a preparation for the CPA examinations and had as instructors three accountants and a lawyer, one each for the four subjects. It seems that the organization was more than an educational institution, because it published a book on each subject prepared by the instructor.

Sketches of the three accountants are here given in tabular form (missing data being represented by dashes):

	HYANS, EDWARD M.	WOLFF, ARTHUR	MOULL, JOHN
Birth date	Nov. 28, 1878	July 23, 1870	—
Birth place	New York, N. Y.	Vienna, Austria	—
School:			
General Public		Comm. H. S., Paris	—
Accounting	Int'l Correspondence Schools	Robt. Lycee, Paris Tipson Course	— Tipson Course
CPA	294, N. Y., 1905 276, N. J., 1908	299, N. Y., 1905 294, Cal., 1923	224, N. Y., 1903
UBI:			
Officer	President and General manager	Director	Director
Teacher	Theory of Accounts	Practical Acct'g	Auditing
Author	Theory, 1905, 4 later	Practical, 1905, 3 later	1903 and later
Early Experience	Bookkeeper	Banking	Arbuckles
Practice	Wolff & Hyans, 1904 Certified Audit Co., 1918	Wolff & Hyans 1904 Certified Audit Co., 1918	Alone —
Member:			
Institute of Accountants	Yes	—	1872
NYSS	1906	1905	1909
AAPA	1906	1905	1909
American Society	Yes	1926	Yes
Died:			
Date	—	Nov., 1946	Feb., 1938
Place	—	Los Angeles	Bloomfield, N. J.

Mayer B. Cushner, who had a degree of LLB and was a member of the New York Bar, taught commercial law and wrote a book on the subject, which was published in 1908. Hyans wrote that Cushner died about 1914.

The Institute's advertising indicated that a prospectus was issued, probably annually, but no copy has been found. Its advertisements in BUSINESS, October to December 1904, the earliest found, said:

> Learn by mail to pass successfully to be a Certified Public Accountant. Subjects: Theory of Accounts, Auditing, Commercial Law, Practical Accounting.

Additional instruction was also offered, according to the advertisement:

> Learn by mail to pass successfully Regents and other Examinations, re Algebra, Geometry, English Composition, Arithmetic, History, Latin, Business Arithmetic, Rhetoric, Physics, Chemistry, Literature, Mathematics, etc.

From January 1905, announcements mentioned accounting subjects only.

The earliest suggestion of its methods was in its advertisement of November 1905: "Our instructors give each student special and personal attention." This personal attention was mentioned through February 1906, the date of the last advertisement found.

The period required for a student to complete the course was stated as six to ten months. The cost of the instruction was described as moderate, and, in December 1905, was permitted to be in partial payments.

The Institute's organization, instructors, scope, and methods having been sketched generally, there remains to be told the little that is known of its students. No registers or statistics of the number are available, and memory is hardly to be relied upon. One person who was connected with the organization wrote in 1943, "perhaps a quarter of a million studying accounting" and again wrote in 1947, "At one time the UBI had over 10,000 students." Even if each student purchased all four books and each book sold was considered to represent one student, that might indicate 2,500 individuals, and even this figure may be too high. It seems that there is no possible means for even approximating the total number of students or of those who took the course either by mail or in residence.

The only ones identified are 42 who signed the Certificate of Incorporation of the Universal Society of Accountants, three others who were named in that document and one nonresident who mentioned the Institute in telling of his studies for the CPA examination. Universal was incorporated January 25, 1909. Its certificate did not state who could be members, but Edward M. Hyans, who was its first secretary, perhaps its only one, wrote that membership was limited to present and past students of the Universal Business Institute, Inc.

Of the 46 members of the Society whose names are known and who had been or then were students of the Institute course, 12 were amongst the 42 signers of the Society's Certificate of Incorporation and some were then or later directors of the Society. They are here listed with the little known about them:

NAME	DIRECTOR	CPA	LOCATION, 1908
Broches, Lee	—	—	New York
Campbell, Edward	—	540, N.Y., 1944	—
Doudera, Emil	1908	—	Winfield
Falconer, Robert M.	1912	—	—
Goldsmith, Herman Ely	—	—	—
Kolstad, Charles A.	1908	—	Brooklyn
Maas, Pieter C.	—	470, N.Y., 1910	—
Robinson, William J.	—	161, Cal., 1920	—
Rose, Charles J.	1908	—	Brooklyn
Ruark, James Fletcher	—	—	—
Save, Leonard T.	1908	—	New York
Seal, Arthur Jr.	—	508, N.Y., 1912	—

Others who were directors but not incorporators were:

Name	Director
Beseler, William A. F	1912
Jaeger, A. H., Jr	1912
Losee, Eugene E.	1912
Weppler, John	1908

Those shown as directors in 1908 were so named in the Certificate of Incorporation. Those shown as directors in 1912 signed Membership Certificate No. 220, which is not dated but was probably issued in 1911, 1912, or 1913.

Probably all incorporators and directors were resident students. The objects of the Society as stated in the second paragraph of its certificate were:

To obtain recognition of accountancy as one of the prime essentials of business.

To maintain the dignity and standard of the profession of accountancy.

To meet at stated intervals for free discussion, solution, lectures, and comments upon any points touching upon the subject of accountancy. . . .

To promote and cultivate good fellowship among its members, professionally and socially.

To obtain and maintain suitable quarters for the conduct of its professional business and sociability among its members and friends.

The last three of these objects probably were of little interest to nonresidents and, even as to the first two objects, nonresidents could have only minor participation in the discussion and formal action.

The only nonresident student who is known as such was Charles Henry Towns of Keene, New Hampshire. While visiting New York he attended one session of the Institute or Society. However, he did not go on with the course but later, after locating in New York, attended New York University's School of Commerce, Accounts and Finance, was graduated in 1917, and became CPA No. 894 of New York in 1920.

Apparently the Institute ceased its operations after the death in 1914 of Meyer B. Cushner, who taught the subject of commercial law. The corporation was dissolved by proclamation of the Governor on March 13, 1926. Probably the Society became inactive soon after the Institute did, because thereafter there would be no more students and therefore no source of membership.

FRANK BROAKER OR THE
TECHNIQUE OF ACCOUNTICS, INC.

In November, 1903, BUSINESS WORLD carried this item:

Mr. Frank Broaker, CPA, has announced that he is now forming a limited class of students for preparation for the CPA examinations. Mr. Broaker was one of the first examiners in New York State and was the senior partner of Broaker & Chapman for many years. He still retains his accounting business at 130 Nassau Street, New York.

That seems to have been the first mention of the class in any periodical and no earlier announcement by other method has been found.

In the January and February 1904 issues of that periodical, the inside front cover carried a full-page advertisement of the course. From August 1904 to January 1906, BUSINESS WORLD carried advertisements of The Technique of Accountics. And the BUSINESS MAN'S MAGAZINE and the BOOKKEEPER of Detroit printed such notices in nearly all issues from May 1905 to April 1906, sometimes by Frank Broaker, sometimes by The Technique of Accountics, but all offering preparation for CPA examinations.

On October 3, 1921, the Regents of the University of the State, pursuant to the Education Law as amended in 1921, issued to Frank Broaker a license "to conduct, maintain and operate the Broaker Accountics Corporation for the purpose of giving instruction in bookkeeping and accounting in the City of New York, State of New York."

Although Frank Broaker had assistants in administration and also in teaching, it seems that the policies as to scope and method were his alone. Therefore, a brief summary of his activities to 1904 may be useful as showing his qualifications for teaching accounting.

Born in Millersburg, Pa., March 10, 1863, he attended public school in Brooklyn and City College in New York for a brief period, and studied bookkeeping at the Y.M.C.A. in Brooklyn at night while employed during the day as a clerk and bookkeeper in an import house. Thereafter, he was employed by John Roundey, public accountant, for a few years and then practiced alone for about eight years and as a partner in Broaker & Chapman.

He became a Fellow of the American Association of Public Accountants in 1891 and served it as Trustee, Secretary, Vice President and President.

He was a prime mover in the enactment of the CPA Law of 1896, was a member of the first Board of Examiners, and prepared the questions for two examinations.

He taught mercantile accounts in the AAPA, New York School of Accounts, 1893-4; prepared and published the American Accountants Manual in 1897; lectured at Koehler's New York School of Accounts three or more times; and a little later, on December 29, 1905, addressed the National Commercial Teachers Association at its convention in Chicago.

The locations of his coaching courses were: first in 1904 in the Tribune Building, 154 Nassau Street; soon thereafter in the Masonic Temple on West 23rd and 24th Streets; in 1915 at 63 Fifth Avenue; in 1933 at Broaker's early address, 150 Nassau Street; and finally at 44 Trinity Place.

His assistants in administration, so far as learned, included Charles A. Fox, registrar in 1904 and perhaps later, T. Oliver Schmidt, secretary (years not learned), who had been a student and also was a teacher and partner in Broaker's accounting practice; and J. M. Gear, a daughter (Mrs. Julia Marie Broaker Gear, now Mrs. Charles R. Perkins), who followed as secretary and later was vice president until 1929.

Besides the four subjects of the CPA examinations, special courses were offered in manufacturing accounts, inventory control, brokerage accounts, and visional control. Apparently these special courses were part of the senior or post graduate courses. As to the course in visional control, a circular cites the Bohemian, Comenius, as a user of "object lessons, pictures, maps, stuffed or live animals." Broaker is said to have taken a class of the deaf and dumb through bookkeeping and junior accounting with this method.

Generally, Broaker's method, probably followed by his assistants, consisted of talks by the teacher and questions to be answered at once by the students. Time for arithmetical calculations was not taken by the teacher or students. He asked students to state the operations for a given presentation of material and to indicate by an *x* where the result should be shown on the appropriate statement.

Broaker's assistants in teaching seem to have been few before 1923, and generally for only short periods while he was ill or out of the city. The only ones known are C. W. Allers, of whom nothing has been learned, and Herman E. Ludewig, who wrote that while on Broaker's staff and later he served as an instructor for him for about three years, perhaps around 1910.

In 1923, when Broaker expanded his courses under the license from the Regents, he used Felix A. Wagner, Frederick A. Wilton, Otto Hummel and Frank Broaker Goree, a grandson, for periods of a few months to two years, as teachers for the classes in bookkeeping and elementary accounting.

Although there are some gaps in the story of the Broaker course where the available data were not as full as desired, the foregoing material is believed to be correct and reasonably complete. But for showing how many students he had during the 12 years from 1904 to 1916, the information is almost wholly lacking. No record was available as to the number of students during the whole period or even during any year, and the names of only 24 were learned and some other facts about 20 of them. Letters from five students telling of the number in the classes they attended have been used for estimating as follows: years 1905 to 1906, one student stated maximum attendance as 12; years 1912 to 1915, four students stated 25, 30, 35, 50; average 35.

Assuming that there was a uniform yearly increase, the average might be 24 and the total number in the 12 years would then be 288. Probably that is too low but nothing has been found to warrant a guess of over 400 for 12 years.

Of the 24 students whose names were learned, 11, or 46 percent, became CPAs, one in New Jersey and ten in New York, and all joined their state societies. But as the 24 names were only 6 percent of the possible total of 400 in 12 years, the 46-percent ratio cannot be considered as applying to all students.

Six students, of whom three became CPAs, gave their opinion of the course and of Frank Broaker. The three who did not become CPAs wrote: "Good opinion"; "Course very practical"; "One of the finest accountants I have known." Two of the CPAs said: "Excellent"; "Excellent teaching of fundamentals." The other CPA who had been a student in 1905 and 1906 wrote: "An able accountant and a good lecturer. Had the faculty of getting his ideas across readily and clearly. Course was well laid out."

END OF THE EARLY COACHING COURSE PERIOD

The discontinuance around 1914 of the Low and Universal courses might have increased the attendance at Broaker's. But besides Koehler's New York School of Accounts, which continued to his death in 1929, there was the New York University School of Commerce, Accounts, and Finance, which had been organized in 1900. In 1906, only two years after the Broaker course was begun, two schools known as Pace Institute and Pace Private School were established in New York and were followed in 1907 by the Accounting Institute of Brooklyn. And in 1910, night classes in accounting were begun at Columbia University. These four institutions were formally organized and more than offset the closing of the Tipson course in 1906. So it seems that 1915 may be taken as the end of the period of early accounting coaching courses. They unquestionably rendered a worthwhile service to the profession.

CHAPTER 3

HISTORY OF THE NEW YORK STATE SOCIETY OF CERTIFIED PUBLIC ACCOUNTANTS

The New York State Society of Certified Public Accountants

ITS GENESIS

By THE COMMITTEE ON HISTORY

While much has been published about the enactment of the first CPA Law on April 17, 1896, and of the events which led up to that result, the published story of the State Society told nothing of what preceded its incorporation.

The Society's *Ten-Year Book*, 1897-1906, after telling on page 13, that "75 certificates were issued in 1896" added "This provided the material from which the State Society was formed."

Then after an explanation of the purpose of the book it stated:

> "After its incorporation on January 28, 1897, the Society was organized at the Hotel Waldorf on March 30, 1897 by the incorporators, John Hourigan, S. Eugene Sargent, Francis Gottsberger, Farquhar J. MacRae and Henry Harney who elected Messrs. Hourigan and Gottsberger temporary chairman and secretary."

The Society's Minutes did not show and the compiler of the *Ten-Year Book* never heard the reason why the first named incorporator and the temporary chairman of the first meeting on March 30, 1987, was John Hourigan of Albany.

But the following extract from *The Financial Record*, page 2, of the issue of January 13, 1897, appears to give the explanation:

> "Mr. John Hourigan, the well-known Albany public accountant, has addressed the following letter to a number of accountants throughout the State:
>
> "'Dear Sir—The passage by the Legislature of 1896 of a law to regulate the profession of public accountants was a very important event to all concerned. Now that the regents have put the law in operation, and issued certificates thereunder, our existence as a legally organized profession may be said to have commenced.

This the second of a series of articles on the History of Accountancy in the State of New York. It was prepared by the Society's Committee on History.

"'In this connection the thought arose in my mind that it might be desirable to have the C.P.A.'s of this State organize into a society similar to that of the physicians, architects or civil engineers. These several societies are certainly of very great value of their members, and I think a society of accountants could also be made of great value to its members.

"'In order to learn what the sentiments of the accountants are, in regard to this question, I have taken upon myself to send a letter similar to this to each certified public accountant. Will you please let me know your views? First: Is it desirable that the C.P.A.'s organize into a State society? Second: If in your judgment it is, where would be the most convenient place for you to have preliminary meeting held? Third: What time would best suit your convenience? If, in your judgment, a State society is not desirable or possible, please let me know. I inclose herewith a stamped and addressed enevelope [*sic*] for reply.

"'All the replies received to this letter I will tabulate and send to each person replying a copy of such tabulation.

Fraternally yours,
John Hourigan'"

If, as appears to be the fact, this letter was the earliest suggestion of the formation of the State Society it is appropriate to record something of its author. The facts here given were supplied by William J. Nusbaum, C.P.A., a member of the Society for many years who has served it as an officer and on committees, and who wrote that he "had the good fortune of having been employed in his office for ten years."

John Hourigan was born in Albany, N.Y., on February 22, 1854. He was educated at the Christian Brothers Academy in Albany, which he supplemented by serious private study. His business life started with the Home Savings Bank of Albany, where he remained until 1890. During this period he had, in 1889, organized the Safety Building-Loan Saving Association and served as its secretary until about 1910. He was influential in putting mutual loan associations on a stable basis.

His resignation from the Bank in 1890 was to devote all his time to "expert accounting," as public accountancy was popularly known in those days, and he continued in practice until about 1920, for many years being the only practitioner in Albany. His practice covered the area to Scranton, Pa., Utica, N.Y., and the Canadian border. He was a conscientious, fearless and able practitioner and, although he shunned publicity, he was an outstanding citizen whose advice was eagerly sought.

He cooperated with the Committee which promoted the CPA Law and his helpfulness in that connection was recognized by a resolution adopted by the Trustees of the American Association of Public Accountants. He received CPA certificate No. 19 in 1896.

As indicated by the letter herein quoted he seems to have been the first to suggest the organization of the State Society of which he was an Incorporator, its first Vice President, and a member of its committees.

In his younger days he had been an enthusiastic oarsmen [*sic*]. He was a prominent Catholic and highly respected. He died July 17, 1932.

The Society's First Annual Dinner

By THE COMMITTEE ON HISTORY

The New York State Society of Certified Public Accountants held its First Annual Dinner on December 28, 1897, at the Waldorf-Astoria Hotel. It is believed that contemporary accounts of this affair will be of interest not only to "veteran" members of the Society but to the younger generation as well. Like so many other activities of the young Society, this dinner was held under the leadership of the Society's first president, Charles Waldo Haskins.

An article of this nature appears to be of unusual interest since a search of the Society archives reveals no mention of the dinner in its publications. Reference is made to the affair, however, in the minutes of the Society meeting on January 10, 1898, which include the following:

> "Motion by Mr. Sells, duly carried: That the Society tender its thanks to the Committee who had charge of the dinner, and recommend to the Board of Directors, the appropriation of a sum of money sufficient to defray the expenses thereof."

The dinner was obviously of no small interest to the public, as current day newspapers and other periodicals carried articles about the affair. Information for this paper was gathered from the New York Times, the New-York Daily Tribune, the magazine Business and the publication "The Second City of the World, New York."

Research in the files of the New York Public Library uncovered the following articles from the New York Times and the New-York Daily Tribune of Wednesday, December 29, 1897:

This is the fifth of a series of articles on the History of Accounting in the State of New York, prepared by the Society's Committee on History.

The earlier articles appeared in the March, May, December 1949, and September, 1950, issues of this publication.

(New York Times)

Accountants at Dinner
Certified Experts in Figures Hold Their
First Banquet as a State Society
Mr. Fitch on City Accounts
The Retiring Controller Traces Their History from the First Ledger and Says
They Are Now Kept Honestly and Well.

The first annual dinner of the New York State Society of Certified Public Accountants was given at the Waldorf-Astoria last night.

Nearly one hundred members and guests were present. The dinner was given in the Myrtle Room of the hotel, which was tastily [*sic*] decorated with flags and potted plants. C. W. Haskins, President of the society, presided. The guests of honor were Chester S. Lord, the Rev. Father Sylvester Malone, Delos McCurdy, R. E. A. Dorr, and S. F. Jarvis.

Father Malone delivered a short prayer when the guests had assembled in the dining room. As the members and their guests sat down, it was announced that Mayor Strong, who was to respond to the toast "City of New York as at Present Constituted" would be unable to attend, as President Haskins said his old enemy, the gout, had kept him at home. Controller-elect Bird S. Coler was also prevented from attending, as was St. Clair McKelway.

C. W. Haskins, President of the society, made a short address. George R. Blanchard, Melvil Dewey, Francis S. Bangs, William H. Baldwin, Jr. and James G. Cannon also spoke.

Controller Fitch responded to the toast, "Municipal Accounts." Mr. Fitch, after paying a compliment to the society on its organization, said:

"The municipal accounts of the city are an interesting study from the first ledger, which was made in 1691, to the present day. While we cannot say the accounts of the city have always been kept honestly, they are kept that way now, and were under Tammany and other rule.

"The first ledger of the city is as clear and better written than these of the present day, yet it may be full of errors, for all we know. They did not have certified accountants then. We have kept the accounts in a way that they can be easily understood. Other administrations have done the same. I am sorry the Mayor is not here to lend his voice to the occasion, as I am that my successor is not present. I have had much to do with public accounts, not only in this city but in Washington, where the accounts are peculiar and intricate.

"We can all be proud of the city we live in. I wish the incoming officers all success. The men at the head of the new administration ought to have the help and support of the people. They will be criticized for what they did and did not do. Let us assist them and give them credit until we know they have not done right."

Chester S. Lord responded to the toast, "The Newspapers."

(New-York Daily Tribune)

Public Accountants at Dinner
The First Feast of the New York State Society

The New York State Society of Certified Public Accountants held its first dinner at the Waldorf-Astoria last night. The society, which received its charter only so recently as March last,* has been formed for the purpose of raising the standard of efficiency in the accountants' profession. This is to be accomplished by means of examinations under the State Board of Regents, and by the imposing upon applicants for certificates requirements as to character and integrity as stringent as those which rule in the selection of members of other recognized professions.

C. W. Haskins, the president of the Society, occupied the central seat at the guest table last night, and placed on either side of him were Controller Ashbel P. Fitch, Melvil Dewey, Secretary of the State Board of Regents; George R. Blanchard, Commissioner of the Joint Traffic Association; Chester S. Lord, Delos McCurdy, Francis S. Bangs, S. F. Jarvis, Jr., the Rev. Sylvester Malone, R. E. A. Dorr, William H. Baldwin, Jr., and James G. Cannon. In his opening address, Mr. Haskins referred to the constantly growing importance of accountants' services, and remarked that the State Legislature, in passing a law creating the certified public accountant, has placed the business of accounting on a professional basis, with all that the term implied, of guaranteed integrity, skill, and single-minded devotion to the interest of the client.

Controller Fitch, speaking on the subject of "Municipal Accounts," said that the city's financial records, which dated from 1691, furnished a most interesting study, and the books for that whole period were legible, clear and well conducted. During all these years, Mr. Fitch said, they had been honestly kept and conducted, and showed to the utmost penny the moneys paid away in behalf of the city government.

The magazine *Business* reported:

Nearly all the members of the Association (sic) were present and the few who were not were unavoidably absent from the city, or, as in the case of Mr. Joseph Hardcastle, confined to a sick bed.

This periodical also named the guests and their callings. From *Business* and other sources we find the following:

Reverend Sylvester Malone, Regent, Pastor of the Church of Saint Peter & Saint Paul
Chester S. Lord, Regent, Editor of the New York Sun
Melvil Dewey, Secretary to the State Board of Regents
Ashbel P. Fitch, former Controller of New York City
George R. Blanchard, Chairman of the Joint Traffic Association

---

*The date of March last evidently alludes to the organization meeting of March 30, 1897, since the Society was incorporated on January 28, 1897.

William H. Baldwin, Jr., President of the Long Island Railroad
Francis S. Bangs of Bangs, Stetson, Tracy & McVeigh
James G. Cannon, President of the National Society of Creditmen and Vice President of the Fourth National Bank

In the same issue, *Business* published the address of Mr. Cannon which he delivered at the dinner.

Reference to "The Second City of the World, New York," published in 1898 by the Republic Press, reveals the subject matter of the addresses given by all speakers at the affair, as follows:

"George R. Blanchard, The Reinforcement of Corporate Integrity;
Hon. Melvil Dewey, The Higher Business Education;
Francis S. Bangs, Value of the Accountant to the Trust Company;
Ashbel P. Fitch, Municipal Accounts;
William H. Baldwin, Jr., The Accountant in Railroad Examinations;
James G. Cannon, Relation of the Accountant to the Credit Man;
Chester S. Lord, The Newspapers;
Rev. Sylvester Malone, Recognition of Society by Board of Regents;
President Haskins, History and Dignity of Accountancy."

The Committee on History believes that this record of the Society's first annual dinner which was the forerunner of its many later celebrations is worthy of permanence.

The Incorporators of The New York State Society of Certified Public Accountants

This paper gives a brief sketch of the life of each of the incorporators of our Society, and suggests that credit for taking the first steps for its organization should be accorded to the Albany CPA, John Hourigan.

The earliest printing of the Certificate of Incorporation under which the State Society was organized—or at least the earliest that has been found by the Committee on History—was that on pages 5-7 of the 1907 Year Book which was published sometime after May 10, the latest date in the book. As there printed, the Certificate was dated January 28, 1897, and bore the signatures of John Hourigan, S. Eugene Sargent, Francis Gottsberger, Farquhar J. MacRae and Henry Harney, and stated that they were to be the directors until the first annual meeting of the Society.

Questions which naturally come to mind at once are: By whom were the five Incorporators selected for this service? Who were these Incorporators who were to be Directors? What were their qualifications for service in such capacities? Two letters printed in the *Financial Record* of January 13, 1897, may serve as a basis for a search for answers to the questions.

An article in the May, 1949, issue of *The New York CPA* told of what seemed to have been the earliest movement for the Society. For those who may not have preserved that magazine it may be sufficient to state that it quoted from *Financial Record* a copy of a letter which John Hourigan had sent all the CPAs in which he suggested the desirability of an association and proposed that on some convenient date a meeting be held to consider his suggestion. The date of his letter was not given in the *Record*. But it must have been after December 1, the date of the earliest certificates, and before January 11, the date when Frank Broaker, Vice President of the American Association of Public Accountants, issued a letter in opposition to Hourigan's suggestion.

This is the tenth in a series of articles on the History of Accounting in the State of New York. It was prepared by the Society's Committee on History.

Whether the proposed meeting was held has not been learned. Even if held, only two who could have attended are still living. Paul A. Hourigan does not have any of his father's papers. And William J. Nusbaum who was with John Hourigan 10 years from 1902 is "sure that all his files were destroyed years ago."

However enough of the replies to Hourigan's letters may have been favorable to his suggestion for him to decide not to wait for his proposed meeting, but to proceed with incorporation before Broaker's opposition might cause some to hesitate. He had started the movement and probably wished to carry it through. And if time seemed important to him—as the execution of the Certificate only 17 days after the date of Broaker's letter suggests—he may have decided to select the Incorporators himself. If so that gives the answer to the first of the three questions.

It is such common practice to take up a group of names in alphabetical sequence—or in the order of seniority—by either of which Gottsberger, like Abou Ben Adhem, would have led all the rest—that both arrangements were here considered. But since the sequence of the signatures may have been planned, not accidental, the Incorporators are here briefly considered in the order of their signatures. For each a brief sketch of his life to the end of 1896 is given with such later facts as may seem to indicate his qualifications and why he was chosen for this service.

John Hourigan

John Hourigan was born in Albany on February 22, 1854, and therefore was nearly 43 years of age at January 25, 1897. His formal education was with the Christian Brothers in Albany and that he supplemented by serious private study. His business life started in the Home Savings Bank of Albany. It seems that while there employed he was interested in banking methods, for the January, 1889, issue of *The Office* (Vol. 6, p. 14) printed his letter of November 15, 1888, relative to Savings Bank Balances and describing his plan for getting correct ones.

The next year, 1889, he organized the Safety Building Loan Savings Institution and was its Secretary many years. In that connection he published in 1894, "Maturity Tables for Building and Loan Associations and other purposes."

In 1890, he resigned from the Bank to devote all his time to public practice. Probably he had practiced part-time before 1890, for the *Financial Record* of October 15, 1897, stated: "He has been practicing as a public accountant for seventeen years."

And while this brief survey of his activities has shown that he was interested in accounting principles and procedures, it is certain that he was also interested in his profession as a whole. At that time there were only two societies of accountants in the State of New York, the Institute of Accounts organized in 1882 and the American Association of Public Accountants in 1886. The title page of his book, published in 1894, shows him as a Fellow of the earlier society. When he became a member of it has not been learned but various references suggest that it was probably before 1890, perhaps in the middle 1880's.

In his younger days he was an enthusiastic oarsman at a time when shells and outriggers were popular on the river. During many years he was the only public accountant in Albany. He was prominent in the community and his church but he never held civic or sectarian office.

Besides the abilities and experience here mentioned there was another activity which may have been an additional qualification for leadership in the formation of the State Society. While there is no record of his having participated in the drafting of either of the CPA bills which were introduced in the 1895 Legislature, he was actively engaged in that effort only a little later.

On March 13, 1895, he attended the meeting in New York when 45 accountants were present including about 20 to 25 members of the American Association of Public Accountants, 7 to 10 of the Institute of Accounts and some not members of either society. A Committee of 14—so called—was created to look after the matter. According to the official record of that meeting Hourigan was not a member of that committee, though in a paper which George Wilkinson read at the Pittsburgh meeting of the American Society of CPAs on September 29, 1927, he listed John E. Hourigan (sic) as one of the non-member group. But Wilkinson was not present at the 1895 meeting and used second-hand information. Perhaps his statement was based directly or indirectly upon a story in *Business* of July, 1896 (Vol. 16, p. 289) which mentioned the efforts made by various individuals and stated: "The Institute was thus represented by its member resident in Albany."

But while the editor of *Business* acknowledged the help given by Hourigan without specifically naming him, merely indicating him by the phrase "its member resident in Albany," the Chairman of the Committee of 14 was explicit and moved:

> "That this Association extends its thanks to Mr. John Hourigan of Albany, Public Accountant, for his services and support in the attempt to pass an act to regulate the profession of Public Accountants, and the Secretary is hereby directed to forward a copy of this resolution to Mr. Hourigan."

The resolution so moved was adopted by the American Association at a meeting on October 8, 1895 (2 Minutes 71).

At the next meeting of the Association Trustees, October 24, there was read a letter from John Hourigan dated October 10,

> "suggesting a meeting of accountants representing different sections of the State in November soon after the election for the purpose of agreeing upon the text of the bill and to select the right Assemblyman and Senator to take charge of the matter when presented." (2 Minutes 74)

The records in 1896 do not mention John Hourigan as often as previously, perhaps because the Association's Vice President Frank Broaker was in Albany almost continuously. But in the July 18, 1896, issue of the *Financial Record* it was stated that Francis Gottsberger—who was Chairman of the Committee of 14—and W. Sanders Davies—who was a member of the Committee—called for Hourigan to accompany them for a conference with James Russell Parsons, Jr., director of the Examination Department of the University. Evidently he was still useful.

This brings his story to the formation of the State Society. Later he was an officer of the Institute of Accounts as well as of the State Society. He retired from practice about 1916 at the age of 62 and died July 17, 1932, at 78.

Sidney Eugene Sargent

Sidney Eugene Sargent was born in 1857, date and place not learned. He came to New York in 1880 and his name appeared for the first time in the New York City Directory of 1897. But it had been shown in three places in 1896. The October issue of *Business* (Vol. 16, p. 443) carried an article copyrighted by him on "How We Will Stand with Free Silver Coinage at 16 to 1." The August issue had on page 383 a list of about 125 public accountants and firms, which showed him as located at 514 Broadway, though his name was not in the similar lists in the June and July issues. And in 1896 CPA certificate #28 was issued to him, it being issued in the second group. And for that recognition he must have shown the Board of Examiners that he had been practicing during 5 years, or since April 1890 or earlier.

The April, 1897, issue of *Accountics* (Vol. 1, p. 14) showed that on April 1 he was elected to the Executive Council of the National Institute of Accounts. He became a charter member of the New York State Society in March, 1897, and through that he came into the American Association of Public Accountants in 1905. In 1897 also he was a charter member of the National Society of Certified Public Accountants. *Business World* of February, 1901, mentioned his removal from 380 Broadway to 85 White Street. And from 1907 the Year Books of the State Society and American Association show him located at 41 Park Row to 1919, and thereafter at 201 West 79 Street, presumably his resident in the Hotel Lucerne. There is no record of his having partners—apparently he practiced alone.

He died in New York February 21, 1932.

Francis Gottsberger

Francis Gottsberger was born in New York July 30, 1833, and therefore was 63½ years of age at January 28, 1897. He was educated at the Old Columbia College Grammar School. His business experience was largely in merchandising and for a considerable period he acted as buyer for large mercantile houses in New York and Boston. While probably he was not the bookkeeper, he came to understand that work. He was listed as a public accountant in the New York City Directory of 1884, but a sketch in the Financial Record of October 15, 1897, stated that he had been in active practice 15 years, or from 1882. That article also stated that "from the first he made a specialty of Surrogate's accounts." As a result of that experience he published in 1902 "An Accountants Guide for Executors, Administrators, Assignees, Receivers, and Trustees."

Apparently he did not join the Institute of Accounts but he became a fellow of the American Association of Public Accountants on September 15, 1893. Only 4 months later he was elected a Trustee, on January 27, 1894, and 2 years later, on January 14, 1896, he was elected Treasurer.

Without any collaboration he drafted an accountancy bill which he read to the Association February 12, 1895, after he had sent it to

Senator Daniel Bradley for introduction in the Legislature. The records do not show that he had been asked to draft the bill and his action seems to have been a surprise to the Association, which, however, at that meeting made him Chairman of the Committee on Legislation.

When the Gottsberger bill collided in the Legislature with one sponsored by the Institute of Accounts, he with W. Sanders Davies issued a call to all public accountants in New York to attend a meeting on March 13, 1895. At this joint legislative meeting he was chosen as Chairman and then also Chairman of the Committee of 14, which against his wishes decided to support the Institute bill.

In 1896, the Vice Chairman of the Association Committee on Legislation, Frank Broaker, who was also Vice President of the Association, took such active steps for the bill that Gottsberger was less prominent, perhaps also less active. Only two references to him in that year have been found. In July he with W. Sanders Davies called for Hourigan to go with them for a conference with the Director of Examinations. And he became CPA #36 in the third group issued. On January 7, 1897, he wrote resigning as Trustee and Fellow of the Association.

He was a Charter Member of the State Society and served it 6 terms as Director and 4 terms as Vice President. He wrote papers on financial and accounting subjects for periodicals. In 1897 he, with Farquhar J. MacRae and John R. Loomis, organized the Certified Public Accountants Company, which however was not listed in the New York Directory and may not have engaged in practice. In 1902 he won a suit for services for which the client had refused to pay more than one-half of the accountant's fee.

He died November 24, 1913, and by his will left $100,000 to his church.

Farquhar J. MacRae

Farquhar J. MacRae was born in Brooklyn April 8, 1862, and was not yet 35 years of age when he signed as Incorporator. He was educated at Erasmus Hall Academy in Brooklyn. Prior to beginning practice on his own account he had been with Howard Bartlett & Co., Selden R. Hopkins and Henry Harney. He was first listed as a public accountant in the New York Directory of 1892 but a sketch in the *Financial Record* of October 15, 1897, stated that he had been in practice for ten years, so that it seems that he began in 1887 or earlier.

Early in 1894 he had John D. Cowan with him as MacRae & Cowan. This firm advertised for assistants, offering $40 per week to those who had five years experience and were members of the Institute of Accounts and only $20 per week to English CAs who "had sufficient experience in this country to render them familiar with modern methods of bookkeeping." This was inspired by William Waddell's help-wanted notices. Later his firm was MacRae, Gardner & Co. with J. A. S. Gardner as his partner, but that was dissolved early in 1897, after which the firm name was Farquhar J. MacRae & Co. In 1897, with Gottsberger and John R. Loomis, he participated in the organization of the Certified Public Accountants Company, with an authorized capital stock of $10,000 par value, which it seems did not continue in practice long if at all.

He joined the Institute of Accounts in 1890 or earlier, had become its Secretary by July, 1892, and was advanced to Fellow on November 9, 1893. On April 1, 1897, he was elected to the Executive Council of the National Institute, and on May 18, 1899, he was in Hartford when that chapter was formed.

He received CPA certificate #23 in the second group issued in 1896, and after signing as an Incorporator of the State Society he became a Charter Member in March, 1897. He was elected a Director in 1897 and 1898, a Vice-President four times beginning in 1899, was elected President on January 17, 1903, for the vacancy resulting from the death of Charles W. Haskins and was reelected three times in 1903, 1904 and 1905.

On February 5, 1903, he became President of the Federation of Societies of Public Accountants in the Untied States, but resigned on June 17, 1904, following the withdrawal of the New York State Society from the Federation. As President of the State Society he, with President Loomis of the American Association of Public Accountants, presided as co-chairman at the dinner on October 4, 1904, which the two organizations gave for the foreign delegates to the Congress of Accountants at the St. Louis World's Fair.

At the age of 85, he died in Brooklyn, March 4, 1947.

Henry Harney

Henry Harney was born in Baltimore, probably about 1835. His early education was by his father E. Rhodes Harney, head of Franklin Square Female Seminary, and in private schools. Later he attended the Baltimore College, University of Maryland. His business experience in

Boston, in a large commercial house in Richmond, and as Chief Accountant in the Bank of Richmond, may have covered about 5 years, 1856 to 1861. During the Civil War he served in the 1st Virginia Regiment and was advanced to a captaincy. MacRae wrote that Harney's northern civilian friends promoted him to a major. He came to New York after the War and during a part of the next 25 years was with Joseph Steiner & Company, a tea house.

He began public practice in 1890 apparently alone, but later as Harney, Cady & Co., Harney, Scott & Co., Henry Harney & Co., having as partners at various times, Charles E. Cady, Herbert W. Hills, William E. Kastendike, John Kastendike, Wilbur A. D. Scott, Edward Glardon, Sylvester E. Strickland and William Cockcroft.

He became a member of the Institute of Accounts in 1886 and a short time later was elected Secretary and, still later, served five successive terms as its president. He was a member of its committee which prepared its CPA bill; perhaps he prepared the first outline for it. He attended the joint legislative meeting on March 13, 1895, and was elected to the Committee of 14 and to its subcommittee of 5. He received CPA certificate #18 in the second group issued, and became a Charter Member of the State Society in March, 1897, but resigned December 14, 1899. He continued his activity in the Institute of Accounts to his death on May 19, 1910.

The foregoing has shown that John Hourigan was active in the efforts to obtain the enactment of a CPA Law; that he suggested the formation of an association of CPAs; that he assumed or was granted the leadership for a society; that probably he believed haste was important because of the opposition by Broaker, Vice President of the Association; that he had many acquaintances in the Institute of Accounts during his membership in it of 7 years or more; that probably he knew fewer members of the Association; that he was well acquainted with Harney and MacRae of the Institute, perhaps also with Sargent, and specially with Gottsberger, then a member of the Association.

These facts do not prove, but they very strongly suggest, that Hourigan selected the Incorporators; and that may have been the reason that he was chosen for Vice President at the organization meeting of the State Society on March 30, 1897.

Others, many others, participated in its growth and development. But unless and until other facts prior to its incorporation come to light it seems that the credit for taking the first steps for the organization of the New York State Society of Certified Public Accountants should be accorded to the Albany CPA, John Hourigan.

[*March, 1953*. Reprinted with permission from *The CPA Journal*, copyright 1953]

MORE ABOUT AN INCORPORATOR

One of the important—yes and pleasant—results of publishing historical articles is that so frequently they bring to light other incidents of which the authors had never heard. The story of The Incorporators of the New York State Society of CPA's in the March, 1953, issue of this magazine had just such an outcome.

Before noon of the day when that issue of the magazine was delivered by the postmen, this Committee's attention was directed to a novel incident—one which had never occurred previously and which could not happen again.

At the Annual Meeting of the Society on May 13, 1946, President Donaldson read a scroll which the Directors had prepared for Farquhar J. MacRae the only living charter member of the Society. The scroll was inscribed as follows: "The Board of Directors of The New York State Society of Certified Public Accountants in the fiftieth year of the Society, awards this Charter Member Certificate to Farquhar J. MacRae, a charter member in recognition of his loyal and continuous membership since the founding of the Society in 1897 and his many contributions to the development of its activities."

—THE COMMITTEE ON HISTORY.

Society Offices and Secretarial Staff

By THE COMMITTEE ON HISTORY

The history of public accountancy in New York State embraces, besides matters prior to the formation of the State Society, at least four subjects, namely: the Society's growth, its development, and its many varied activities; its relations with other organizations, both accounting and others; the individual accountants who have served it and the profession; its administrative personnel and equipment for its activities.

Much of the first two classes has been told briefly or in detail in its publications which have included addresses at meetings; occasional reports by committees on specific subjects; and its several publications, *Year Books* from 1907, supplemented in 1948 by its *Ten Year Book, 1897-1906*; its series of Bulletins begun in 1923; *The New York CPA* from October, 1934; and the *CPA News* issued since October, 1949. The Committee on History has not had any part in the preparation of these and cannot claim credit for them.

But now after its life of about five years the Committee has reviewed its work for *The New York CPA* and classified it as follows:

Re: State Society and Profession Generally	
Early Developments in New York State	March 1949
The State Society—Its Genesis	May 1949
Incorporators of the State Society	March 1953
Society's First Annual Dinner	March 1951
Re: Educational Institutions	
N.Y. School of Accounts—Koehler's	December 1949
Pace Institute	September 1950
School of Commerce, Accounts and Finance of New York University	April 1953
Re: Individual Accountants	
Joseph Hardcastle	September 1951
Frederick George Colley	May 1952

This is the twelfth in a series of articles on the History of Accounting in the State of New York. It was prepared by the Society's Committee on History.

Charles Ezra Sprague	July 1952
Robert Lancelot Cuthbert	November 1952

Although no definite preliminary program had been planned, this classification of the eleven articles that have been published suggests that the stories were fairly well distributed among three of the subjects for accountancy history stated here in the introductory paragraph.

But this resume of the history written by others and of that compiled by the Committee on History caused some of its members to wish that more were known as to where and by whom the administrative work of the Society had been performed. The result of research for those facts was of such interest that they have been assembled with this story which the Committee believes will be informative to the members of the Society and hopes may also be found interesting. And this will give one story upon the fourth subject of such history.

The Society offices and a little about the secretarial staff are taken up first because there were so many changes and the available records of them are so meager.

From March 30, 1897, when the Society elected its first officers to May, 1898, its Minutes do not mention an office or headquarters. Therefore, it seems probable that during the first 13 months the Society's records of its membership, committee appointments, etc., were at the office of the Secretary, Arthur W. Teele, 11 Wall Street, which now is the location of the executive offices of the New York Stock Exchange.

From April or May, 1898, to May 1, 1902, about 4 years, the Society had headquarters in the Johnston Building at 30 Broad St., thus:

May to November, 1898	in Room 1224,	Rental not recorded
Nov., 1898 to May, 1899	in Room 1232,	Rental not recorded
May, 1899 to May, 1902	in Room 1105,	Rental $500 per annum

For this headquarters the Directors authorized the purchase of furniture, cost not recorded, but the Treasurer was told to borrow $400.00. A directory of accountants in *Business* of July, 1896, shows that at that date Haskins & Sells, Patterson & Corwin, and Veysey &

Veysey had offices at 30 Broad Street and only 2 of 119 listings were north of the financial district.

Beginning in 1898 the Society had a House Committee and, when the Broad Street headquarters were taken, the Directors employed Mrs. E. E. Schmitt at $200 per annum to take charge. No title for her position was stated at that time but later her position was stated as Librarian. In April, 1898, the Library Committee had reported a gift of some 50 volumes and other gifts were reported later. Though it seems that the collection was not large, her duties may have included that of recording books loaned and returned. Also, as the Society maintained a form of employment agency, she may have had duties for that. No other mention of Mrs. Schmitt has been found except that she resigned February 28, 1901, having served nearly three years. On June 28, 1901, she offered to sell her typewriter to the Society.

Miss A. L. Farrell followed Mrs. Schmitt and served a little over four years from February 28, 1901, to April 30, 1905, the first fourteen months at the headquarters in the Johnston Building. But the House Committee on April 14, 1902, reported that it had given up the room in the Johnston Building, where the Society had been located for four years and one month, and had rented a room in the Edison Building, 44 Broad Street at $325 per annum. This change was approved by the Society and a few days later the Directors appropriated a sum for more furniture and authorized the installation of the Society's first telephone.

The office at 44 Broad Street, Edison Building, was discontinued on April 30, 1905, after the House Committee had reported that the rent, salary of stenographer, telephone and other expenses were costing about $600 per annum, whereas it was used only for the Director's meetings and for the Registration Bureau. The office furniture was then sold for $73 and two cases of books were stored at Winans, 407 Greenwich Street.

In this account of the Society's effort to establish and staff an office during the seven years 1898-1905, as compared with its 1953 offices and its 1952 membership of over 6500 and its 1952 income of over $207,000, it should not be forgotten that in those early years the Directors were planning for the future and using for the foundation such available materials as the Society then could afford.

Although during May, 1905, the Society referred to the Directors "a suggestion that instant measures be taken whereby it should have headquarters," that action was not taken for 20 years during which the administrative work of the Society was conducted at the offices of the Society Secretaries which were as follows:

1905-1908, 3 years at Office of Leon Brummer	277 Broadway
1908-1909, 1 year at Office of Samuel D. Patterson	55 Liberty St.
1909-1914, 5 years at Office of Samuel D. Patterson	141 Broadway
1914-1915, 1 year at Office of James F. Farrell	150 Broadway
1915-1920, 5 years at Office of James F. Farrell	120 Broadway
1920-1925, 5 years at Office of James F. Farrell	110 William St.

Two incidents of the 20 years may deserve mention. The door of the office of S. D. Patterson at 141 Broadway indicated that it was also the office of The New York State Society of Certified Public Accountants. Apparently many records of the early years of the Society were lost long ago. While it is not known when or where this happened, it has been said that they had been stored in a basement and thereafter lost by a flood.

After twenty years (1905-1925) as the paying guest of its Secretaries, the Society again established headquarters of its own on the 18th floor of 110 William Street under a 5-year lease with an annual rental or $2,900. Possession seems to have been taken about the middle of 1925 and the event was of such importance that the planning for it was given a paragraph in the President's report for 1924-1925 and its completion was noted in the President's and Secretary's reports for 1925-1926. An action of importance near the end of this period, while James Francis Farrell was Secretary, was the creation of the position of Assistant Secretary.

William Alcorn Brown, who was the first Assistant Secretary and served from December 1, 1922, to July 6, 1936, was born in Bethel, Ohio, on November 28, 1878, the son of Dr. Quincy Adams Brown. He was graduated A.B. from Oberlin College in 1909 and thereafter taught English in the High Schools at Sandusky and Cleveland for two years.

During 5 years, 1911-1916, he was Assistant Educational Director of the 23rd Street Y.M.C.A. in New York, and for 6 years, 1916-1922, he was Secretary of the New York Chapter of the American Institute of Banking. During his service for the State Society the membership increased nearly fourfold, from about 625 in December, 1922, to 2365 in May, 1936. After about 30 months in the office of

Secretary Farrell, he supervised its removal to its own office in the same building in May, 1925; and 7 years later in 1932, he moved it to 30 Broad Street. He died July 7, 1936.

Wentworth Flagler Gantt, successor, was appointed August 10, 1936, as Assistant to the President. During the year 1940-1941 the title of the position was changed to Executive Secretary and so remains. As Mr. Gantt still holds that position no sketch is included.

Arthur Wellington Teele, the first Secretary, served the Society a little over 2 years from its organization on March 30, 1897. He was born June 16, 1867, in Medford, Mass., but his parents soon moved to nearby Watertown, where he attended the grade and high schools and where he got his first instruction in bookkeeping. Then or later he studied at Eastman Business College, Poughkeepsie. His experience was first as a bookkeeper in his father's retail hardware store, continued in a wholesale hardware in Boston and with a manufacturing hardware company; and then as a traveling salesman for three years until, because of an accident, his doctor advised him to give up travel. Teele became CPA #13 in 1896, one of the first group certified.

In 1891, he began public practice in New York, apparently alone, but during the next decade the practice was conducted under various names. In 1893, he joined with William Trenholm who had started a practice about 1890 and was a Trustee of American Association of Public Accountants. The firm name was William Trenhold [*sic*] & Teele. The next year, 1894, it became William Trenholm, Teele & Dennis, when Rodney Strong Dennis came in. Dennis was CPA #5 in 1896, was a member of the Board of CPA Examiners in 1898, and remained in the firm until his death on March 9, 1904. Trenholm withdrew in 1895 to resume practice alone, and the firm name was shortened to Teele & Dennis and so stood for about five years to 1900. Then Teele & Dennis was consolidated with Patterson & Corwin, which was slightly senior in practice, under the title Patterson, Teele & Dennis. Andrew Stuart Patterson, CPA #41, twenty-odd years older than Teele or Dennis, remained in the firm until his death on April 2, 1903. Through all the changes in the firm names Teele continued a partner and after the withdrawal of Trenholm in 1895, and the death of Patterson in 1903, and of Dennis in 1904, he was the senior partner in the practice which he had begun alone in 1891.

Following his service to the State Society as its Secretary he was elected a Director and served 2 years from May 8, 1899. He had joined the American Association of Public Accountants January 6, 1893 but withdrew the next year, the reason for which action has not been learned. However, through the New York State Society he was again in the Association in 1905. And he was a member of its Committee on Department Methods of the Government (U.S.) 2 years, 1907-1908, and of its Committee on Federal Recognition also 2 years, 1914-1915.

He was a member of the New York State Board of CPA Examiners 2 years, 1905-1907, and was the first Chairman of the Institute Board of Examiners which he served 5 years, 1916-1920. He was then elected a Vice President of the Institute in 1921 and during the 18 years, 1922-1939, he was its Treasurer, thus having served it as an officer continuously for 24 years from 1916. Even this does not recount all his service to the Institute, for among other services he was a member of its War Committee 2 years, 1917-1918, and during his successive terms as Treasurer he was on its Executive Committee.

With attention to the practice of his firm's offices in New York and other cities and with the services he gave to New York State, the United States and the professional societies it might seem that he was fully employed. However, he had a social nature as shown by his membership in many clubs in New York and elsewhere—he served the New York Athletic Club in many ways and was its President in 1925, when it acquired its property at 7th Avenue and 59th Street. He was fond of sport, especially golf and yachting, and it is understood that he gave much time and thought to the operations of his farm on Long Island.

Leon Brummer, the second Secretary, 1899-1908, was born in New York in 1868. He was educated at The College of the City of New York, where he was a member of the Phi Sigma Delta fraternity. He became CPA #88 of New York in 1896, and under the resolution adopted by the State Society on October 9, 1899, he was one of the five members who were named as a committee to confer with Columbia and New York Universities for the establishment of a school of accounts. Upon the organization of the School of Commerce, Accounts and Finance in New York University, he was appointed to its Faculty as Professor of Practical Accountancy, serving to 1915, and during its first two years, from 1900 to 1902, he was also Secretary of the Faculty.

Whether he had other employments between his attendance at City College and his start in the public practice of accountancy has not been learned. But if there were such employments they could not have been of long duration because the issue to him of a certificate by waiver indicates that he was in practice at the latest by 1891, while an item about him in *The Financial Record* of June 15, 1899, suggests that he may have started by 1889 when he was only 21. In 1892, he was a member of the firm of Bergtheil, Horley & Co.; during 1892-1895, of Bergtheil, Cook & Co.; in 1896, of Brummer & Co.; and during 1897-1899, of Horley, Brummer & Co. Thereafter, he may have practiced alone except for an uncertain period beginning in 1904, when he was a member of Hertle, Cook, Brummer & Haag, and again from 1923 to 1927, when his firm was Leon Brummer & Becker.

He was an early member of the New York State Society (in July, 1897), which he served as Secretary for 9 years, 1899-1908, and later as a director; and through it he became a member of the American Association in 1905 and of the American Institute in 1916. At the 10th Anniversary of the Society he gave a short history of the Society's activities to that date.

Samuel Duncan Patterson, the third Secretary, who served from 1908 to 1914, was a descendant of Andrew Patterson who emigrated from Perth, Scotland, and on September 5, 1685, settled at what now is Perth Amboy, New Jersey. Samuel Patterson was born in New York on September 19, 1855.

The brief sketch of his first 70 years, which he prepared for the 1925 edition of Accountants' Directory and Who's Who, stated as to his education only that he attended the public schools. However it seems that he extended that education, presumably by reading and surely by experience, because he became New York CPA #176 on July 17, 1901. He was a member of the faculty of the School of Commerce, Accounts and Finance of New York University as Professor of Executorship Accounts from 1907 to 1928, and was a member and secretary of the New York State Board of Examiners during the 8 years from April 1, 1909, to April 12, 1917.

Nothing has been learned of his occupation during the 15 or 20 years after his attendance at school, but the issuance to him in 1901 of a waiver certificate (under the law of that year which did not widen the field of possible applicants but only extended the period during which applications might be filed) indicates that he had begun the public practice of accountancy by 1891 to earlier. Generally his was an individual practice though it seems that he may have been a member of

Rea & Patterson in 1897, and a letter from Farquhar J. MacRae stated that he was a member of Glardon & Patterson for two or more years from 1898. In 1907 and 1908, perhaps earlier, his office was at 55 Liberty Street but from 1909 to 1929, when he retired, it was at 141 Broadway.

Patterson was a member of the Institute of Accounts and was its Secretary for a time, but the dates of his membership and of his tenure of the office have not been learned. He was admitted to the New York State Society of CPA's in October 1901, soon after he was certified and, as already noted, was its Secretary during 6 years, 1908 to 1914. He was a member of the committee which arranged the celebration of the Society's 25th Anniversary in 1922. Through the State Society he became a Fellow of the American Association of Public Accountants in 1905, and in 1916 of the American Institute of Accountants. He joined the American Society of CPA's very early, perhaps in 1921.

He died December 30, 1938.

James Francis Farrell, the fourth Secretary, was born in Jersey City in 1879. He completed the parochial school course in 1894, at the age of fifteen. Eleven years later, in 1905, he extended his formal education by taking the course in accountancy and business administration at the newly organized Pace Institute, being the third student to enroll in it. In 1909 he became New York CPA #436. And for eight years, from 1910 to 1917, he was a member of the faculty of Pace Institute. Even that did not end his contact with accountancy education, for he served three years, 1925-1928, on the New York State Board of Examiners.

Before beginning the practice of public accountancy he spent over twenty years in business, first with the Erie Railroad, rising from office boy to manager of the Department of Eastbound Accounts. Then for about ten years he was with Charles M. Higgins & Company, ink manufacturers, advancing from its bookkeeper to the position of assistant to the manager. And for about three years from 1910, he was office manager for Pace & Pace.

Leaving business to take up the public practice of accountancy in the latter part of 1913, with the late James Francis Hughes (CPA #545) he formed the firm of Hughes & Farrell, with offices at 150 Broadway. A year later the firm's offices were at 120 Broadway, where Charles F. McWhorter, CPA #361, and David E. Boyce, CPA #459, were also located. In 1915 these four joined forces as McWhorter, Boyce,

Hughes & Farrell, but after about two years McWhorter withdrew, after which the practice was continued as Boyce, Hughes & Farrell though Boyce died on October 1, 1918.

Farrell joined the New York State Society in February, 1912, and served as its Secretary from 1914 to 1925, which period of eleven years was longer than any other secretary served either before or after him. In 1925, 1928, and 1929 he was elected Vice President.

Through his membership in the State Society, James Farrell became a member of the American Association of Public Accountants in 1912, and of The American Institute of Accountants in 1916; he also became a member of the American Society of CPA's.

He died in Brooklyn, October 15, 1932.

Martin Kortjohn, the fifth Secretary, served 5 years, 1925-1930. He was born in Germany on October 15, 1878, and in 1892 he came to the United States. The sketch which he prepared for the 1920 edition of the Accountants' Directory and Who's Who stated that he was educated in the public schools. As he was 14 years of age when he came to America, his early schooling probably was in Germany. Later he took courses of the International Correspondence Schools and the N. Y. Preparatory School. With that preparation before or by 1909 he passed an examination of the U.S. Civil Service Commission. He completed the course at Pace Institute by January, 1915, and in June of 1915 he passed the New York CPA Examination. In September 1916, be *[sic]* became a teacher of Accounting at Pace Institute and continued during several years. On December 3, 1917, he became New York CPA #750.

Of his occupations to 1915, a story in the *Pace Student* of January, 1918, stated "he secured a job whenever and wherever he could, making no stipulation except that it be honorable and honest"; and during that period he was employed by the Borden Company 3 years, and in the Customs Service at New York from 1909 to 1915.

In 1915 he joined the staff of Fedde & Pasley, remaining there until some time in 1917. He then began practice on his own account, apparently at 154 Nassau Street until July, 1920, when he moved to 15 Park Row. On August 1, 1922, the practice became Kortjohn & Tripp but by 1925 it had become Martin Kortjohn & Company, which firm in 1940 removed to 10 East 40th Street.

He became a member of The New York State Society of CPA's in October, 1920, where besides his service as Secretary, 1924-1929, he was a Director from 1933 to 1936. He joined The American Society of CPA's in 1925 or before, and the American Institute of Accountants in 1929. Also he was a member of the National Association of Cost Accountants and the Society of Industrial Engineers.

He died at his home in the Bronx on October 10, 1949.

Fred Lucius Main, the sixth Secretary, served three years from 1930 to 1933. He was born in Titusville, Pennsylvania, January 24, 1881, and was graduated from the High School there. Then he attended a Business College in Oil City, commuting daily from home. Before completing that course he was employed as a messenger for a short time by the Second National Bank of Titusville, going from there to the Commercial Bank of that city and starting in what proved to be a long connection though broken for a relatively short time by his first experience in public accounting. This was with Main, Squires & Co., of which firm Frederick W. Squires, New York CPA #250 was the New York partner and Frank Wilbur Main, New York CPA #295, was the partner in Pittsburgh.

However this interlude was not long and he returned to the Commercial Bank as cashier, his total service with that bank being more than ten years. In 1917 he returned to New York with Main, Squires & Co., but was away again for service with the Red Cross in World War I. When Main, Squires & Co. was dissolved about 1919, he became a partner in Main & Co. as the head of its New York office, and so remained throughout his life. He became New Jersey CPA #106 in 1919, and New York CPA #1454 in 1924. He joined the New Jersey Society of CPA's in 1919, the American Institute of Accountants in 1922, and The New York State Society of CPA's in 1924. He died at his home in Upper Montclair, New Jersey, on November 9, 1950.

George Charles Hurdman, the ninth Secretary, 1937-1941, was a nephew of Frederick Harold Hurdman and was born in Ottawa, Ontario, Canada, on September 25, 1900. After attending the public schools and Collegiate Institute in Ottawa, he entered the Royal Military College of Canada at Kingston in 1918 and, upon completing its short course, he received a commission as lieutenant in the Royal Canadian Engineers. Later he took a correspondence course in accountancy with the Walton School of Commerce of Chicago and was graduated. He became CPA #2319 of New York on November 29, 1927.

Following his course at the Military College he spent six months on a timber survey in northern Ontario. Following that he came to New York and, for a short period, was with the National City Bank after which he joined the staff of Hurdman & Cranstoun and became a partner in 1935, spending several years in charge of the firm's office in White Plains.

He served as an officer of several hospitals and many social service organizations and was a member of several clubs in Westchester County and New York, The Accountants Club among the latter.

He joined the American Institute of Accountants in 1931, and the Municipal Finance Officers Association in 1936; but earlier, on May 10, 1929, he became a member of the New York State Society of CPA's. After his service as Secretary during the four years, 1937-1940, he served as Director during 1942-1945 and as Vice President during 1946-1948.

He died after a short illness on February 19, 1948.

Franklin Cornelius Ellis, the twelfth Secretary, 1945-1947, was born in Brooklyn October 23, 1894. He attended the public schools and Drake Business School in Brooklyn, and the New York Preparatory School and Pace Institute in Manhattan, and became New York CPA #2075 on December 6, 1926.

Before turning to public accountancy he had spent 7 years in the insurance field, 3 years with a firm of insurance brokers and 4 years with two insurance companies; and he was in the U.S. Army Air Service as a 2nd Lieutenant during a large part of 1918. Late in 1918 he became a member of the staff of Patterson & Ridgeway, and in 1924 he was admitted to the partnership.

He joined the American Institute of Accountants in 1933, was also a member of the National Association of Cost Accountants and of the National Tax Association. On October 1, 1928, he was admitted to The New York State Society of CPA's. Prior to his election as Secretary he had served as Director for one term of three years, 1938-1941, and immediately after his retirement as Secretary he was elected a Vice President for the year 1947-1948.

He died October 13, 1949.

This completes the stories of eight of the Secretaries who have died. There were seven others who are here listed:

7th—William J. Forster, of Harris, Kerr, Forster & Co.	2 years	1933-1935
8th—William R. Donaldson, of Crafts, Carr & Donaldson	2 years	1935-1937

10th—S. Carlton Kingston, of Stern, Porter, Kingston & Coleman	1 year	1941-1942
11th—Charles H. Towns, of Loomis, Suffern & Fernald	3 years	1942-1945
13th—Harold J. Beairsto, of Beairsto & Co.	3 years	1947-1950
14th—Edward J. Buehler, of Patterson & Ridgway	2 years	1950-1952
15th—Raymond J. Ankers, with Lybrand, Ross Bros. & Montgomery		1952-

A Greek philosopher of the second century of our era, in speaking through one of his literary characters, advised: "not to speak evil of the dead." Perhaps later with more experience he might have added: "avoid saying anything of the living." The preparation of biographical sketches of these Secretaries and of the present Executive Secretary are therefore left for a later story by the Committee on History.

CHAPTER 4

BIOGRAPHIES

Joseph Hardcastle

By THE COMMITTEE ON HISTORY

The outstanding facts concerning the career and writings of Joseph Hardcastle, eminent author and respected member of the faculty of the New York University School of Commerce, Accounts and Finance in its early days, have been collated in this biographical note concerning one of the earliest leaders of our profession.

A conversation with almost any member of the early classes of the New York University School of Commerce, Accounts and Finance, is very likely to bring reminiscences of early teachers. It is generally agreed that, for a school in a field which was almost entirely new, its faculty was remarkable. One of its members is still with us; others lived long enough for some of us to know them; and book-length biographies or shorter articles have told of others. So few facts have been assembled about one of its outstanding members, however, that the History Committee felt an urge to know more about him and to learn why memories of him were so vivid for those who knew him. This story has been pieced from many publications.

Joseph Hardcastle was born April 22, 1827, at Skipton in Craven, Yorkshire, England. In 1840 he was admitted to the Free Grammar School where, in 1843, he competed for and won a scholarship to York and Ripon Diocesan Training School. There, and by private study, he acquired a knowledge of the classics and mathematics besides German, French and Italian. The quality of his learning is indicated by his success in the above-noted competition in 1843; in that for a position in Belize in 1855; and in the examination for New York Public School teacher in 1858 and for the New York CPA Certificate in 1896. There is a tradition that he was offered a waiver certificate but he preferred to sit in the examination. That his confidence was warranted is shown

---

This is the sixth of a series of articles on the History of Accounting in the State of New York, prepared by the Society's Committee on History.

The earlier articles appeared in the March, May, December, 1949, September, 1950, and March, 1951, issues of this publication.

by his ratings of 87 in Theory, 80 in Practical Accounting, 85 in Auditing and 95 in Law. This was a simple average of approximately 87 whereas the corresponding averages of the two others who were successful were 85 and 79. One other passed three subjects but failed in Law and the fifth failed in four subjects.

His teaching experience covered seventeen years, 1847 to 1864. It included three years in the Training School from which he had just been graduated in 1847; four years in his own school at Peterhead, Scotland, where one of his pupils won the mathematical prize of £60 at Marschall College in Aberdeen; one year at Leith, Scotland; about three years as Superintendent of Schools at Belize, British Honduras; and six years as first assistant principal in Grammar School No. 38 at New York. The thoroughness of his teaching and its effectiveness with his pupils is evidenced by the suggestion of one of them, a son of Peter Gilsey, that his father consult him on a problem in income tax requiring a knowledge of sinking funds. The suggestion was followed and his solution was accepted by the Income Tax Commissioners.

The New York position was his last in teaching for many years, but his ability was recognized by his selection as the first Chief Examiner of the Institute of Accounts in 1882; by his chairmanship for many years of the Institute's Committee on Lectures; by his lectures to the students of Koehler's New York School of Accounts; and finally by his appointment in 1901 to the faculty of the New York University School of Commerce, Accounts and Finance, as Professor of the Principles and Practice of Accounts, which post he held until his death in 1906. His lectures on the accounts of executors and testamentary trustees were published by the school as one of their "Studies in Business."

His experience in public practice probably began in 1864, with his engagement by Peter Gilsey for whom and whose estate he acted as Accountant for forty-two years. While nothing has been learned concerning his other public accounting activities, it seems certain that they were of sufficient scope for the Board of Examiners to recommend him for certificate No. 104 in 1896. It declined to recommend a certificate for another able accountant who had no experience in public practice.

His interest in accountancy was shown by his membership in the Institute of Accounts of which he was a charter member in 1882; in the New York State Society of Certified Public Accountants which he joined in 1897 soon after its organization; and in the American

Association of Public Accountants of which he became a member in 1905 through the New York State Society.

His authorship indicates the wide range of his reading, and a list of his writings is impressive as showing his industry. It seems that he was not only a scientist in accounting and a philosopher about it, but that he was also a practical bookkeeper and interested in the mechanics of that activity as well as in its philosophy.

No complete list of his writings has been found. The Accountants Index lists twenty-five titles of which the earliest was published in 1890 in three issues of *The Office*, but he began contributing to such periodicals in 1882. The list of sixty-one titles appended to this article is probably not complete because it does not show any items between those in *American Counting Room* of June, 1884, and in *The Office* of June, 1886. During the intervening two years it seems probable that he wrote for *Treasury* of which no copy has been found.

Many of these titles were published in instalments. Some were parts of one general subject like chapters of a book. His "Accounts of Executors and Testamentary Trustees" was developed from his lectures at New York University as the lectures were based on his earlier articles. The six issues of "Accountics" were to have formed part of another book. Sometimes a series was interrupted and an unrelated article was published, perhaps because it was thought to be more timely.

His qualifications were recognized by his teachers who recommended him for positions; by at least one pupil who suggested that he might solve a problem which others could not; by the Gilsey interests who retained him professionally throughout his life; by the societies which continued to invite him to speak at their meetings; and by the editors who found that their readers wanted his articles.

The Committee on Honorary Degrees of New York University also appreciated his ability and on April 24, 1905, recommended him for a degree. At commencement, the citation included some of the biographical facts given herein and continued:

> "He has taken a prominent part in the elevation of accounting to the rank of a profession. For many years a contributor to the periodicals of his profession and writer of text books recognized as authoritative in their field. Teacher, author and leader in his profession, he is recommended for the honorary degree of Master of Letters."

But perhaps there was a still greater tribute. Students often are critical of their teachers and are not hesitant in voicing their judgment of individual members of the faculty. The first issue of *The Commerce Violet*, student annual of the School of Commerce, Accounts and Finance at New York University, said of him:

> "Beloved by every student and most highly respected by members of his profession."

He was the victim of an accident on June 8, 1906 and died on June 16, 1906.

The following list of his published articles probably is not complete but it includes all which have been found and is more extensive than any other published list.

LIST OF WRITINGS OF JOSEPH HARDCASTLE

(*Note:* Items are listed in chronological sequence of publication except that items published between sections of a series are listed after all instalments of the series.)

Title	Year	Month	Periodical	Vol ume	Page
Origin of Calculation Deduced from xx Language	1882	Oct. 24	"Bookkeeper"	5	336
Is Capital Account a Liability?	1882	Dec. 19	"	5	397
On the Theory of Life Insurance	1883	Jan.-Mar.	"	6	17, 35, 89
Equating Payments	1883	Aug.-Nov.	"American Counting Room"	7	79, 219, 281
Calculating Interest on Bonds	1884	March	"	8	158
Accounts of Real Estate	1884	June	"	8	226

(No file or even a single issue of "Treasury" has been found)

Trade Discounts	1886	June	"The Office"	1	3
Bonds as an Investment	1886	July	"	1	21
Trade Discounts	1886	August	"	1	46
Amount of an Annuity	1886	Sept.	"	1	59
Installment System	1886	October	"	1	80
Calendar—Old and New Style	1886	November	"	1	111
How to Count the Ballots	1886	December	"	1	131
Common Standard for Interest	1887	January	"	2	4
Interest	1887	Mar.-Apr.	"	2	43, 66
Credits	1887	July	"	3	123
Prices & Profits, a Chapter in Accountics	1888	Jan.-Mar.	"	4	15, 39, 49
Building & Loan Associations	1888	November	"	5	225
An Ideal Building Association	1889	March	"	6	44
Building Association, Reply to Critic	1889	May	"	6	82
Uniform Methods of Building Associations	1889	July	"	7	112
Cooperative Building & Loan Associations	1889	October	"	7	180

Talks on Accounts, I to III	1890	Aug.-Dec.	"	9	227, 251, 325
Talks on Accounts, IV	1891	May	"	10-11	97, 183
Talks on Accounts, V to VI	1892	Mar.-June	"Business"	12	98, 131
A Corporation Issues Bonds	1892	February	"	12	26
Renewal of a Loan	1894	April	"	14	136
Accounts as Tools of Business	1895	Jan.-Dec.	"	15	
Sparks from an Accountant's Anvil	1896	Jan.-Dec.	"	16	
Sparks from an Accountant's Anvil	1897	Jan.-Feb.	"	17	
Theory of Accounts, I to IV	1897	Mar.-June	"	17	80, 112, 141, 173
Answer to Bond Question	1897	May	"	17	149
Logismography	1897	July-Dec.	"	17	203, 235, 273, 303, 335, 366
Review of a Review	1897	December	"	17	361
Cost Prices I to IX	1898	Jan.-Sept.	"	18	
Realization of Profit	1898	Oct.-Nov.	"	18	625, 689
Problem and Solution	1898	December	"	18	753

Partnership	1899	Jan.-Feb.	"	19	37, 110
Purpose in Accounts	1899	March	"	19	139
Negative Accounts	1899	April	"	19	242
Old and New	1899	May-Sept.	"Business"	19	
Units of Use	1899	Oct.-Dec.	"	19	626, 691, 756
Business Statistics	1900	January	"Business and Public Accounting"	20	28
Bookkeeping of Quantities	1900	February	"	20	87
Science of Practice of Instalments	1900	Mar.-Dec.	"	20	
Science of Practice of Instalments	1901	Jan.-May	"	21	
A Personal Theory of Accounts	1901	June	"	21	224
What is Business	1901	July	"	21	276
Investment by a Private Individual	1901	August	"	21	306
Partnership in Liquidation	1901	Sept.-Oct.	"	21	347, 386
Balancing Accounts in One Operation	1901	November	"	21	428
Depreciation in its Application	1901	December	"	21	470
Adjustment & Regulating of Entries & Accounts	1902	January	"Business World"	22	28
An Analysis of the Ledger	1902	February	"	22	76

Statement of Affairs & Deficiency Account	1902	March	"	22	124
Administration and Business	1902	Apr.-May	"	22	168, 216
A Proprietor's Business	1903	February	"Commerce Accounts and Finance"	5	5
Two Principal Theories of Accounting	1903	June-July	"Business World"	23	268, 327
A Question of Annuities	1903	November	"	23	530
Origin of By and To in Double Entry Bookkeeping	1903	November	"	23	534
Accounts of Executors and Testamentary Trustees	1903	December	"School of Commerce, Accounts and Finance, Studies in Business, First Series, No. 2."	75 pages	
Dignity of Accounting Profession	1904	April	"N.Y. Accountants' and Bookkeepers' Journal"	3	104
Accountics, I to VI	1905	Mar.-Oct.	"Business World"	26	
Single Entry	1905	June	"Journal of Accountancy"	2	202
Problem in Executors Accounts	1905	August	"	2	311

Frederick George Colley

By HENRY E. MENDES, C.P.A.

This a brief biography of the only New York CPA to receive a grade of 100% in all four subjects of his CPA examination, taken at one sitting. It recounts the more important activities in the professional and industrial life of an early leader in our profession.

Frederick George Colley, born on March 7, 1872, at Monks Coppenhall, Crewe, County of Cheshire, England, was one of the many Britons who, coming to America towards the latter part of the nineteenth century, helped to mold what was then the comparatively small but fast-growing profession of public accountancy in the United States. Although he may not have been at all times during his varied career prominently in the forefront in professional activities, he left a definite imprint on the profession, nevertheless, in many important respects. As this biographical sketch attests, he had a most active and interesting life and, as is known by those who were acquainted with him intimately, not without its tribulations.

In his youth, Colley attended the British National School and the Mechanics Institute, both at Crewe, and upon graduation in 1888 he entered the employ of the London and North Western Railway at Crewe. In 1889, Edwin Waterhouse, of the London firm of Price Waterhouse and Co., offered him a position in their London office,

---

This is the seventh in a series of articles on the History of Accounting in the State of New York. It was prepared by Henry E. Mendes, C.P.A., at the request of the Society's Committee on History.

Mr. Mendes is a member and former Vice-President of our Society. He is also a member of the A.I.A. and the N.A.C.A. He is a member of the Society's Committee on Statewide Activities and Vice-Chairman of its Committee on Cooperation with Other Accounting Societies. He is a former Chairman of the A.I.A. Board of Examiners and of the New York Board of CPA Examiners.

Mr. Mendes is a partner in the firm of Touche, Niven, Bailey & Smart. Mr. Colley was his former partner in the predecessor firm of Touche, Niven & Co.

which he accepted; he eventually became the private secretary to Mr. Waterhouse, which position afforded him a wonderful and unique opportunity to become versed in accountancy at a high level, an opportunity of which, as evidenced by his subsequent accomplishments, he must have taken the fullest advantage. He left England in September, 1892, upon being transferred to the firm's first branch office—or agency—in America, which Lewis D. Jones had opened two years earlier at 45 Broadway, New York City; at that time the personnel of the organization consisted of Jones, William J. Caesar (in charge of the Chicago office), Sandys B. Foster, Edwin Chapp and Colley.

He resigned from Price Waterhouse & Co. sometime during 1895 to accept an important executive position in industry, i.e., he became secretary and treasurer of W. & J. Sloane, the well-known carpet merchants, where he remained until the latter part of 1898. He was engaged by Haskins & Sells on January 23, 1899, and remained with them until November of that year, at which time he left to accept the position of secretary and treasurer of the Bickford & Huffman Company at Macedon, New York. That Company was merged in 1903 with the American Seeding Machine Company, of which Colley then became a director and the secretary and general auditor. In 1906, he returned to W. & J. Sloane in their San Francisco organization, remaining with them until sometime in 1908. From 1908 to 1911, he was president of the Anglo-American Button Company at Seneca Falls, New York, and on August 14, 1911, he returned to Haskins & Sells where he remained until November 30, 1912, leaving them to go with Touche, Niven & Co.

Colley became associated with Touche, Niven & Co., which was then operating as a corporation, on January 1, 1913, as a director with a participation in the earnings. Upon dissolution of the corporation as of October 1, 1913, he emerged, along with the others who were interested in the practice, with full partnership status. Among the matters which came under his aegis during his short connection with that firm was the opening, on October 17, 1913, of their Chicago office, at No. 10 South LaSalle Street, of which he was in charge for a short period pending the appointment of a resident manager. Colley withdrew from the firm as of July 31, 1917, to assume the comptrollership of the Pierce Oil Corporation. Due to internal dissensions, his stay with the Corporation was short-lived; it appears that he resigned sometime during 1918, after which he entered the practice of public accountancy on his own responsibility, having desk room for a while with Charles S. McCulloh, the then secretary of the New York State Board of Certified Public Accountant Examiners. Some time prior to or about August, 1919, Colley then associated himself with Arthur Young & Co. as a partner in the local New York partnership of the firm, and when the united firm embracing all offices was formed in 1921 he became a member of that firm, of which he remained a partner up to the date of his untimely decease on September 2, 1933, at the age of 61, in his native England, at Wimbledon, where he had gone that summer to spend his vacation.

It was rather inevitable that Colley, being the aggressive personality that he was, coupled with his wide and diversified experience and the many positions he held both in the profession and industry, developed into a proficient and accomplished accountant. He had a keen mind, able to perceive the significance of business transactions and financial results with almost uncanny correctness, was master of the written word and, being blessed with an abundance of energy, was an indefatigable worker; above all, he was an intensely practical accountant and an inspiration for anyone who had occasion to meet him. He sat for the New York C.P.A. examination in June, 1912, and was given a rating of 100 per cent in each of the four parts of the examination, as a result of which there was issued to him New York C.P.A. Certificate No. 586, dated August 20, 1912, to which a blue seal inscribed "100%" was attached with the legend "With Honor" appearing alongside the seal. Subsequently, in 1923, Colley was the recipient of Wisconsin C.P.A. Certificate No. 187.

Immediately following receipt of his C.P.A. certificate, Colley was admitted to membership in The New York State Society of Certified Public Accountants as of August 30, 1912, and, by reason of that membership, became automatically, pursuant to the scheme then in vogue, a member in the American Association of Public Accountants, the earlier name of the American Institute of Accountants. Colley participated actively in the affairs of these professional organizations, having been, between 1913 and 1917, a member of the Legislation, the Arbitration and several other committees of The New York State Society; and, between 1916 and 1924, he was a member of the committee on Education (for two terms) and the Committee on State Legislation—of which he was chairman, 1922-24—of the American Institute. Also, he served as auditor of the Institute for the year 1921-22. He had been a member of the National Association of Cost

Accountants since its inception in 1919, and at one time (1923) was a member of the American Society of Certified Public Accountants.

Colley was one of the prime movers in the formation of The Accountants Club of America, Inc. He attended the first organization dinner at the old Waldorf-Astoria Hotel in New York City, preceding the Club's incorporation, and was one of its incorporators. At the time of his death he was Chairman of its Advisory Board. Shortly after his decease, the Board of Governors passed a resolution in recognition of his loyalty to and his untiring efforts on behalf of the Club with an expression of "its sorrow at the great loss which the Club had sustained in the death of its esteemed member."

It should be chronicled, also, that Colley was interested in other organizations outside of the profession, notably, the American Society of Mechanical Engineers, of which he was an associate; the American Geographical Society, of which he was a fellow; and The American Association for the Advancement of Science, of which he was a regular member.

While Colley was not as prolific a writer as some other well-known accountants, he made some worthy contributions to the literature of accountancy. Of his more-important papers, six are listed on page 250 of the Accountant's Index, 1920, and two others on page 164 of the Second Supplement, 1923-1927. The first appearance of Colley's writings in the public prints, according to these lists, deserves special mention, revealing, as it does, an interesting and characteristic angle of his basic thinking and attitudes at the time he sat for the C.P.A. examination. It is a communication addressed by him to the "Editor, Journal of Accountancy", on July 15, 1912, in which he expressed his opinion regarding C.P.A. examinations in general, but more particularly describing his impressions regarding the June, 1912, New York C.P.A. examination. For anyone who may wish to read the communication, it may be said that its significance lies largely in the fact that it was written shortly after he had sat for the examination but before knowing that he had passed with such signal honors as already reported herein. The communication appears under the title, "An Appreciation of the New York C.P.A. Examinations" on pages 148 to 150 of the August, 1912, issue of The Journal of Accountancy. However, for the benefit of anyone not having readily available back issues of the Journal and who may not care to read the whole letter, its two opening paragraphs, the really salient ones, are quoted in full below:

> "As a candidate who took the June examination for certified public accountant in the state of New York, and before knowing the result, I desire to express my appreciation of the character of the questions in all of the first four subjects. I believe I am a practical accountant, for I first entered the office of a chartered accountant in London nearly twenty-four years ago, and have had a varied experience in American offices for twenty years. Circumstances have prevented my trying for the C.P.A. degree until this year, but I have watched the examination questions in many states, and particularly New York, for many years. I have heard the examinations in the past criticised as being "theoretical," "academic," and no real "test of a practical man." Surely this criticism cannot fairly hold against the recent examination. Whether I, personally, have been successful or not, I submit that the questions were eminently practical, covering a wide and proper range in all four subjects,—a fair and and [*sic*] excellent test of a man's right to practice as a C.P.A., and comparing well with the best examination ever held for certified public accountants in the United States or for chartered accountants in Great Britain—and I have read the questions set at the majority of them from the beginning of examinations to date.
>
> "The refreshing feature of the examination is the evident purpose of the board of examiners to maintain, and to hold candidates to, standards. Practical accountants have preached for years of the necessity for standardizing nomenclature, classifications and forms, etc., yet when the Interstate Commerce Commission comes out as an authorized supreme court of last resort, possessing all the final authority of law, and imposes upon the profession a classification of accounts for steam roads, for instance, some of these same accountants 'howl' because said classification does not meet their narrow views in some particular. Likewise with the Public Service Commission and its accounting rules for various public utilities. These men overlook the fact that these governmental bodies have honestly sought and obtained the opinions of the very best practical men in the offices of railroads and other enterprises concerned."

The remainder of the communication deals almost wholly with a discussion of some of the questions and problems—placing special emphasis on the relationship of the theory questions to the practical problems—that were comprised in the several parts of the June, 1912 examination.

This biography, being restricted to Colley's business and professional activities, does not attempt to cover his private life; but, it might be well to mention, in passing, that he married Effie M. Cushman in August, 1898, and that they had one child, Dorothy E. At one time the family had a modest estate at Lake Mahopac, Putnam County, N.Y.

In conclusion, Colley, beyond his aggressive and, what to his intimates sometimes appeared, irascible and emotional disposition, was of a generous and understanding nature. He was always ready to render assistance and impart sage advice to those seeking help—not only as it related to professional matters but, also, concerning problems of a strictly personal character. All those who knew him regretted keenly his passing at his early age, fully aware that they had lost a true and loyal friend.

Charles Ezra Sprague—Public Accountant

By The Committee on History

This article points up three important but less widely known aspects of the later career of this early leader of our profession: (1) his relationship to the earliest effort to provide specialized formal education for the public practice of accounting; (2) his preparation of the first CPA law; and (3) his service upon the first State Board of CPA Examiners.

The 67-page biography of Colonel Sprague by Helen Scott Mann, which New York University published in 1931, is very interesting and in some respects quite satisfactory. The author told of his parentage and boyhood; of his four years at Union College where he was graduated (A.B.) in 1860 when he was 18 years of age, receiving an A.M. in 1862 and his Ph.D. in 1896, and becoming a Life Trustee in 1906; of his enlistment in the Union Army in May, 1862, being wounded at Gettysburg, and discharged a Colonel in March, 1864. The story continues, after his wound had healed sufficiently, with his teaching in the military academies in Yonkers, Peekskill and Poughkeepsie. His biographer recited incidents of his marriage and family life, their travel, his interest in the artificial languages, Volapuk and Esperanto, and his love of music particularly that of Sousa's and other bands. Though necessarily brief, this recital seems to be complete as to these phases of his life, except that it does not mention his "teaching in what is now Greenwich Union Academy, remaining there a year and a half" which Colonel Sprague included in a sketch for a Union College publication in 1907. And of less importance, it did not mention his adoption of simplified spelling of which he was an advocate and which he used in some of his writings.

The biographer very properly told of his 41 years in the Union Dime Savings Bank, and gave more space to his service in the School of Commerce, Accounts and Finance of New York University, and to

---

This is the eighth in a series of articles on the History of Accounting in the State of New York. It was prepared by the Society's Committee on History.

his authorship, but told only incidentally and largely by quotation, of his participation in accountancy as a profession.

Without minimizing in any degree the importance of his activities in the fields covered in the Mann biography it seems that his experience in bookkeeping and accounting was a major factor in preparing him for the more spectacular services he rendered during his last ten or fifteen years.

In the chapter on his authorship the biography stated:

> "In addition to writing articles for business magazines, such as *Business* and *The Office*, he took an active part in the publication of two, acting as associate editor of *The Bookkeeper* and *The Journal of Accountancy*." (Chapter 5, page 57)

While no confirmation has been found of such association with the *Journal*, he was connected with *The Bookkeeper* and the story of that relation introduces the reader to his activities in accountancy.

The publication of *The Bookkeeper* was begun July 20, 1880, and in its issue of August 31, 1880, page 64, it said of itself:

> "The First and only Publication of its character in the world."

As published for the groups he addressed that was true. *The Accountant*, London, was first published in October, 1874, but it was addressed to public accountants.

To the first issue of *The Bookkeeper* Sprague contributed the first of four installments on the "Algebra of Accounts," and in the fourth issue, August 31, he began a series on "Bank Bookkeeping" which he carried through 25 installments to December 31, 1881. Before that series was completed, the editor, Selden R. Hopkins, announced in the issue of August 2, 1881, that Charles E. Sprague

> "will henceforth share the duties and responsibilities of the editorial department of *The Bookkeeper*."

That relationship continued through June 19, 1883, when the name and format were changed and, instead of a bi-weekly as *The Bookkeeper* had been during 3 years, it was published monthly as *American Counting Room* from July, 1883.

Apparently these magazines like others in limited fields had financial difficulties. As of January 1, 1884, the periodical, which up to that time had been the property of Hopkins, was incorporated as the Counting Room Company, Limited, with Sprague as President, George S. Parker as Vice President, and Hopkins as Secretary-Treasurer. But in March following, Hopkins withdrew and as a result no issues were published during April and May, but Sprague brought out an issue for April-June 1884. His editorial explanation of the delay indicated that the publication would be continued, but no later issue has been found. Since it appears that he was the largest stockholder, probably because of loans to Hopkins prior to 1884, it is not unreasonable to suppose that he, as a banker during the preceding decade, realized that the publication could not be made to pay its way.

But his connections with these publications during 3 years as contributor and editor were not Sprague's only relation with them. He was also an advertiser. *The Bookkeeper* in October 26, 1880, page 128, with other notices carried the following:

"Charles E. Sprague
Accountant
Address, by mail, Union Dime Savings
Institution
Broadway and 32nd St., New York, N.Y."

At that time, after 7 years as a clerk in the Savings Bank, he had become its Secretary. The public practice for which he offered his services, was probably a side vocation but almost surely one in which he was greatly interested. His professional card was continued throughout. And the February 27, 1883, issue (page 77) said:

> "The editors of The Bookkeeper will undertake the audit, adjustment and examination of accounts of corporations, public officers, manufacturers, merchants, etc., in any part of the United States. They may be consulted on questions of accountancy, and will advise in the organization and the opening and closing of books of account."

Of course this may have been the beginning of Sprague's practice as a public accountant, but since Hopkins had been practicing since 1868, it seems probable that the association of Hopkins and Sprague in editorial work and public practice was based upon a longer experience of Sprague's. He was listed as a public accountant in the New York Directory of 1885.

Quoting from the introduction by John R. Loomis in the fifth edition of "The Philosophy of Accounts," the biography, on page 63 in referring to the Institute of Accounts and American Association of Public Accountants, said that Sprague was

> "among the earliest to assume membership in these organizations."

That was incorrect as to the Association, in which his membership dated from the entrance of the New York State Society of C.P.A.'s. in 1905.

However, it was correct as to the Institute, which he joined fairly soon after its organization in 1882. Frequently he lectured at its meetings and he was its President on December 15, 1886, when the Institute had Edwin Guthrie of Manchester as its guest. He joined the New York State Society of C.P.A.'s. in May, 1897.

As his Army service had prepared him for his teaching in the three military academies; as those years with his earlier teaching in the Greenwich Union Academy had equipped him for the art of instruction; and as his clerical work in the bank had provided the knowledge which he put into his many articles in *The Bookkeeper*; so these experiences, coupled with that from his public practice, his editorial work, and his membership in the Institute of Accounts, prepared him for other services barely mentioned or not at all in the Mann biography.

The first of these and the one of which the least is known was his relationship to the earliest effort in the world to provide specialized formal education for the public practice of accounting. Early in 1892, the American Association of Public Accountants sent to the Regents of the University of the State of New York, a petition for a charter for a College of Accounts. A hearing thereon was held in Albany on June 8, 1892, when those who met with the Regents Committee included 14 officers and members of the Association, Melvil Dewey, Secretary to the Regents (in many ways corresponding to the present Commissioner of Education) and a long-time friend of Dewey, Charles E. Sprague. There are no records of his participation in the meeting—he seems to have been only an observer—but it also seems that he may have told his friend Dewey that the purpose was important, but the proposal then made was too ambitious. If so it is highly probable that Dewey passed the advice on to the Regents.

The next instance was in the matter of CPA legislation and as to that we have Sprague's own statement. *Business* for July, 1896, page 320, printed Col. Spragues' [*sic*] letter of July 10, thus:

> "The above is a copy of a bill prepared by me and introduced in the Legislature in January (actually March) 1895, including Section 4 which was withdrawn in committee. I prepared the bill as a member of a committee of the Institute of Accounts. This copy has been in my possession ever since January 24, 1895 until today. C. E. Sprague."

As is common knowledge the bill was defeated in the Senate in 1895, but was passed almost unanimously in 1896. The success in 1896 seems to have been due to the Association's Committee and especially Frank Broaker. But the scope and wording of the bill were Sprague's, no doubt with advice from Dewey, but Sprague must have the credit for having a good advisor.

The third instance, that of his service on the State Board of Examiners was briefly mentioned in the biography and in his autobiographical sketch prepared in 1907. There are records as to the reasons for the selection of the other two members appointed in 1896, but not as to the selection of Colonel Sprague. It seems quite possible that he may have been suggested by a formal resolution of the Institute of Accounts. That is not known, however, because no trace of the Institute's records has been found. But even if the Institute did or did not suggest him for appointment by the Regents it is almost certain that the Regent's Secretary Melvil Dewey, who had opinions as to the administration of the CPA Law which he knew were contrary to the hopes and expectations of most public accountants, wanted on the Board of Examiners one whom he had known for long and on whose judgment he felt he could rely.

To Certified Public Accountants, while recognizing the value of his authorship and teaching, it seems that his preparation of the first CPA Law and his service upon the first State Board of Examiners were the most important services of Charles Ezra Sprague.

Robert Lancelot Cuthbert

By THE COMMITTEE ON HISTORY

Orrin Bishop Judd once wrote, "Biography is the fountain-head of history. As the waters of a thousand springs run, in confluent streams, from mountain-heights to the ocean; so the lives of individuals, coalescing in families, communities and nations, are merged in, and make up the general history of mankind." This is the brief story of the only member of our Society to make the supreme sacrifice in World War I.

As one leaves the elevator car at 677 Fifth Avenue to enter the offices of The New York State Society of Certified Public Accountants, he may see on the wall directly in front of him a bronze plaque which below an eagle bears the following legend.

"In memory of the
following members of the
New York Society of
Certified Public Accountants
who made the supreme
sacrifice in World War II

* * * *

Charles Daum
Vernon L. Denby
William Coros
William Combrinck-Graham
Jack Hauser
Irving Levine
Alexander Saladuchin
Leo Taub
Richard C. Whitelocke

* * * *

This is the ninth of a series of articles on the History of Accounting in the State of New York, prepared by the Society's Committee on History.

and in honor of the
904 members who served
in the armed forces."

At September 30, 1945, about the end of the fighting, the membership of the Society was reported to be 4,892. Nearly 19% of that number were or had been in the armed services. And the losses by death of the 9 for whom the above described memorial was made were 1 out of 544 of the total membership.

At the end of World War I the membership was between 372 as at May 10, 1918, and 400 as at May 12, 1919, perhaps midway at 386. The number in the services was not reported. But the records show that of them one life was lost out of the membership of 386.

This is an appreciation of that single member who in that earlier conflict made the supreme sacrifice—

ROBERT LANCELOT CUTHBERT

What he was may be suggested by facts of his biography and confirmed by what was said of him by those who knew him well.

His father, Hugh Cuthbert, son of a well-known ship-owner of Greenock, Scotland, and his mother, Anne, daughter of Col. Sir Thomas Wilkinson, Knight Commander of the Star of India, were the parents of six sons and two daughters. One of the daughters and all six sons were in active military service, two sons in the Boer War in South Africa and four in World War I in which 2d. Lt. Reginald Vaux Cuthbert of the Seaforth Highlanders was killed in action.

Robert, the oldest child, was born in Greenock, Scotland, on June 19, 1868. He was educated at Wimbledon School near London and the University of Edinburgh. In continuation of his education he served as an apprentice of A. & J. Robertson, Chartered Accountants of Edinburgh, from 1886 to 1891. Then upon an examination of the Scottish Institute in 1891, in which he was a prizeman, he became a Chartered Accountant of Edinburgh. Based upon this educational background and upon his experience in practice, which will be told a little later, he became New York Certified Public Accountant #16 in 1896, being one of the second group for which the examination was waived.

He came to New York probably early in 1894 and soon took out his papers for naturalization when about 26 years of age.

Before coming to the United States he had been employed by public accountants in London, perhaps Deloitte's from 1891 to 1893. Here in New York he practiced alone about 4 years, 1894-1897. In 1898 he and Frederick W. Menzies, CA, founded Cuthbert, Menzies & Co., which early in 1899 became Cuthbert, Boughey and Menzies (upon the addition to the firm of Frank M. Boughey, CA, CPA) to March 31, 1900.

From April 1, 1900, he resumed his practice alone through 1904; then was a partner in Deloitte, Plender, Griffiths & Co., from 1905 to 1911; and then of Arthur Young & Co. during 1912 to about May 1914, after which for a few months he resumed his individual practice. In 1914 he visited Great Britain and his practice of accountancy was ended. But it should be noted that beside his membership in the Society of Accountants in Edinburgh dating from 1891, he became a member of The New York State Society of CPAs, April 1897, and through that, of the American Association of Public Accountants in 1905, retaining all these memberships throughout his life.

But he was not one of the kind of accountants described by Elbert Hubbard. Though he never married, he mixed with men. His clubs were the Garden City, National and St. Andrews Golf Clubs, the City Club and St. Andrews Society of New York; and two yacht clubs, the New York and the Seawanhaka-Corinthian. Probably his greatest sports interest found expression in yachting, especially in small boats of which he owned several and raced them himself.

While Cuthbert was vacationing in London in the summer of 1914, World War I broke out. There is no record of his consideration of what that meant to him. Perhaps he thought of his grandfather in India, or of his two brothers who served in South Africa, or of his three brothers and a sister who then were or soon were to be in the present conflict. Was not that enough for one family? Besides, he was 46 years of age, and an American citizen. But persuasive arguments to the contrary, *noblesse oblige*.

There is a record that "to do his bit for the land of his birth he applied to a recruiting Sergeant who refused to believe he was as young as he stated. Cuthbert contended that no matter what his age was, he was physically able to endure the hardships of a soldier's life. The Sergeant, admiring his persistence, agreed to accept him if he could pass the doctor, and he did * * * he joined the 2nd King Edward's Horse, attached to the 1st Canadian Division, then in training at

Windsor, and there he spent the winter and spring until his regiment was sent to France."

From there his story is short. "While engaged in particularly hazardous scout duty in Flanders he was shot on July 6, 1915 and died the next day."

Perhaps it was the result of their training or of some inherent disposition to stick to facts of record and to avoid statements of their own impressions, that accountants have said so little of him. The president of The New York State Society of CPAs in his annual report dated May 18, 1916, said: "Death has again claimed toll of our society and I have to announce the loss of four of our esteemed members during the past year." He named them, one being Robert L. Cuthbert. No officer of the American Association of Public Accountants reported the losses by death which that society had sustained. The obituary in the *Journal of Accountancy* told only a little of his professional life and of his enlistment and death. The editor of *The Pace Student* went a little further and wrote that "Cuthbert's friends among American accountants will be greatly pained to learn the sad news."

But others outside his profession did not have such inhibitions. "His fellow soldiers spoke most highly of his courage and gallantry as a soldier and they missed him as a true friend and companion. His sunny disposition was always a help to his fellow soldiers." Those fellow soldiers had known him during only a few months. Extracts from records of a few of the organizations with which he was connected in New York reflect earlier opinions of him.

The Trustees of the Seawanhaka-Corinthian Yacht Club recorded:

> "His untiring energy and interest in the Club and its best attainments over a period of twelve years, as well as his enthusiasm and interest in the sport of yachting will long be remembered and appreciated, but the qualities which now truly endeared him to us were those of loyal friendship and true sportsmanship which makes his death so keenly felt by us. Therefore Resolved in his passing the members have lost a warm and loyal friend, an enthusiastic yachtsman, a keen sportsman and a charming companion."

The New York Yacht Club's Committee on Resolutions said:

> "In his death this Club has suffered an irreparable loss; he was an enthusiastic yachtsman, the master of his vessel, a corinthian. In the private relations of life his loss will be felt by those who best knew him. Always courteous, generous and mindful of the comfort and pleasure of others, it is

> not strange that he kept the affectionate regard of all with whom he came into contact. The members of the New York Yacht Club have lost a friend."

The Council of the University Settlement Society resolved:

> "Mr. Cuthbert had an interesting personality. He was a man of high character, great energy and unusual capacity; he had the warmest of human sympathies and an abounding generosity. He was capable of close friendship and had many friends. His many acts of unsolicited kindness to them will not soon be forgotten. His sense of duty was unusually keen . . . While a member of the Council, the Settlement enjoyed the benefit of Mr. Cuthbert's zealous, unselfish and effective work and it is fitting that this minute be made in testimony of the service he rendered, of the appreciation of the Council of his character and of its sincere sorrow on account of his untimely death."

Robert Lancelot Cuthbert, we, of those for whom you died, salute you!

[*November, 1952*. Reprinted with permission from *The CPA Journal*, copyright 1952]

The First Woman C.P.A.

By THE COMMITTEE ON HISTORY

This paper sketches the professional career of Christine Ross, the first woman CPA (New York) in the United States. Briefer mention is also made of the careers of Harriett B. Lowenstein and Theodora Daub, the next two women to receive CPA certificates from New York State.

Even as late as the 1930's a news item about a woman who passed the CPA examination in almost any state was likely to include an assertion that she was "the first woman CPA." Such an assertion not only reflected a lack of information about women's interest in accounting, but no doubt was also influenced by a regrettable state of public ignorance about the accounting profession in general.

Accountancy and the functions of the CPA are receiving wider publicity in an era in which their contribution to the general welfare is recognized if not always understood. That women have been interested in accountancy from the earliest days is not equally well known.

One of the difficulties of research about women arises from the fact that names are not always an index. Florence, for example, though predominantly a feminine name, is occasionally bestowed upon male offspring as well. So when we find Florence Crowley listed as an accountant in the New York Directory in 1797 at 237 Water Street, in 1798 at 59 Cherry Street, and in 1802 at 16 Banker Street, and Florence Crowdy similarly listed in 1801 at 9 Frankfort Street, we cannot be sure that Florence Crowley, or Florence Crowdy, was a woman. About Margaret and Viola there is less uncertainty. We are therefore probably safe in assuming that Margaret Barrow, listed as an accountant in the New York Directory of 1897-1900, and Viola D. Waring, similarly listed in 1898-1899, were women.

About Christine Ross we can be sure. Although there are some gaps in the record, it seems clear that she not only practiced public accounting but was the first woman in the United States to pass the

---

This is the fourteenth in a series of articles on the History of Accounting in the State of New York. It was prepared by the Society's Committee on History.

examination for the CPA certificate. Newspaper and magazine articles published around the turn of the century, supplemented by information obtained from a former employer, from the superintendent of the building in which she had her office, and from a few persons who remember her, together with data contained in the files of the State Education Department, furnish both a story and a modicum of background.

Christine Ross was born in Nova Scotia, possibly around 1873, perhaps earlier. She had a taste for mathematics and logic and is reported to have studied law, though whether or not she ever attended law school for the purpose is not known.

Her accounting experience dated from 1889, but where her experience before 1902 was had and what it consisted of is not known. The State Education Department around 1899 had a record of an address for her at 70—31st Street, Milwaukee. It is possible, however, that this was a temporary address, since the other available information places her in New York both before and after this date. In 1902 she had offices with the Manning Yacht Agency at 45 Broadway, and later had an office at 17 Battery Place. An article in *The Business World* of April, 1902, stated that in addition to acting in several public capacities and besides the services rendered to Manning Yacht Agency, she performed accounting services for a clientele which included many women of wealth, women of fashion, women in business, and societies of women.

The exact date of the CPA examination which she took has not been established, but it can be placed within a period of thirteen months.

On April 17, 1896, New York became the first state to adopt a CPA law. Because the New York State Capitol fire in 1911 destroyed certain records of the early examinations, it is not certain whether Christine Ross took the examination in June 1898, December 1898, or June 1899, but it is certain that she took and passed one of these examinations and that she received certificate No. 143, dated December 27, 1899.

The difficulty in establishing the date on which she was examined arises not only from the loss of records in the State Capitol fire but from a few discrepancies in other sources of information.

In its July, 1899, issue, *The Public Accountant*, a Philadelphia publication, used the word "recently" in noting that she had passed the examination and had requested that a certificate be granted her. This might have referred to the examination of June 13-14, 1899 (the sixth examination), although it seems rather soon for the matter to have been ready for comment in a July magazine, or it may have referred to the fifth examination, which was given on December 13-14, 1898.

In its February, 1900, issue, *The Book-keeper* of Detroit referred to her application as having been made a year before. If so, it probably was for the fifth examination, that of December 13-14, 1898. The article also stated that there were twelve candidates, of whom she was No. 3. *The Business World*, New York, stated in its April, 1902, issue that her name was second on the list of those who passed the examination in December, 1898.

The minutes of the Board of Examiners show that for the sixth examination there were only six candidates, of whom two passed. For the fifth examination, that of December, 1898, the minutes record that No. 3 was the third highest of those who passed all subjects. Ratings of No. 3 were: law, 84; theory, 89; practical accounting, 75; and auditing, 90.

Since the article in *The Business World* was based on an interview with Miss Ross and since the minutes of the Board of Examiners tally fairly well with the statements made in the article, the assumption at this point is that it was the December, 1898, examination which she took.

But there is a further complication. In the minutes of a meeting of the Board of Regents held December 21, 1899, we find this record:

> "Voted that the full C.P.A. certificate be granted to Christine Ross, who successfully passed the professional examination in June, 1898."

This was the fourth examination. The minutes of the Board of Examiners do not record the number of candidates who took this examination or their ratings. Could the minutes of the Board of Regents have been in error as to the date? One can only conjecture as to the date of her examination, but this much is clear: She was the first woman to pass a CPA examination and the first to receive a CPA certificate. On March 29, 1899, Pennsylvania had become the second state to adopt a CPA law. It gave its first examination in November, 1899, and, according to the *Accountants' Directory and Who's Who*, 1925, issued a certificate to Mary B. Niles in 1900. As we have seen,

Miss Ross took her examination in New York no later than June, 1899, and received her certificate as of December 27, 1899.

Another matter which is clear is that there was an interval of eighteen, twelve, or six months between the time of the examination and the date of the issuance of her certificate. The story of this delay is told in the public prints of that time.

In July, 1899, *The Public Accountant*, Philadelphia (Vol. I, No. 10, page 115), carried a lead editorial as follows:

> *"The New York Examination Controversy*
>
> "An amusing incident occurred recently in New York, amusing to the accountants in other States, but the New Yorkers fail to see the joke, and very rightly, too.
>
> "The facts of the case are these: It seems that a certain New York accountant (whom we will call Jones, because that is not his name) had some difficulty or other with the Regents of the State of New York. How this trouble arose or the merits of either case is not to the point here; sufficient be it that there was trouble and that Jones made the remark that 'the examination questions set by the Regents were too easy and that any old woman, who never had any actual experience, could pass the examination.' This the Regents denied. Jones made no contradiction of this, but he immediately set himself about coaching a person, who had never handled a set of books. This person took the examination, and passed away up and now desires that a certificate be granted, when lo and behold, the said person turns out to be a woman, a relative of Jones' typewriter. Then the fight commenced. The Regents offered to give her a junior certificate, but Jones seriously demurred to this, saying, 'The person is of full age, has passed an examination set by you, and she is entitled to a full certificate.'
>
> "There the matter rests.
>
> "Jones and the Regents are at worse loggerheads than ever and the time for healing the breach seems as far off as ever.
>
> "Like all other innovations, the Examining Boards in New York and Pennsylvania have to put up with many difficulties until proper amendments can be determined on and passed. This woman affair is only one of the many pitfalls which could not be foreseen when the acts were passed.
>
> "The editor refrains from comment on the above case but leaves it to the accountants to determine whether Jones was right or wrong."

A sequel to this editorial appeared in the next issue, that of August, 1899, on page 127 of Volume I, No. 11:

"A Correction

"In the last month's issue of *The Public Accountant* there appeared an article on the editorial page entitled 'The New York Examination Controversy,' in which mention was made of a woman who had passed the examination entitling her to a certificate from the Regents. The facts on which this article was based were supplied by a New York accountant of known integrity, but, it seems, there is a mistake somewhere, as the following letter will show:

"Editor of *The Public Accountant*,
Philadelphia, Pa.

"Dear Sir:—My attention has been called to your July editorial, entitled 'The New York Examination Controversy,' and as I am the 'person' who figures in this 'amusing incident,' I trust you will grant me the courtesy of a short space in your next issue to correct some of your 'facts.'

"I have had ten years' practice in accounting. I was not coached by a man whom you call Jones. I am not a relative of his typewriter. I know nothing of trouble between the Regents of the State of New York and the man whom you call Jones; but so far as I am concerned, your only 'fact' is: 'This person took the examination, passed away up, and now desires that a certificate be granted.

Yours very truly
Christine Ross
45 Broadway, New York

July 31, 1899

"To say the least, the editor was startled to receive such a contradiction, but, with the idea of ascertaining the exact state of affairs, he communicated with several correspondents and found to his sorrow that a rather grave mistake had been made and that the injured one was a lady. He therefore makes all the reparation possible under the circumstances by publishing the history of the whole matter. The fact that the editor at the time of writing had no idea of the identity of the lady who took the examination is the only extenuating circumstance in the case.

"As Miss Ross is the only woman who has taken the C.P.A. examination in New York, she must necessarily be the one referred to."

Two further articles tell us more about Miss Ross. The first appeared as an editorial in *The Book-keeper*, Detroit, on page 94 of the issue of February, 1900, Volume XII, No. 8. It reads in part as follows:

"The postman who delivers mail in a Broadway office district gave into a young woman's hands one day last month a document so distinctly a cause for congratulation that she has had a smile and a bright word for him ever since. The document was postmarked Albany. Before it came the young woman was just a plain, everyday bookkeeper—a good bookkeeper, but merely one of the rank and file. Now she is a C.P.A., a Certified Public Accountant, and the only one of her sex who has won, or indeed, applied for the degree. The document was the certificate awarded by the Regents to show that she had successfully passed an examination in the following matters: Theory of accounts, practical accounting, auditing and commercial law, and is otherwise fitted for the profession of expert accountant. . . .

"* * *

"The candidates are known to the examiners only by numbers, and a year ago, when the young woman book-keeper made her application, her identity was not disclosed until her examination papers had been passed upon. There were twelve applicants in that class and when the person whose examination number was 3 applied by name for her certificate the board was non-plussed. She had passed an exceptionally good examination, but women had not been thought of as members when the association was chartered. The matter was therefore held over for further deliberation. The eleven men who passed the examination got their certificates promptly, but the young woman waited. A few days ago her triumph came, and now she is free to start out as the pioneer in an entirely new field for women."

The second is a full-page article in *The Business World*, published in New York in April, 1902, Volume XXII, page 175. As has been stated, this article was based on an interview with Miss Ross and is the source of some of the biographical data appearing herein. It quoted her as saying, "I think women should have equal opportunity with men to earn an independent living in any business or profession they choose to enter." It also contained her photograph, the likeness of a pleasant-faced woman.

Of her later history not much was discovered, except that she married a man named Barker and is believed to have returned, with him, to Canada and afterward removed to the Pacific Coast.

There are now around 150 women CPA's in New York State and around 900 in the United States, but for seven years Christine Ross was the only woman to hold a full New York CPA certificate. In 1907, another woman was certified, one junior certificate having been issued in the meantime. The junior certificate, which was issued in 1905, went to Mary E. Slater, the full certificate to Harriett B. Lowenstein.

Mary E. Slater studied accounting at Koehler's New York School of Accounts. She was employed by I. Newman & Sons, Inc., as a private accountant and may never have entered public practice.

Harriett B. Lowenstein became a CPA (certificate No. 351) in 1907, and was admitted to the practice of law in the same year. It appears, therefore, that she was the first woman to be both a New York

CPA and a member of the New York Bar. In her examination she received a perfect rating in practical accounting. She was the first controller of the Federation of Jewish Charities and of the American Joint Distribution Committee and installed the accounting system in each of these organizations. From 1913 to 1920 (the date of her marriage) she was philanthropic advisor to the late Felix M. Warburg of Kuhn, Loeb & Company.

She was the first woman employed as an attorney in the law department of the City of New York, where, on assignment to the Appeals Division of the Corporation Counsel's office, she prepared a three-volume index and digest of cases in which the city appeared. She also did some briefing in the Appeals Division.

In 1920 she married Jonah J. Goldstein, who was then an attorney and is now a Judge of Court of General Sessions of the County of N. Y.

Theodora Daub had also passed the examinations in 1907, but her junior certificate received at that time (No. 356) did not become a full certificate until 1909. She was born in New York in 1879, and attended Yonkers High School and New York Preparatory School, and in 1904 joined the staff of Theodore Koehler, CPA, whom she later married. She was associated with him in the conduct of his New York School of Accounts and was co-author with him of several books on accounting.

Of the three women who, by 1909, had received full CPA certificates from New York State, two, Harriett Lowenstein and Theodora Daub, joined the New York State Society of Certified Public Accountants, thereby establishing a pattern for those who came later in far greater numbers.

Robert H. Montgomery, C.P.H.

By The Committee on History

This article deals with the lifelong hobby of the late Col. Montgomery—trees

No, the final letter of this caption is not a printer's erratum. It is properly an H and the three letters indicate a degree or license which he earned—*Confirmed Persistent Hobbyist.*

He made fun of himself and said he was lazy. But the truth was that he gave his time and himself to play with the same zest that he had shown in the work just completed.

Robert Hiester Montgomery was not only an accountant—as to which adjectives are superfluous—but also a teacher, a student in order to keep, as he said, one day ahead of his class, a collector of old books of account to illustrate his teaching and, as an outgrowth of his teaching, an author. His autobiography, issued in 1939, carried a picture of him at his desk which showed more than forty volumes bearing his name.

At some time during that period of teaching and writing he became a collector of old books on accounting. His zest in that activity resulted in the Montgomery Library, which he gave to Columbia University.

To enlarge their qualifications as accountants he advised others to study law as he had done. And then, by admission to the Bar, he had a new tool and used it in practice as an attorney.

Early at the outset of the Spanish-American War he enlisted in the Infantry, where he was soon made a lieutenant. But to better his prospect for getting to the front, he again enlisted as a private in a battery of light artillery. It was not his fault that he did not fight. His transport got stuck in the mud at Ponce.

Early in 1917 he was called to Washington on war work. There he was made a lieutenant colonel and was given not only medals for service in the Spanish-American War but a number of full-time jobs which did not end with the cessation of fighting. As a result of this

---

This is the fifteenth in a series of articles on the History of Accounting in the State of New York. It was prepared by the Society's Committee on History.

experience he later formed the Accountants Post of the American Legion.

From 1899, when in Philadelphia he was one of the founders of the Pennsylvania Institute of Certified Public Accountants, he held offices in many societies of accountants. He was treasurer and later secretary of the Federation of Societies of Public Accountants in the United States of America and served as president for two years each of the American Association of Public Accountants, the New York State Society of Certified Public Accountants, and the American Institute of Accountants. He had an active part in planning the first Congress of Accountants at St. Louis in 1904. He represented the American Institute at the Congresses held abroad and was president of the 1929 Congress in New York.

Perhaps this is as good a place as any to mention the Accountants Club, of which he was an organizer and the first president.

However, it seems proper to consider that teaching, authorship, collecting old books and almost continuous office holding in accountants societies, and even his organization of the Accountants Post of the American Legion, all were developments in varying degrees from his basic activity in public accountancy. Probably no other accountant covered so much ground and cultivated it so deeply. But many have settled upon portions of those fields and raised and harvested good crops.

Although these activities probably were hobbies, they did not fit in with his philosophy on the subject as stated years later and based upon his experience. He wrote:

> "Any hobby, even a poor one, will add years to one's life. A hobby which takes one out of doors, if taken on cheerfully at any time before fifty, will add at least ten years."

Of his early activities before he reached these conclusions, he said:

> "Some of my early collections were rather pitiful attempts but I always had a thrill over each new acquisition. I did get tired of some of them surprisingly soon, but usually because I found something new, and of course something vastly more important and interesting."

Apparently his hobby had to be one where horse and rider were fitted.

The hobby which fitted was trees, but as to why and how:

> "I'll never know why I selected trees as a hobby. Of course I loved them—most people do. I think it must have been because they are alive and have their moods and change from day to day."

If that tells the why perhaps the how is:

> "As far back as I can remember I have liked trees. I like the woods and the forests. I particularly like the forests in France. When I dashed off there for a change after working days, nights, and Sundays to finish a tax book, I would spend days in driving through their wonderful, well-kept forests."

So then in the late 1910's, perhaps, he got his first impulse to take trees as the hobby he would ride.

He was then in his forties. To arrange his time-table to his theory that one should have his hobby before fifty it was necessary for him to act before 1922. As he told it:

> "After a long search in 1920 I found, thirty miles from New York in Connecticut, something better than I had expected to find, viz., a primeval hemlock forest, with ravines and ponds and a house. The house wasn't much but the forest was and is the only one of its kind near New York."

Anyone who has built his home, and especially one who has bought an old place, will know that at once the Colonel began to plan and do things. That is what we get homes for. In his "Fifty Years" he did not tell whether the place had a name when he bought it. But as "Wild Acres" it was soon known to his friends. All who know New England and New York will remember—if old enough—that early in this century all chestnut trees were killed by a blight. Although his book does not mention this, his friends recall his telling of his efforts to develop chestnuts which were immune to the blight. Not succeeding in that he brought and planted trees from China. Mrs. Montgomery tells the story thus:

> "The Chinese chestnut trees were already growing at Wild Acres when Bob and I were married. He had planted them after the blight killed the American chestnuts. They bore well and for several years we enjoyed great quantities of them. Then the neighboring children discovered them and we got very few thereafter. I used to fuss about this but Bob, in his philosophical way, defended the kids by saying to me, 'Didn't you ever steal apples when you were a kid?'"

This and other replacements or improvements to make good the depreciation or ordinary wear and tear of prior years seem to have been his hobby for several years. Then, in 1928, he read an article in the *Atlantic Monthly* written by George P. Brett about his pinetum. The Colonel's own story is too good to abridge.

"I found that a pinetum is a collection of cone-bearing evergreens. It was well written and, why I don't know, it made me feel as if I would like to start one at once. Soon afterwards the New York Botanical Garden sent me a booklet describing more than 100 different species and varieties growing in The Bronx. So I started. I found that Mr. Brett was President of The Macmillan Company and had a country house in Fairfield, not far from Greenwich. I wrote and asked him if I might see his conifers. He gave me a cordial invitation to lunch. Thus I met George Brett, whose memory today is a precious thought. He gave me good advice which I followed. With the frenzy of a collector, I was not satisfied until I had one or more specimens of every procurable variety. I visited all the nurseries in New England, New York, New Jersey, Pennsylvania, Delaware, and Maryland. I sent to England, France, and Holland. I built a special greenhouse 25 feet high to house the tender species. I found out how many different kinds there were in the Arnold Arboretum, the Rochester Parks, and The Bronx, and left no stone unturned until I passed them all. I now have about 700 different species and varieties growing and am advised that there is no other collection nearly as large.

"Mr. Brett was a horticulturist; I am not. He got more out of his trees horticulturally than I did out of mine, but I had more excitement than he had. I was annoyed at times to find that trees were exactly alike though bought under different names.

"I spent about a year trying to organize a Conifer Society. I wanted some authoritative body to settle disputes in nomenclature. About 200 signed up but it wasn't enough, so I dropped the idea. I still think that it has more possibilities than some of the other horticultural societies which exist.

"I spent much time in looking for new species and varieties of conifers. Mr. Little and I drove through most of the New England states, and visited as well many of the leading nurseries in New York and New Jersey. In this way I obtained many new species and fine specimen trees which cannot be duplicated. In some cases owners refused to sell rare or unusual trees which they had treated as pets for many years. But later on, in 1931 and 1932, many nurseries were hard pressed for money and I had rare trees offered to me not previously for sale. In this way I obtained my lovely weeping hemlock. A nurseryman sold it to me for $500 not so long after he had refused $1,200 offered by some one else.

"In my search for new varieties I found no one nursery which specialized in rare and unnamed specimens. My superintendent who had accompanied me on many buying trips agreed with me that a nursery which confined itself to rare varieties should make money. The business attracted me. I found that nurserymen were, with one solitary exception, a fine class of men. So I started the Montgomery Evergreen Nursery, Inc. We bought thousands of young trees and propagated many more. We were about to fill some good orders when F. D. R. closed all the banks and the orders were cancelled. I decided to take my loss and quit. It was a real loss in money and great disappointment."

This story of the pinetum at Wild Acres was published by R. H. M. in 1939. Probably he continued to expand the collection in quantity and variety. While no facts as to its growth thereafter are available, there are records of two acts by its owner as to the disposition of parts of the collection.

The first was on May 26, 1949, when the Colonel gave the New York Botanical Garden more than 200 species of conifers selected from the 700 or more at Wild Acres. About one-quarter of the gift was of native trees, but over 150 were foreign varieties. The gift was accepted and landscaped over an eight-acre area at the south end of the grounds. Each tree was labeled by Henry Teuscher of the Montreal Garden and all is known as the Montgomery Conifer Collection. At its dedication a new dwarf spruce was christened. It was named R. H. Montgomery and he gave to the Garden a young plant which he had raised from a cutting from the parent plant. The Colonel spoke, telling of the beauty of the conifer under all conditions. As a part of his talk he said:

"Through a microscope the winter buds of conifers are as beautiful as any rose, and in spring the color of the trees makes a wonderful picture."

It became known on the publication of his will in May, 1953, that on October 30, 1952, Robert Montgomery executed a codicil to his will reading in part as follows:

"I have now concluded that this property known as 'Wild Acres' should not be disposed of in any way which would destroy its unique beauty. . . .

"I therefore give and devise the aforesaid real property, including the buildings and improvements thereon owned by me, and located in the Town of Greenwich, Connecticut, to the TOWN OF GREENWICH, CONNECTICUT on the condition that the TOWN OF GREENWICH shall agree that the portion of the property comprising the hemlock forest, waterways, lakes, the pinetum and such other land as may be necessary to form a logical park and such as a landscape architect would consider necessary to form a harmonious whole shall be used and maintained as a public park or garden. Since some name for the park or garden is necessary I suggest MONTGOMERY PINETUM as most suitable."

The codicil also provided that the proceeds of sales of the remaining acreage not required for the park should be placed in a special fund and used exclusively for the care, maintenance and further beautification of the park. Thus he not only continued his deep interest in an early result of his hobby but also provided for its future when he would not be here to look after it.

Colonel Montgomery gave George P. Brett credit for advice as to how he should proceed as a collector of conifers and also for the suggestion that he become a collector of palms. He had spent three winters in Mountain Lake, Florida, where he had made a heavy investment. But in the summer of 1930, when he and Mr. Brett were at lunch, Mr. Brett talked to him of palms. He said there was not a good collection in the United States and that though he had started a collection he could not hope to live long enough to get together a creditable one. R. H. M. was not enthusiastic but promised to think about it. The following March he visited Mr. and Mrs. Brett in Coral Gables. He was convinced. He got experienced help to select a place, bought seventy acres, and arranged for building a small house for overnight visits and one for a caretaker. Then in March, 1932, he and Thomas A. Fennell spent a week motoring through Florida, buying palms.

> "When I left the place in March, 1932, it was a barren wilderness. When I saw it next in December it was a complete estate, fully planted, with gorgeous flowering vines and flowers and a superb lawn."

The first tree had been planted in August 1932. One must read the Colonel's own story to get an idea of his enthusiasm. Here it is possible to mention only a few of his experiences.

He had sought all available varieties of palms in Florida and wished also get them from foreign countries. But as quarantine restrictions forbade the importation of living palms he proposed to get seeds from tropical gardens abroad. Then he learned that most such gardens are not allowed to sell seeds—they could only exchange them. And a further bar was that they could exchange only with similar institutions. So besides being successively an accountant, auditor, student, teacher, author, and officer in a variety of organizations, he became an institution and named himself "Coconut Grove Palmetum". This seems to have provided the necessary introduction, though it had one unexpected result. In Paris he called on the Vilmorin firm and presented a list of the palms he had and requested seeds of all other species. The person he had met spoke no English and apparently he and R. H. M. didn't speak the same kind of French. The outcome was that instead of learning what seeds he could buy he was told what seeds Vilmorin would buy from him. However, he got seeds from every tropical country, and in 1939 he stated that he had growing about 400 different species, the largest private collection of palms in the world. In 1935, at the Palm Beach Flower Show he exhibited only palm flowers and seeds and stole the show.

Although he was still intensely interested in his Florida place, he

> "could not afford to buy more land and raise more and more hundreds of tropical things, and yet I wanted to do just that more than anything of that nature I had ever wanted. Maybe it was the same urge I had had scores of times. Anyhow I had it. I considered what might be done and decided that there must be thousands of others who, as much, or almost as much, as I would like to see in the continental United States the finest tropical garden in the world. And so I organized it."

And thus began the Fairchild Tropical Garden. As the garden grew with the most expert advice and administration, he had time to laugh at his experiences and to make mental blueprints of possible extensions of some of his minor hobbies. Perhaps one of his satisfactions was in recalling the organizations he created as subsidiaries to his major hobby, including the Montgomery Evergreen Nursury [*sic*], Inc., the Coconut Grove Palmetum, and the Fairchild Tropical Garden. Our imagination is not stretched to believe that these were the inspiration for his and his wife's last holiday card in 1952 [*appended next page*]:

Christmas and New Year Greetings
from
the firm of Montgomery and Montgomery
Coconut Grove, Florida
Dealers in Flowers and Trees

Any Quantity, Any Kind, Easy Credit Terms
Our Balance Sheet for the Year Ending December 25, 1952

ASSETS	LIABILITIES
Good health. Kindly feelings. Love of nature. Realizing we can do only so much and no more.	Regrets for not sending 1951 Christmas Cards. Too lazy or too tired after long trip gathering seeds.
Warmest greetings to all our friends.	Inability to change what we don't like.
General Manager, Secretary NELL	Chairman of the Board BOB

Automation—1894

By THE COMMITTEE ON HISTORY

In assessing the wonders of today's computing machines let us not overlook the impetus given to machine bookkeeping by Charles Ezra Sprague, CPA, banker, teacher, author of the First CPA law, and member of New York State's first Board of Examiners.

A brilliant student, he had an aptitude for languages and is said to have spoken sixteen, including Esperanto and the somewhat less publicized Volapuk, on which he wrote a book. His usefulness as an interpreter got him a job as clerk in the Union Dime Savings Bank in 1870, when he was around twenty-eight years old. Twenty-two years later he became president of the bank and remained in that post until his death in 1912, at the age of seventy.

According to the biography of Colonel Sprague written by Helen Scott Mann, published by New York University in 1931, he fathered many improvements in savings-bank bookkeeping, but none more revolutionary than the machine, known as a *teller's machine*, which was developed under his guidance.

The biography tells that, because of his liking for a young reporter in need of copy, he outlined his idea of a machine that would make bookkeeping entries, and found himself so deluged with inquiries from prospective users that he was obliged to do something about it. So he took his ideas to a machinist and around 1894 or 1895 the first savings-bank-teller's machine was born. In one operation it made the necessary entry in the depositor's passbook, recorded it for the bank's records, and accumulated the day's total. Rather dismayingly called an *automalogothotype*, it was the first savings-bank-teller's machine, though not, of course, the first adding machine. The Union Dime Savings Bank is said to have had two of them, one for deposits and one for withdrawals. It appears that this was the machine described in United States patent No. 570,620, issued to Leicester Allen of Brooklyn, N. Y., on November 3, 1896, on an application filed October 15, 1895.

This is the sixteenth in a series of articles on the History of Accounting in the State of New York. It was prepared by the Society's Committee on History.

These seem to have served the bank's purposes until about 1908 or 1909, when Colonel Sprague negotiated with The National Cash Register Company for the development and purchase of newer machines to replace the Allen-type machines. The first NCR machine, their class number 1200, bearing the factory number 872,430, was delivered to the bank in August, 1910. It is fully described in United States patent No. 1,198,418, issued to William A. Chryst on September 19, 1916, on an application filed September 21, 1911. This was the first of ten machines which were built and delivered to the Union Dime Savings Bank between 1910 and 1917.

According to information supplied by Carl Beust of the patent department of The National Cash Register Company, who was present at the installation of the machine in August, 1910, no other machines of this type were ever built by the company for any other bank.

In October, 1955, the Union Dime Savings Bank put on display in its Madison Avenue office one of these old machines, flanked by a portrait of Colonel Sprague.

Orrin Reynolds Judd

By THE COMMITTEE ON HISTORY

Orrin Reynolds Judd, a Certified Public Accountant for over fifty years, was born in Kingston, New Jersey, on November 4, 1870, the son of the Reverend Orrin Bishop and Susanna Reynolds Judd. Most of his working life was spent in banking, but he was active as an independent accountant in two different stages and was always interested in the affairs of accountants, and participated in the work of the accounting societies.

Mr. Judd's first job was with the People's Bank on Canal Street, in 1885. He received $3 a week for working on their books of account and was increased to $4 a week within a year. He continued his education at night while working for People's Bank and its successors, and received his certificate as a Certified Public Accountant in 1902.

Election Day in 1891 fell on November 3rd and gave rise to an interesting incident. Mr. Judd was eager to cast his first vote, but his right to register was challenged by the election officials. The Corporation Counsel of Brooklyn ruled that, since the law disregards fractions of days, he became twenty-one on the last day of his twenty-first year, and should be permitted to vote.

He was graduated from New York University School of Commerce, Accounts and Finance in 1902, as a member of its first class. Continuing at N. Y. U., he was awarded the degree of LL.B. from the Law School in 1904 and was admitted to the New York Bar. He decided to stick to banking and use his legal knowledge in trust work. He taught evening courses at the N. Y. U. School of Commerce until 1909, as well as serving as a teacher for the American Institute of Banking.

When he received his C.P.A. certificate, he was employed in the personal trust department of Knickerbocker Trust Company. A year later, in lieu of a salary increase, he was given permission to do outside accounting work, beginning with one of the estates the Trust Company was handling. He founded Nassau Audit Company and served a variety

---

This is the nineteenth in a series of articles on the History of Accounting in the State of New York. It was prepared by the Society's Committee on History.

of mercantile clients until 1910, when it became necessary to devote full time to the trust work of Columbia Trust Company, which had merged with Knickerbocker after the 1907 panic. The accounting practice was taken over by Cornwall and Firth, who had been associates in the Nassau Audit Company.

Columbia Trust Company in turn became involved in a series of mergers. In 1923, it became Irving Bank-Columbia Trust Company, and Mr. Judd was made a Vice-President. He was later made head of the personal trust department of Irving Trust Company. In 1933, he was honored with election as Vice-President of the Corporate Fiduciaries Association of New York, and the same year retired from Irving.

There followed two years of independent accounting from his own office. In keeping with the depression economy, he specialized in mortgage reorganizations, and was appointed a temporary Trustee of Series F-1 of New York Title & Mortgage Company by Justice Alfred Frankenthaler.

In 1935, he was invited by Jacob C. Klinck, President of Kings County Savings Bank, to help out for a year while Mr. Klinck was Grand Master of Masons of the State of New York. Beginning a new banking career as Cashier, Mr. Judd stayed on through the terms of three succeeding presidents, becoming a Vice-President, a Trustee, and then Executive Vice-President, the position he held at the time of his second retirement in 1953.

Mr. Judd belonged to The New York State Society of Certified Public Accountants and had been a chairman of its History Committee. He was a member of the American Institute of Accountants. He also belonged to The Accountants' Club, of which he was an honorary member, and the Downtown Association, the Society of Colonial Wars, and the New England Society of New York.

New York University continued to occupy a large place in his life. He was active in its alumni affairs and in 1934 was given the Alumni Award for Meritorious Service. He had been elected to the Council of the University in 1931, and served as its Secretary from 1938 to 1951. He retired as a member of the Council in 1953, but continued as an Associate until his death on March 5, 1954, at the age of 84.

Mr. Judd was also active in administrative affairs of the Baptist Church and of Colgate University. He was President of the Young Peoples Baptist Union of Brooklyn in 1898-99, and a Trustee of the Baptist Educational Society of New York from 1901 until his death. In addition to service as deacon and Sunday School superintendent of his own church, First Baptist of Williamsburgh and later Emmanuel Baptist, he served as Treasurer of the Baptist State Convention of New York (1906-25), Treasurer of the Northern Baptist Convention (1926-36), and President of the Baptist Church Extension Society of Brooklyn and Long Island (1924-40). Colgate University elected him a trustee in 1923. He served on the Board until 1946, and continued as a Trustee emeritus to his death in 1954.

Mrs. Judd, the former Bertha Grimmell, whom he married in Brooklyn, New York, on October 4, 1905, was also active in Baptist and interdenominational church affairs. She died in 1947. They had three children, two of whom died during the influenza epidemic of 1918-19, after World War I. A son, Orrin G. Judd, who survived, was Solicitor General of New York State from 1943 to 1946, is the author of articles and legislation on trust accounting, and is currently a member of the law firm of Goldstein, Judd & Gurfein.

[*July, 1956.* Reprinted with permission from *The CPA Journal*, copyright 1956]

J. Lee Nicholson

By THE COMMITTEE ON HISTORY

The man whom we know as a pioneer in cost accounting and founder of the National Association of Cost Accountants was born Jerome Lee Nicholson in Trenton, New Jersey, on September 24, 1863. Though his formal education was limited to that obtained in grammar school, he must later have studied extensively and to good advantage, for he became in time a lecturer and a widely published author in his special field.

When he was still a boy, his family moved from Trenton to Virginia and from there to Pittsburgh, where he worked as an office boy for Keystone Bridge Company. From office boy he advanced to a job as accountant for the Pennsylvania Railroad, and in 1885, when he was twenty-two years old, he embarked upon a selling career. For four years he traveled as a salesman for S. Katz & Company of New York, making his home in New York City. Here he used his diverse talents to supplement his income. Because he was an exceptionally fine penman his friends employed him to write business cards. He also studied bookkeeping and accounting in his spare time and profited from his new knowledge by writing up books and accounts in his evening hours.

In 1889, he decided to set up a public accounting practice of his own and opened an office on Broadway above Grand Street, near the old Prescott Hotel.

He early availed himself of the newly-provided opportunity to acquire the CPA certificate, which New York State was the first to offer, and in 1901 became the holder of CPA Certificate No. 190W. No doubt he had followed the early beginnings of the New York State Society of CPA's with interest, for he became a member in 1902, at which time the Society had been in existence for about five years. As early as 1906 he held membership in the American Association of Public Accountants, the predecessor of the American Institute of Accountants.

This is the twentieth in a series of articles on the History of Accounting in the State of New York. It was prepared by the Society's Committee on History.

Perhaps it was his work in the drafting department of the steel mill at Pittsburgh which led to his interest in costs. At any rate, in 1909 he published a major work on the subject, a book entitled *Factory Organization and Costs*, brought out by Kohle Technical Publishing Company. As an authority in the increasingly important field of costs, he was engaged in 1911 to lecture on cost accounting at the School of Commerce, Accounts, and Finance of New York University. He also served as instructor and lecturer on that subject at Columbia University from 1912 to 1917.

During this period his interest in and knowledge of the subject increased steadily, and in 1917 he published, through Ronald Press, his second book, *Cost Accounting—Theory and Practice*, to be followed in 1919 by the Nicholson-Rohrbach volume, *Cost Accounting*, also published by Ronald Press.

In the meantime, he had been contributing to the work of the New York State Society. After serving in 1913-1914 as a director and member of the complaint committee, he became a first vice-president of Society and held that post from 1914 to 1917. In 1917, when World War I was in Progress, he was called by the Government to be Chief of the Division of Cost Accounting (war contracts) in the Bureau of Foreign and Domestic Commerce, became a consulting cost specialist for the Federal Trade Commission, and on November 15, 1917, became a Major, Ordnance Department, Officers Reserve Corps, with the title of Supervising Accountant.

The war over, his strong interest and wide experience in costs led him to call a small group of men together for an organization meeting in Buffalo on October 13 and 14, 1919. Thirty-seven people were present. Those who attended from New York were, besides Mr. Nicholson, Walter S. Gee, Harold Dudley Greeley, and Alfred J. Stern. At this meeting the National Association of Cost Accountants was founded and Major Nicholson was chosen its first president. The stated object of the association was to "advance the science of cost accounting through such avenues as research, discussion, and acquisition and diffusion of cost accounting knowledge."

In memory of the founders of NACA, and especially of Major Nicholson, whose career was centered around the subject of costs, the Spot Club presented a bronze placque [*sic*] to NACA in November, 1949.

He died in San Francisco on Sunday morning, November 2, 1924, not long after the publication by Ronald Press, in 1923, of his last book, *Profitable Management*. He was sixty-one years old at the time of his death.

The Society's files contain this resolution, which is a fitting testimony to a colorful career in accounting.

> "On November second (1924) through the death of Major J. Lee Nicholson, one more has passed from our active membership, where for a long time his name was inscribed. Through all these years we who knew him had learned increasingly to admire him for his character and accomplishments, not the least of which was the service he so cheerfully rendered his country.
>
> "We learned to believe in him and were glad for the broad recognition which was given to his abilities—we followed with our respect and support his efforts and lead in the organization of the National Association of Cost Accountants, which is a monument to his special achievements, and we record our own sense of our own loss through his death.
>
> "To his partners and to his family we express our deep and abiding sympathy."
>
> "For the committee:
>
> (*Signed*) John F. D. Rohrbach
Harold Dudley Greeley
Edward L. Suffern"

The years spent by Jerome Lee Nicholson in studying cost problems and in arousing an interest in the development of cost analysis provided a major contribution to accounting history. His published works, together with the huge store of literature built up through the association which he founded, are a reservoir widely drawn upon in the management, operation, and control of business enterprise.

[*September, 1956*. Reprinted with permission from *The CPA Journal*, copyright 1956]

Norman Edward Webster

By THE COMMITTEE ON HISTORY

Norman Webster well earned the title of Historian of American Accountancy. His patient, tenacious exploration of every possible source of facts about accountants and their organizations has greatly enriched the literature of the profession.

His approach to history was essentially biographical. He believed fully that every lasting institution is the lengthened shadow of a man. History, to him, was the story of the lives of persons, both natural persons and the artificial persons that live in the form of associations or societies.

A reason for this—perhaps *the* reason—is that he was always a man of friendships. To him, human contacts were necessary. People were what he thought, talked, and wrote about.

He knew that progressive developments of accountancy were expanding the basic concept of the accountability of stewardship into areas where accounting controls were aiding modern management of enterprises of all sorts to shape their day-to-day progress. He was fully aware that new methods of record-keeping and new mechanical devices provided modern tools for the modern accountant which were not known to the founders of our accounting associations. He knew that other historians should, and probably would, in time, write the story of these developments. He urged his friend A. C. Littleton to carry on the work he had begun with his *Accounting Evolution, to 1900.* But Norman Webster knew that, for him, the search for facts, forgotten or never formally recorded, about those men who began the building of professional accountancy, was both a vocation and an avocation.

Historical Works

His first published historical work was *The Ten Year Book* of the New York State Society of Certified Public Accountants. For the first ten years of the existence of the Society there was no connected and

---

In preparing this article, the Society's Committee on History (Jennie M. Palen, Chairman) was provided with material by Henry A. Horne, C.P.A., a past President of our Society and one of Mr. Webster's partners.

coherent record of activities. Thereafter there was an annual succession of *Year Books*. Mr. Webster set himself the task of assembling all possible data relating to Society activities during the initial decade and of arranging them in narrative form.

The success of this effort imposed on his active mind the idea of a similar history for the national association of professional accountants. That aim was realized in 1954, when the American Institute of Accountants published his volume *The First Twenty Years of The American Association of Public Accountants*. The preparation of this work took much more time, much more ingenuity, and very much more by way of correspondence and personal interview than the earlier volume for the New York State Society.

Many of his writings have appeared in the magazines of the profession. His address presented at the Fiftieth Anniversary convention of the American Institute of Accountants was published in *The Journal of Accountancy*. Of the twenty-two historical articles that have appeared to date in *The New York Certified Public Accountant* eleven were the work of his hand.

Family Background

Born in the small village of Decatur, Michigan, on March 26, 1869, he thought of himself always as a son of "the Middle Border". His father, Norman Earl Webster, was a carpenter. The family was part of a farming community, though not actively sharing in agriculture. During all the long years of his maturity which were lived in Washington and New York, he never lost his appreciation of his early years in rural surroundings.

His mother, Jennie Chavileer Webster, was a small, active, vivacious woman and her only child inherited largely from her. Both parents were descendants of early American families. The Webster family came to New England early in the seventeenth century, moved to Vermont, to New York State, to Ohio, and on to Michigan. The Chavileer family was believed to be of the French Huguenot migration to the New World. Probably the name was "Chevalier" originally, the altered spelling being a conformance to the accepted pronunciation.

Religious Affiliations

The family were members of the Presbyterian Church, the father holding an office as a layman in the local congregation. Norman Edward Webster became a member of the church in Decatur. He was transferred later to a church in Kalamazoo and still later to the Church of the Covenant in Washington, D.C. That church and congregation is now known as The National Presbyterian Church and is the church attended by President and Mrs. Eisenhower.

In the last year of his life he joined the New York Collegiate Church of The Reformed Church in America, West End congregation, a church with a Presbyterian form of government, the oldest church organization in New York, and probably the oldest Protestant church organization in the Western Hemisphere. All these features appealed strongly to Norman Webster's veneration of the old and to his affection, through tradition, for the Presbyterian polity.

Early Education and Training

His early education was received in the Decatur Graded School, which carried him through what are now known as "the grades" and also into "secondary school" studies, which now would be defined as those of high school rank. In that school he came under the influence of a man of strong character and high ideals, a Professor Henry Upton. Professor Upton's impact on the life of the boy Norman Webster continued until the end of life. Another teacher of that country school who left a strong impression on him was Miss Abigail Pierce. Apparently the bright, fun-loving boy was a favorite with both of these early teachers.

At the end of his schooling he was employed as a clerk and as a bookkeeper, by the Decatur Manufacturing Company. In various job changes his pay-check came successively from Hinckley Stave Company and Michigan Buggy Company. At that time (1885-1893) Michigan industry was based largely on lumbering and wood-products. The manufacture of wooden horsedrawn vehicles was the field in which Norman first learned about business.

Early in 1893 he procured a scholarship to Union College, Schenectady, New York. He attended for one semester and was inducted into the mysteries of Beta Theta Pi. At the opening of the summer vacation season he learned that he could get employment at the Chicago World's Fair—The Columbian Exposition. The work of that summer fastened in his mind the need for financial auditing as well as some of its techniques. His duties required him to obtain sales data from the polygot [*sic*] concessionaires in the exposition grounds. As Bret Harte's phrase has it "For ways that are dark and tricks that are vain. . . ." Well—young Norman learned a few tricks, also.

Government Service

At the close of the exposition, one of Norman's boyhood friends who had secured a civil service position convinced him of the advantages of work in Washington. Young Webster took an examination, gave up the idea of completing his college course, and became a bookkeeper in the office of the U.S. Treasury Department that had the responsibility for the audit of the Post Office Department. He had been employed in the Treasury Department office for over ten years when he learned that a new position was to be created in a relatively new bureau in the Department of the Interior. During the administration of Theodore Roosevelt it became apparent that there were large areas of our western states which could be rendered fertile and productive if water could be made available. The U.S. Reclamation Service undertook to provide the water, and in so doing it found that some accounting knowledge was needed. An examination for the position of Chief Accountant was prepared by the Civil Service Commission. Mr. Webster took the examination and was the successful candidate. During the succeeding six years he traveled over much of the West, planning for and supervising the financial transactions of the Reclamation Service.

Incidental to his work for this organization he took, successfully, the first CPA examination given in the State of Michigan. He was one of the first group of Michigan CPA's. He could not be "Number One", because his name places him close to the end of any alphabetical listing.

While in the Reclamation Service he was named a member of a committee of conference with a committee from the American Association of Public Accountants, which had been asked by President Theodore Roosevelt to examine and report on certain governmental administrative functions. These conferences brought him into friendly contact with some of the leading professional accountants of the day. Particularly, he cherished his acquaintance with Arthur Lowes Dickinson, Elijah Watt Sells, and Henry Anderson Niles.

Professional CPA Practice

Mr. Niles offered him a partnership in the firm of Niles & Niles in New York. Aware that the bringing in of a partner from the outside would have a disrupting effect on the morale of the staff, Mr. Webster accepted on the condition that he be permitted to be a staff employee for one year. A year later, on January 1, 1911, he began a partnership relation that was to last more than sixteen years.

The change of residence from Washington to New York meant a severing of relationships built up during sixteen years. On December 17, 1895, his childhood sweetheart, Rose Rezeau, became Mrs. Webster. They had been together for almost sixty years when she died on May 25, 1955. Mr. and Mrs. Webster had been active in the Christian Endeavor Society of the Church of the Covenant, in Washington. The Reverend Doctor Teunis Hamlen, an alumnus of Union College, was the minister of this church. He took a strong liking to the young Websters. Knowing of Norman's attendance at Union and being desirous of beginning, in Washington, an Alumni Society for the sons of Union College and a University Club for all college men living in the city, he pressed Norman into service as his administrative assistant. As a result, Norman Webster was one of the founders of the University Club of Washington, continuing his membership until the day of his death.

The Washington years were put to good use. Evening attendance at National Law School earned for him his bachelor's and his master's degrees (LL.B.; LL.M.). He was admitted to the bar of the District of Columbia. He was active in the organization of the Association of Government Accountants and was elected to its presidency. His success in the discharge of his various governmental duties, his activities in alumni and university matters, and (probably) the friendship of Doctor Hamlen, caused his Alma Mater, Union College, to bestow on him the honorary degree of Master of Arts (A.M.).

In New York City a new career began. He presented himself for the New York CPA certificate and was successful in all subjects on his first examination. In later years he was a member of the New York State Board of CPA Examiners and for most of his long term of office was Chairman of the Board.

Participation in Professional Societies

His period of active participation in professional public accountancy, which began in November, 1909, included many important engagements involving large financial affairs. During that period, also, he gave of himself liberally to the work of the professional societies. In the American Institute of Accountants he was a vice-president and a member of council, in addition to long years of service as Chairman of the Committee on History. In the New York State Society of CPAs he was a vice-president, a director, and, for many years, a member of its Committee on History.

On May 1, 1927, with a small group of fellow accountants, all old friends, he organized the accountancy firm now known as Webster, Horne & Elsdon, then with offices in New York and in Hartford, Connecticut.

During the Second World War he was asked to lend his prestige and support to the war effort and was appointed to be the Chief Supervising Auditor of the Third Naval District, whose headquarters were in the Port of New York.

The Chapter of Beta Alpha Psi at Syracuse University made him an honorary member of the fraternity and of that Chapter. It is fair to say that Mu Chapter of New York University had adopted him also.

The opening of the office in Hartford suggested application for a Connecticut CPA certificate, which was granted promptly. The Connecticut Society of CPAs welcomed him as a member. The University Club of Hartford also brought him into its fellowship.

When The Accountants Club of America was organized he became one of the charter members. Later, for five years, he was president of the club, a position for which he was by temperament particularly adapted.

Soon after the organization of the National Association of Cost Accountants in 1919, he became and remained thereafter an active and interested member of the association and of its New York Chapter.

For many years and until his death he was a member of the American Accounting Association, which succeeded the former Association of University Instructors in Accounting.

He was one of the group that organized the National Association of Certified Public Accountant Examiners and he remained actively interested in that association continuously thereafter.

His membership in the Michigan Association of CPAs was continuous from the date of its organization until the end of his life.

Cultural and Social Interests

Though history was his dominant interest, it was not his only one. He was one of the earliest members of the National Geographic Society, having joined it in Washington in the 1890's. He was also a member of the American Geographical Society of New York. His cultural instincts led him to membership in The Metropolitan Museum of Art and The American Museum of Natural History. As might be expected, he was an interested and active member of The New York State Historical Society and of The New York Historical Society of New York City. In New York City he was a member of the Lawyers Club. In the country he enjoyed membership in the Sleepy Hollow Country Club, in the area that is full of the memory of Washington Irving. In political affiliation he was a Republican.

A Full and Rewarding Life

After the death of his wife in May, 1955, Mr. Webster's health failed substantially. In January, 1956, he had a severe illness, primarily pneumonia, but seriously complicated by a chronic heart weakness. Thereafter he could not recover strength. Continuous medication sustained him until July 15, 1956, when, without pain or struggle, in the eighty-eighth year of a full and rewarding life, he died.

His library of accountancy history materials he gave to the American Institute of Accountants Foundation, with the intention that it should be available at the library of the American Institute of Accountants. His personal library will go to a library in his native village of Decatur, Michigan. His will provides that the residuary estate be used for the building and maintenance of that library.

John Thomas Madden

By EARLE L. WASHBURN, C.P.A.

"John," as he was affectionately known by his contemporaries, was born in Worcester, Massachusetts, October 26, 1882. Perhaps his personality is best described by the dedication in the 1916 year book of the School of Commerce, Accounts and Finance of New York University. It reads, in part: "John Thomas Madden, Scholar, Friend, Man." As a small boy he is remembered as being round and good natured. These characteristics remained with him through life. In his early years he also acquired a reputation for business acumen and he is said to have been expert in trading jackknives.

Educational Background

Following his graduation from Worcester Classical High School in 1899, he entered the employ of Swift & Company, where his duties were principally of an accounting nature. In 1909 he enrolled in the School of Commerce, Accounts and Finance of New York University. While pursuing the course of study, he was employed in the office of William Leslie, a chartered accountant, so that upon passing the CPA examinations in the summer of 1911 he was able to furnish the experience qualification and to have his certificate issued to him. Simultaneously, he received the Bachelor of Commercial Science degree from New York University, suma [*sic*] cum laude. In later years he received the degree of Master of Arts (Hon.) from Holy Cross College and the degree of Doctor of Science (Hon.) from the University of Newark.

Best Remembered as Dean of the N. Y. U. School of Commerce

He engaged in public accounting in his own name in New York City and became an instructor in accounting at New York University

---

EARLE L. WASHBURN, C.P.A., is a member of our Society's Committees on History and on Membership, and a past chairman of the Committee on Institutional Accounting. Mr. Washburn is the Controller of New York University. This article was prepared by the author as part of the continuing program of history studies undertaken by the Society's Committee on History (Jennie M. Palen, Chairman).

in 1911, assistant professor in 1913, professor and head of the Department of Accounting Instruction in 1917, and Dean in 1925, in which position he served until his death in July, 1948. It was in his capacity as Dean that he is best remembered. His kindly yet dynamic personality made him beloved of students, faculty, and alumni. No matter how many problems occupied him, he always found time to lend his aid to any who sought it. This often took the form of financial assistance; and while the nature of such relations is a closed book, it is fairly well established that there was never a default in repayment.

Honors and Professional Affiliations

His mind was quick and logical; his versatility such that his talents were frequently requisitioned for use in a wide variety of endeavors which earned for him, among other honors, the decoration of Commander of the Order of the Crown (Rumania). King Albert of Belgium dubbed him Commander of the Order of Leopold II. In 1929 he was elected President of the Alexander Hamilton Institute, President of the International Accountants Society, and Public Governor of the New York Curb (now the American) Stock Exchange. He was a member of numerous organizations, including the American Institute of Accountants, the New York and New Jersey State CPA Societies, and past President of the American Association of University Instructors in Accounting. Four fraternities claim him as a brother: Delta Mu Delta, Theta Mu Epsilon, Alpha Kappa Psi, and Beta Gamma Sigma. In all except the first he served terms as national president.

Human Qualities

He had the happy knack of combining wit with a profound knowledge of his subject and his succinct remarks caused him to be always in demand as a speaker at dinners and other functions. He was very human and very likeable, as a host of friends and former students in the accounting profession will testify, and endowed with a sound and practical philosophy. He was always quick to praise others, a favorite aphorism being, "a little taffy during life is better than a lot of 'epitaphy' afterwards." Another of his much quoted maxims was, "the penalty for good work is more good work to do." But probably the best indication of his basic character was his impatience with what is disparagingly labeled "educational bookkeeping," namely, the mere accumulation of academic credits without enthusiasm, direction, or purpose.

Publications

With all these activities, he was still able to spare the hours necessary for research, writing, and editing for publication. His first book, "Principles of Accounting," appeared in 1918; in the next year "Accounting Practice and Auditing"; and in 1920, with the collaboration of Arthur Rosenkampff, "Elementary Accounting Problems." With the co-authorship of Marcus Nadler, he published two books—"Foreign Securities" in 1929 and "International Money Markets" in 1934. In 1936, with the collaboration of Marcus Nadler and Harry Sauvain, he published "America's Experience as a Creditor Nation." "Auditing," which he wrote with P. E. Bacas and Arthur Rosenkampff, appeared in 1937.

An Outstanding Contribution to Accounting Education

It is difficult, of course, to summarize and evaluate the life of any person. In the case of Dean Madden, it is most evident that he made an outstanding contribution to the raising of the standards of accounting instruction on the university level throughout the United States.

New York State Tax Forum

Benjamin Harrow, C.P.A., J.D., initiator of this department in February 1947, and its editor continuously in the ensuing eleven years, died on January 26, 1958. In place of his usual department, Max Block, Chairman of the Society's Committee on Publications, has written the following tribute to his memory, in recognition of his prodigious services and his great devotion to this department, to the magazine, to our Society, and to the accounting profession as a whole.

—The Editor

In Memoriam—Benjamin Harrow
(1892-1958)

Ben Harrow is no more, but he has left a cherished heritage of memories and works to the members of the New York State Society of CPAs, and to the accounting profession as a whole. It can be truly stated that he was selfless in his devotion to his profession and fellow men, and that he gave unstintingly of his physical self, his time, and of his great talents.

Many men will mourn for him as their great teacher, the man who inspired them to achieve excellence of character as well as technical excellence. For this some have referred to him as an "architect of character." Many members of the profession will remember him as a prolific author and lecturer who added so much to their store of knowledge and helped solve so many of their technical problems. Those who were close to him in the State Society and the Institute will grieve for him as a friend who endeared himself to them by his friendliness, character, and gentility, and whom they respected for his competence, erudition, and devotion to his profession. His family, of course, will miss him as a devoted husband, and as a kindly father who helped in the intellectual and spiritual development of his daughter and two sons. To all of the aforementioned, Ben Harrow's way of life and his achievements will always be a cherished memory, and to succeeding generations they will be goals for emulation.

Prior to entering the professions of accountancy and law, Ben Harrow was a teacher. For a while he was a teacher of English at the De Witt Clinton High School. There he endeared himself to his pupils by virtue of his inspirational qualities, the masterful lucidity of his teaching, and the humane and sympathetic consideration of the pupil as an individual. Thereafter he transferred his interest to the professions which became his life work, and for over twenty years he was a member of the faculty of St. John's University where he lectured on some accounting subjects but more importantly on tax law. At the time of his death he had the rank of Professor Emeritus of the St. John's University School of Law. There, too, his personal traits and competence endeared him to his students. Many members of our Society remember him well as their high school teacher or college professor, all with pleasure and gratitude.

Members of our Society knew Ben Harrow as the editor of the monthly New York State Tax Forum Department of THE NEW YORK CERTIFIED PUBLIC ACCOUNTANT, as well as the author of many articles on various federal and state taxes which appeared in THE NEW YORK CERTIFIED PUBLIC ACCOUNTANT and in THE JOURNAL OF ACCOUNTANCY. In 1949 his tax department in our Society's magazine was the recipient of an Award of Merit certificate in the Eleventh Annual Editorial Competition conducted by Industrial Marketing magazine for an outstanding series of articles among the Class, Institutional and Professional papers.

Very few realize how much time and effort was involved in the research, writing, and careful checking and editing to produce these articles and departmental material. Ben was not one to talk about it, nor to complain. Realizing that many accountants would base decisions and actions on his pronouncements, he exercised most meticulous care in checking and rechecking every position he took in his New York State Tax Forum Department, regardless of the cost in time and effort. As a result of his position as departmental editor, and as a renowned authority, his office was always "open house" for Society members and others who, by telephone and by mail, presented problems to him that arose in their practices, and requested his advice and counsel. The demands on his time were very considerable in the aggregate, each month, yet he carried on uncomplainingly and willingly.

His most outstanding literary work is his book entitled "New York State Income and Franchise Taxes." Despite the changes wrought by time, this book is still a recognized guide to New York State tax law and procedures.

Those who had the pleasure and privilege of being associated with him in the Society's affairs, and in his other activities, quickly came under the spell of his personality. He will be sorely missed at State Society and American Institute meetings and conventions, which he attended faithfully, often as a member, often as a speaker, giving of his time and knowledge generously and cheerfully. He illumined every group in whose midst he was present. His ready, warm smile made one feel welcome and at ease immediately. The light in his eyes beamed kindliness and humility. His handshake was the sincere clasp of a friend's hand.

Ben Harrow was not one to be a passive member of his State Society even with respect to its administration. In the face of his many commitments, not to mention his own economic and social obligations, he nevertheless made time to volunteer for active Society duty. In recognition of his competent and devoted services he was elected to high position in the Society and was appointed to important posts. He was elected to the Board of Directors for a three-year term and a few years later to the position of Vice President. He served as chairman or as a member of these committees, apart from various special assignments: Committees on Education, Legislation, Cooperation with State Education Department, Cooperation with the Bar, Federal Taxation, State Taxation, Meetings, Committee Operations, Publications, Awards, Nominations, and a few others.

His membership in the American Institute of CPAs was also not passive. For two years he served as a member of its Council and he was a member of their Federal Taxation Committee for eight years and served on the Social Security Act committee.

In all of these undertakings he performed as was natural for him, with initiative, intelligence, competence, and dependability. No self-interest, pride or egotism ever colored his judgment or actions. For these reasons his views were sought out and respected.

Ben Harrow's compassion for mankind made it possible for him to hurdle the very high barriers of preoccupation with the cited activities and to find time for active service in welfare organizations. There were many such organizations to which he gave of his time, money, and physical self. Outstanding in this area of activity was his response to the urgent need of his foreign co-religionists for a place of safety and spiritual growth. His extensive personal efforts to aid in the development of the State of Israel received the commendation of his co-religionists and of humanitarians generally.

There is much more that could be said of this unusual man, whose life was so deliberately devoted to the service of his fellows. Long ago

Plutarch stated that "The measure of a man's life is the well spending of it, and not the length." By that standard Ben Harrow's life measured up to the highest potential.

Robert H. Montgomery

By THE COMMITTEE ON HISTORY

Robert Heister Montgomery, accountant, lawyer, author, teacher, bibliophile, horticulturist and leader of the accounting profession from the earliest days of the twentieth century, exemplified the courage, vision and intellectual honesty found in those stalwarts who have carried the profession to the position of eminence and respect in which it is held today. This article is not only a recital of his accomplishments in the field of accounting; it is also an attempt to reveal his characteristics, his foresight, imagination, and above all, his insistence upon integrity. He had a strong dislike, indeed a deep-rooted antipathy toward anything that savored of sham or pretense. He minced no words either in conversation or in his writings where he felt intellectual honesty called for criticism. For example, he said: "Success (taking the word in its usual meaning) is often achieved through bunk. Success in a finer sense is often achieved by merit alone."

He was born in Mahanoy City, Pennsylvania, on September 21, 1872, the son of a Methodist minister. His formal education was limited, as the family had to move from one place to another every two or three years, usually in March, because of the custom of reassignment prevailing in the Methodist Church. The environment of a prelate's children, however, with its association of sermons, speeches, and articles to be read and consulted, served as a stimulus for knowledge. This background, coupled with his native ability and supplemented by intensive study at night, was a contributing factor toward the later successes of Robert H. Montgomery.

Financial considerations and the illness of his father forced him to take his first job at the age of fourteen. On February 4, 1889, after serving a year in several jobs, he became an office boy for John Heins, who at that time was President of the American Association of Public Accountants.

In the Heins organization were William M. Lybrand, T. Edward Ross and Adam A. Ross, who later became his partners. While

---

This article was prepared as part of the continuing program of history studies undertaken by our Society's Committee on History, Leo L. Tauritz, Chairman.

working with them as an assistant, he was guided through the intricacies of accounting and auditing. Here began a friendship which was terminated only by death. From 1889 to 1898, when the firm of Lybrand, Ross Bros. & Montgomery was founded, Robert Montgomery's public accounting experience covered every phase of commercial, financial, professional, philanthropic, and public service, and all other branches of human endeavor in which accounts are kept.

In the summer of 1898 he enlisted as a private in Battery A, Philadelphia Light Artillery, Pennsylvania Volunteers, U. S. A., and saw service in Puerto Rico. On June 15, 1899, he was awarded his Pennsylvania certificate as a Certified Public Accountant; in later years he was granted certificates to practice in New York, Missouri, District of Columbia, Michigan, Ohio, Illinois, Kentucky, and California. He was admitted to the Philadelphia Bar in 1900, and to the New York Bar in 1904.

Early in his career, he felt that the major benefit he derived from attempts to teach others was the pressure on himself to gain enough knowledge to keep on teaching; in other words, to educate himself. His teaching activities began in his firm's Philadelphia office in 1902 and he taught one of the evening classes there until 1904. He continued his teachings at the University of Pennsylvania, where evening classes were started in 1904 under the sponsorship of the Pennsylvania Institute of Certified Public Accountants. In the winter of 1905-06 he lectured not only before the Evening School of Accounts and Finance of the University of Pennsylvania, but at New York University as well. Evening classes were not established at Columbia University until 1910. Robert Montgomery taught the first class there and obtained instructors to take over the additional classes.

One of the difficulties he encountered in his teaching activities was that most of his students had never seen a set of accounting records. Accordingly, he acquired a dozen or more sets of books of account, chiefly of bankrupt concerns, which he used and which he called an Accounting Laboratory. In a pamphlet which he published in 1914, "An Accounting Laboratory—The Connecting Link between Theory and Practice," he pointed out the possible advantages from what he was starting. Typical of the author is one of the phrases in the pamphlet. . . "It serves to emphasize what I frequently have told the students of my accounting classes, viz., 'Practical accounting cannot be taught, it must be learned'."

In 1915 he was appointed Assistant Professor of Economics at Columbia University and in due course, as the number of classes increased, was in 1919 made a full Professor of Accounting of the School of Business and for a time was a member of the Administrative Board of the School.

That Robert Montgomery practiced what he preached to his clients is illustrated by his action at the opening of the firm's New York office in September, 1902, at 25 Broad Street. While this office consisted of only one room, he sublet part to two lawyers who had just started a practice. He stated that it was necessary to lessen the first year's overhead as he did not intend that expenses should exceed gross income.

He was one of the sponsors of the first International Congress of Accountants held in St. Louis in 1904, where he delivered his paper, "The Importance of Uniform Practice in Determining the Profits of Public Service Corporations Where Municipalities Have the Power to Regulate Rates." This talk attracted most favorable attention. In that same year, he received permission from Professor Lawrence R. Dicksee to publish the American edition of *Auditing: A Practical Manual for Auditors*. As he could not find a publisher willing to take the risk, he had it printed at his own expense in 1905. A revised edition was published in 1909.

The year 1905 witnessed several events indicative of his efforts on behalf of the profession. He was largely instrumental in organizing a corporation and obtaining funds for publishing *The Journal of Accountancy*. He wrote for the first number, issued in November, 1905, an article entitled "Professional Standards—A Plea for Co-operation among Accountants." This article, which served as a forerunner of present-day rules of professional conduct, is as current today as it was over fifty years ago and exemplifies his great vision. He also enlisted the aid of other outstanding accountants as contributors to the first issue. In 1905 he became a member of the American Association of Public Accountants, when the Federation of Societies of Public Accountants, of which he had been Secretary, merged with the Association.

In the years 1907 to 1911, Robert Montgomery was especially active at the annual meetings of the American Association of Public Accountants, acting as toastmaster, working on by-laws, rules of professional ethics and the like. In 1912 he was elected President of the

American Association of Public Accountants, predecessor organization of the American Institute of Accountants, and was re-elected in 1913.

By 1912, experience had demonstrated that the American revision of *Dicksee's Auditing* had in effect outlived its usefulness, primarily because many of its features were not adaptable to American practice. Accordingly, Montgomery determined to bring out his own book, which was better suited to the requirements of students of accounting and of the profession in this country. Seven other editions have been published since 1912, the latest in 1957 under the title "Montgomery's Auditing." As authoritative reference works these books are found in schools and offices of accountants, not only throughout this country but in other countries as well, translations having been made into many foreign languages.

Commencing with the year 1917, editions of Montgomery's *Income Tax Procedure* (presently entitled *Montgomery's Federal Taxes*) have been published almost yearly. These books have been quoted time and again by the several courts in many instances in support of their own opinions, primarily because of their clear interpretation of the various Revenue Acts.

In 1917, as Chairman of the Committee on Federal Legislation of the American Institute of Accountants, Montgomery, together with George O. May and Harvey S. Chase, at the request of the Federal Trade Commission, prepared a program for audit procedure. This was approved by the Commission and transmitted to the Federal Reserve Board, was published in the Federal Reserve *Bulletin*, and reprinted in pamphlet form for general distribution under the title, "Approved Methods for the Preparation of Balance Sheet Statements."

Commissioned a Lieutenant Colonel in March, 1918, he became a member of the War Department Board of Appraisers and Price Fixing Committee, War Industries Board. In September, 1918, he was appointed Chief of the Price Fixing Section of the Purchase, Storage and Traffic Division of the General Staff and served until January, 1919.

Shortly after his inauguration in 1921, President Harding appointed Albert D. Lasker to the chairmanship of the United States Shipping Board, the most controversial agency left from World War I. Colonel Montgomery became Assistant to the Chairman in charge of finance and accounts. The Board had no inventory of the property it owned, and the Comptroller General had disapproved vouchers amounting to

$700,000,000. In the words of Chairman Lasker, it was the "worst accounting mess in history." No one inclined to weigh the risks to professional reputation would have dared to face this situation. Here, again, was an evidence of courage, for under Colonel Montgomery's direction, procedures were established whereby a physical inventory was taken of the property owned by the Board on the Atlantic, Pacific and Gulf seaboards, the planning for which was so thorough that it was quickly completed. In addition, a financial statement of the realizable assets and liabilities as of June 30, 1921 was prepared which necessitated gathering financial information from widely scattered points. New accounting methods and procedures were established which, for the first time, made possible the preparation of monthly statements for the vast organization with complete comparative analyses of operating and administrative costs. Robert Montgomery and his staff devoted approximately five months of intensive efforts to this work. Despite the magnitude and complexities of the undertaking, the engagement was brought to a successful conclusion.

Elected as President of the New York State Society of Certified Public Accountants in 1922 and re-elected in 1923, he started a campaign to bring together the American Institute of Accountants and the American Society of Certified Public Accountants. The latter organization was formed in December, 1921, because of divergent viewpoints of the separate organizations. Progress toward merging the two organizations was slow and it was not until 1936, the year following his election as President of the Institute, "upon a clearcut platform of merger," that agreement for the merger was reached.

As a result of efforts on the part of the American Legion, Congress in June, 1930, created a Commission to study and consider amending the Constitution of the United States to provide that private property might be taken by Congress for public use during war, to devise methods to equalize the burdens and remove the profits of war, and to make a study of policies to be pursued in the event of war. Through the suggestion of Bernard M. Baruch and Hugh Johnson, and at the urgent request of Secretary of War Patrick J. Hurley, Colonel Montgomery was elected Executive Secretary of this Commission. Every known phase of war and preparation therefor was considered and explored. He worked closely with Secretary Hurley, Acting Chief of Staff Moseley and Major Dwight D. Eisenhower. His relations with Messrs. Moseley and Eisenhower were among the most pleasant memories of his life and his contacts with them were daily, sometimes hourly, over a long period. Because of the change in administration in 1933, little attention was given at that time to the Commission's Report to the President of the United States. It constitutes, however, an important and lasting contribution to war preparation planning.

Colonel Montgomery always contended that any decent hobby would add years to one's life. He felt that a hobby enlisted both the intellect and the emotions and was progressive in its nature. For many years before World War I, he circularized many sources all over the world and gathered a really fine collection of old publications on bookkeeping, among which was the first book containing a description of double entry bookkeeping, *Summa de Arithmetica*, by Lucas [*sic*] Pacioli, published in Venice in 1494. In 1926, he gave the entire collection to Columbia University where it would be available to everyone interested. While this hobby was closely associated with his profession, in later years he expanded his ideas to the end that if they added to knowledge, created beauty, or in some way rendered social service, such hobbies were more worthwhile. So he selected horticulture, which became his supreme interest during the last twenty-five years of his life. He had always loved trees. The forests of France had a particular attraction for him. After a long search, in 1920 he acquired an estate in Cos Cob, Connecticut. In 1945, he donated a part of the fine conifer collection located on this estate to the New York Botanical Garden; and in 1947 approximately 200 specimens of pine, spruce, hemlocks, yew and cedar trees were transplanted to a two-acre plot at the Botanical Garden. His estate was willed to the town of Greenwich, Connecticut, for use as a public park and as a preserve for the fine hemlock forest and other rare conifers that grow there.

His interest in horticulture was not confined solely to Connecticut. In March, 1938, the Fairchild Tropical Garden at Coconut Grove, Florida, was dedicated. It was made possible by a contribution from Colonel Montgomery which included 83 acres of land. Through the generosity of his partners, a gift was made to the Garden which enabled it to provide a library and museum building. Many thousands of tourists and others visit this garden each year and enjoy the tropical plantings.

Dickinson College, Carlisle, Pennsylvania, conferred an honorary LL.D. degree upon him in 1941. The bestowal of this degree was especially fitting in view of the fact that his father was graduated from Dickinson College in 1848. A signal honor was bestowed upon him in 1950, when Ohio State University recognized his outstanding contributions to the accounting profession by naming him one of the first of three men to be elected to its Accounting Hall of Fame.

Funeral services were held in the garden of his home in Coconut Grove, Florida, on May 6, 1953. Those present were deeply impressed by the beauty of the scene and by the sermon of the Pastor of Plymouth Congregational Church, who conducted the services. Expressing the spirit of his living, the pastor said, "Truly it can be said of him as it was said of the historian, Gibbon, 'He died climbing'."

Colonel Montgomery's passing created a vacancy in the accounting profession which will be difficult to fill. His character and accomplishments will not be forgotten by those who knew him. In the words of the Bard of Avon "He was a man, take him all in all; I shall not look upon his like again."

[*February, 1959*. Reprinted with permission from *The CPA Journal*, copyright 1959]

DeWitt Carl Eggleston

By HENRY LIEBERMAN, CPA

DeWitt Carl Eggleston, engineer, accountant and educator, was born in Chagrin Falls, Ohio, on May 5, 1880. Son of DeWitt Clinton and Mary E. Eggleston, he was descended on his mother's side from Alexander Hamilton.

After graduation from high school in Greenwich, Connecticut, he attended Brown University from which he received an M.E. degree in 1905, and was licensed in New York State as a mechanical engineer. He received a CPA certificate from Connecticut in 1908, one from New York in 1923, and one from Virginia in 1943; he also received an LL.B. degree from LaSalle Extension University in 1923.

He married Sara Burroughs McLaughlin on October 28, 1909, and they had one child, Dorothy, who later became Mrs. Chandler Withington of Riverside, Connecticut.

In 1914 he joined the staff of The City College of New York, on a part-time basis, to teach accounting subjects and taught there until his retirement in 1945, at which time he held the rank of Assistant Professor.

He became a member of the New York State Society of Certified Public Accountants in 1923, serving as director (1934-1936), as a member of its Committee on Amendments to By-Laws (1930-1933), and as chairman of that Committee (1933-1935). He served on its Publications Committee (1937-1939), Professional Conduct Committee (1947-1949), Textile Accounting Committee, as chairman (1924-1935), Committee on Accountants' Office Procedure (1931-1939), and as chairman (1935-1936), Committee on Stock Brokerage Accounting (1934-1937), and Committee on Local Taxation (1937-1939).

With his training and experience, and with a self-discipline which enabled him to schedule his writing time carefully, Professor Eggleston

---

HENRY LIEBERMAN, CPA, is a lecturer in accountancy at the Baruch School of Business and Public Administration, The City College of New York.

This article was prepared by the author as part of the continuing program of history studies undertaken by our Society's Committee on History, Leo L. Tauritz, Chairman.

was the author of the accounting textbooks, "Municipal Accounting,"[1] "Problems in Cost Accounting,"[2] and "Business Costs,"[3] this last in collaboration with Frederick B. Robinson. In the preface to "Business Costs," Professor Robinson wrote as follows:

> Educated as an engineer, Professor Eggleston was able to understand the mechanical process of production, and as a certified public accountant he was competent to analyze the financial books of any concern. Thoroughly prepared in these two essential branches of knowledge, he spent a number of years as an expert of the United States Tariff Commission, examining the production plants and books of a great many concerns in various lines of industry in order to report on the details of costs that might affect tariff legislation. This experience was subsequently amplified by extensive work as a cost consultant in private practice.

Professor Eggleston also prepared a volume entitled "Cost Accounting" which was part of a five-volume series "Business Accounting."[4] Several years later his "Auditing Procedure"[5] was published. In the preface to "Auditing Procedure," the author noted that the position held by him as chairman of the Committee on Accountants' Office Procedure afforded him an opportunity for exchanging ideas and information which he further developed in the textbook.

In 1930 he published two volumes entitled "Modern Accounting Theory and Practice."[6] Volume I dealt with general theory and Volume II with the accounting of corporations, estates and foreign exchange organizations. "Wall Street Procedure"[7] was published in the same year

---

1. Published by The Ronald Press Company in 1914.

2. Published by D. Appleton and Company in 1918.

3. Published by D. Appleton and Company in 1921.

4. Published by The Ronald Press Company.

5. Published by John Wiley & Sons, Inc. in 1926.

6. Published by John Wiley & Sons, Inc.

7. Published by Greenberg, Publisher, Inc. 1930.

and "Department Store Accounting"[8] in the year following. His experience in auditing the records of large retail stores qualified him as an expert in this field.

He also had a distinguished career in public accounting. He was a partner in the firm of Klein, Hinds & Finke from 1919 to 1936. From October 15, 1936 to April 14, 1943, he was on the staff of Haskins & Sells. On April 15, 1943, he became a member of the firm of Wilfred Wyler & Co., with which firm he was associated until his death on September 6, 1950.

In his later years Professor Eggleston adopted art as an avocation, and some of his work hangs in the homes of friends.

He died in the New Haven Hospital at the age of 70 from the effects of a stroke suffered on the train while traveling from his summer home to his New York office.

According to Dr. Stanley B. Tunick, Chairman of the Accountancy Department of the Baruch School of Business and Public Administration, a departmental resolution prepared at the time of his death reads in part, "DeWitt Carl Eggleston will be long remembered with affection by his colleagues and students as a learned, enthusiastic, sincere, kindly friend and mentor."

8. Published by Greenberg, Publisher, Inc. 1931.

Society Release

Dedication of Haskins Memorial Room

Resolution of Dedication

WHEREAS, Charles Waldo Haskins was appointed a member of the first State Board of Certified Public Accountant Examiners and at the Board's first meeting was named President, a position he retained until his death, and thus became one of the founders of the profession in the State of New York, and

WHEREAS, Charles Waldo Haskins, realizing that any profession must be organized and self-regulating to further its aims and aspirations, was instrumental in founding The New York State Society of Certified Public Accountants and became its first President, and

WHEREAS, Charles Waldo Haskins, recognizing the profession's need for formal preparatory education, conferred with the Trustees of New York University and finally achieved the establishment on October 2, 1900, of its School of Commerce, Accounts and Finance, of which he was named Dean and Professor of the History of Accountancy, and

WHEREAS, the Board of Directors of The New York State Society of Certified Public Accountants, after full deliberation, in acknowledgment of the debt owed to Charles Waldo Haskins for his contribution to the profession in securing legal recognition and regulation, in establishing self-imposed disciplines, in providing suitable preparatory education, and for his constant inspiration and continuing influence, it was

RESOLVED: That the Board of Directors formally authorize the dedication of the meeting rooms of the Society as the Haskins Room in perpetual memory of the man to whom so much is owed, and

BE IT FURTHER RESOLVED: That a copy of this resolution, suitably engrossed, be presented to the Haskins and Sells Foundation in honored memory of Charles Waldo Haskins and in grateful commemoration of this occasion.

IN WITNESS WHEREOF we hereunto subscribed our names and affixed the seal of The New York State Society of Certified Public Accountants.

HOWARD A. WITHEY
President

EDWARD L. LAWSON
Secretary

April 15, 1959

Charles Waldo Haskins

BIOGRAPHICAL SKETCH

CHARLES WALDO HASKINS was born January 11, 1852 in Brooklyn, New York. Graduated at 15 from Polytechnic Institute of Brooklyn. Predictions were for a future in civil engineering, his parents' choice of profession for him, but this became less alluring as he considered it.

He secured a position in the accounting department of the old and highly reputed importing house of Frederick Butterfield & Company, New York City. There he served five years, which was his apprenticeship in accounting.

To determine for himself what he wanted to do, he then went abroad. He spent two years in Paris studying art, for which he had both taste and talent, and made a tour of Europe.

He returned to New York and entered Wall Street, forming a temporary connection with his father's banking and brokerage firm. In his earlier business experience he had seen the relationship of accountancy to foreign trade and all its multiform phases and problems. Now, in Wall Street the figures were connected with finance and the rise and fall of stocks. He was soon to see the spell that figures exercised in relation to railroad construction, transportation activities and business enterprises, with their multiplicity of details, all finally expressed in a series of figures.

Accountancy was in its infancy in the United States. It required a man of vision to see what it might become. Mr. Haskins had this vision. With the imagination of a poet and the intuition of a prophet, he realized what accountancy could become, and he determined to do his part toward vitalizing it to the fulfillment of its destiny.

A red-letter day in his life was that day in 1886 when he opened an office of his own in New York City and entered the profession of public accountancy. In the several years following, he also held numerous important executive positions. He served as secretary of the Manhattan Trust Company and of the Old Dominion Construction Company, as comptroller of the Ocean Steamship Company, of the Chesapeake and Western Railroad, and as receiver of the Augusta Mining and Investment Company.

In 1893, Charles Waldo Haskins and Elijah Watt Sells met in Washington. Two men of strong individuality and of differing characteristics, previously unaware even of the existence of the other, met almost by chance and formed a life-long friendship and rare kind of mutually motivated partnership.

With a third expert, these two men had been selected to assist the "Dockery Commission" which was created in 1893 by Congress and authorized to investigate the status of laws organizing the Executive Departments, to examine the operation of employes [*sic*] and methods and to recommend improvements. The work required not only accounting ability and business knowledge and experience in relation to the conduct of great corporations—for they were investigating the accounting system of the United States Government—but also keen analysis, clear judgment, and infinite tact and wisdom in the handling of men and measures.

Investigations had been many, had come and gone with no results, and were considered expensive but harmless. One Senator expressed the general view: "Oh, it's all right; it amuses Dockery and doesn't do any harm."

The atmosphere soon changed. The Joint Commission proved itself a real force. The recommendations of the experts were so clear, final, and self-evident in their business common sense that one bill after another reported by the Commission to Congress went through, or became in force by regulations or orders. Many reforms were put into effect in all departments, especially in the Treasury, Post Office and the Interior Departments, at savings of several hundred thousand dollars annually.

During the closing weeks of their work on behalf of the Commission, Mr. Haskins and Mr. Sells discussed their future plans, and on March 4, 1895, they opened an office at No. 2 Nassau Street, New York, under the firm name of Haskins & Sells.

Mr. Haskins was one of the leaders in the profession of accountancy who were responsible for securing the passage in New York in 1896 of legislation regulating the profession of public accountants, providing for a class of public expert accountants to be known as "certified public accountants" with exclusive right to use the three letters "C.P.A." and authorizing the Regents of the University to establish examinations and issue certificates.

Mr. Haskins' partner, Elijah Watt Sells, was convinced that Mr. Haskins should continue his work for the strengthening of the young profession and believed that Mr. Haskins should be on the new Board of Examiners. He set in action a plan which resulted in the Regents being confronted with an overwhelming stack of telegrams, endorsements of Mr. Haskins from the most influential men in New York. Mr. Haskins was unanimously elected by the Regents. At the first meeting of the Examiners, Mr. Haskins was made president, a position he retained until his death.

In the spring of 1897, he helped to organize the New York State Society of Certified Public Accountants and became its first president.

There was a recognized need for a school of accountancy. At a Society meeting in November 1899, President Haskins was requested to confer with the Trustees of New York University for the purpose of arranging for a class for technical study in accountancy and related subjects. After much struggle the matter received consideration and finally resulted in the foundation of the New York University School of Commerce, Accounts, and Finance. To Mr. Haskins, more than to any other one man, is due the credit for carrying it through.

On Tuesday, October 2, 1900, the new school began its pioneer work in the University building in Washington Square, New York. A number of excellent speeches were delivered by Chancellor MacCracken, Colonel Sprague, and other members of the faculty. Then the first Dean of the School, Mr. Haskins, gave his first lecture as Professor of the History of Accountancy. There were about fifty matriculants in attendance at this opening session.

Soon after this the University conferred on him the degree of Master of Arts. The Chancellor told him that, because his relation to the school had to do with business and not with the recognized sciences, his acknowledgment of the degree in English would be acceptable. However, Mr. Haskins preferred to conform to the tradition of the University and gracefully acknowledged the honor in Latin.

He was deeply interested in the history of accounting, tracing it back almost to primitive man. From the notched stick, the knotted string, or the scratched piece of clay to the elaborate modern systems of accounts is a wondrous process of evolution. The subject was never a dry one to Mr. Haskins or to those who heard his lectures, addresses and informal talks. He loved the subject and planned to write an elaborate History of Accountancy.

Mr. Haskins has been described as "of stalwart physique, vital, pulsing with health and good spirits, kindly, cordial and hearty in manner, magnetic in personality, making friends readily and holding them strongly, as was attested by the popularity he won in the twenty or more clubs, societies and associations of which he was a member."

His firm has moved steadily forward, the School of Commerce has flourished beyond any dream of his, and the State Society has increased in size and stature. No man who does real work for the world ever sees the full fruitage of his efforts. He does not realize the seeding of purpose, initiative, influence, and inspiration that mean constant new harvests after he is no longer present to see and to know.

On January 9, 1903, Mr. Haskins' death followed a short sudden illness. He was buried on January 11, his fifty-first birthday anniversary.

Ferdinand William Lafrentz (1859-1954)

By ABRAHAM HOROWITZ, CPA

On April 21, 1947, the Board of Directors of the New York State Society of Certified Public Accountants, as part of its celebration of the Fiftieth Anniversary of the founding of the Society, presented a testimonial to Ferdinand William Lafrentz. In its resolution, the Board of Directors, on behalf of the Society, extended its congratulations in the following words, "we express our sincere and heartfelt appreciation of his services to this Society, to the profession and to the community which he has served for over a half-century. . .fully realizing. . .that the history of our profession and of our Society for this first half-century would not be complete without this recognition of his great contribution to their advancement and development." At that time Ferdinand W. Lafrentz was 88 years of age.

Yet, in 1896, when he was granted CPA certificate number 20, in the second group issued by the State Board of New York, Lafrentz was already well known in accounting and business circles.

Ferdinand William Lafrentz was born in 1859, of German parents, on a small island off the Jutland Peninsula, then under the dominion of Denmark. He arrived in the United States at the age of fourteen and settled in Chicago. Attending the Bryant and Stratton Business College in that city he soon won attention, and after completing his studies won a post as assistant professor at a competing school. He later returned to his alma mater as assistant, and later department head, of the Practical Business Department.

An invitation to handle a special assignment for a Chicago banking firm turned Lafrentz's eyes to the opportunities then available in the western United States. He joined the headquarters force of a cattle company in Wyoming, in charge of the company's financial affairs. After several years, his abilities won him a seat in the Territorial Legislature, where he introduced the joint resolution requesting that the

This is one in a series of historical studies of outstanding figures and institutions of our profession. It was prepared by the Society's Committee on History under the chairmanship of Henry Lieberman.

territory be admitted into the Union. Wyoming entered the Union in 1890.

In 1889 Mr. Lafrentz moved to Ogden, Utah and set himself up in the practice of public accounting. During this time he also studied law, winning admission to the Utah Territorial Bar in 1893. He moved to New York City later in 1893, having accepted a position as claim adjuster for the American Surety Company.

Accountancy was a profession still largely in the embryo stage and only a man with widely recognized talents in business and finance could win recognition in the field. But such a man was Lafrentz. By 1899 he had organized The American Audit Company, devoted to the independent practice of accounting, and set up his first offices at the Waldorf-Astoria, then at Fifth Avenue and 34th Street.

In the meantime he had begun an active role in furthering the development of the profession. He was instrumental in the passage of the first CPA law in the United States, enacted by the legislature of the State of New York in 1896. He was active in the American Association of Public Accountants, predecessor organization of the American Institute of Certified Public Accountants, serving in various executive capacities, including a term as president from 1901 to 1903. When the New York State Society of Certified Public Accountants was organized in 1897, Ferdinand Lafrentz was one of its first members.

By 1899 it had become evident to the Society that "it is expedient and necessary to the development of the profession of Public Accountancy that the same be established upon an educational basis as in the case of other professions." A series of conferences were held with the trustees of what is now New York University. On October 1, 1900, the School of Commerce, Accounting and Finance of the University commenced operation with a faculty including F. W. Lafrentz, CPA, as an instructor in Auditing. This relationship with the School of Commerce continued for many years as a lecturer and trustee, Lafrentz finding ample scope for his abilities in that direction.

From 1903 to 1907 and, again, from 1917 to 1925 he was a member of the New York State Board of CPA Examiners. In 1916, when the American Institute of Accountants came into being, he served on its first Council. By 1923 the character of public accountancy had changed greatly, having achieved a high level of acceptance as a business science and as a profession. The American Audit Company then became F. W. Lafrentz & Co.

Ferdinand W. Lafrentz died on July 15, 1954 at the age of 95, leaving a rich legacy in his services to his chosen profession. To this day it is remembered in the symbolic form of the F. W. Lafrentz Gold Key and Scholarship Fund at the New York University School of Commerce and Finance, established by his associates on the fiftieth anniversary of his CPA certificate. The award is made to the male evening session student, majoring in accounting, who receives the highest averages grades in English through his junior year.

Walter A. Staub

(1881-1945)

By WILLIAM J. NEARY, CPA

Walter A. Staub, President of The New York State Society of Certified Public Accountants in 1933 and 1934, was during his forty-five year career in public accounting one of that distinguished group whose tireless and unselfish devotion to the advancement of the accounting profession has helped to bring it to its present level of competence, dignity and public service.

As a boy in his native city of Philadelphia, his road was not an easy one. Born on February 27, 1881, he was not yet five years of age when his father died. The family lived in very modest circumstances. At the age of nine he was admitted to Girard College, a school for fatherless boys founded by the merchant and philanthropist, Stephen Girard. He graduated with honors in 1897. This terminated his formal education but with a strong desire for knowledge he continued to study on his own. Throughout his life he maintained an active interest in Girard College and in 1934 was the recipient of the Stephen Girard award as one "whose outstanding qualifications in his chosen field of activity reflect credit and honor upon Girard College."

After graduation he took a position in the office of an electrical contractor and, in 1899, became an assistant to the accountant for the Girard Estate. In 1901, he came to the attention of Robert H. Montgomery who, three years earlier had, in association with William M. Lybrand, T. Edward Ross and Adam A. Ross, founded the firm of Lybrand, Ross Bros. & Montgomery in Philadelphia. Mr. Montgomery was impressed with the accounting knowledge and the mature judgment of this young man of twenty. In short order, Walter Staub became associated with the new firm, an association which was to last until his death almost forty-five years later.

The firm of Lybrand, Ross Bros. & Montgomery grew quickly and in 1908 Mr. Staub was assigned to set up and manage a new office in Pittsburgh. In 1911 he became a partner, the second partner to be

---

This is one in a series of historical studies of outstanding figures and institutions of our profession. It was prepared under the auspices of our Society's Committee on History.

admitted to the firm since its founding. At that time he assumed charge of the Chicago office. In 1914 he transferred to New York and was a resident partner there until his death.

In 1903, Mr. Staub passed the Pennsylvania CPA examination and received his certificate. In later years he became certified in a number of other states, including New York.

In 1904, the first International Congress of Accountants was held in St. Louis. Mr. Staub won the prize offered by the Congress for the best paper by a clerk in an accountant's office on "The Mode of Conducting an Audit." It is noteworthy that in 1943 his winning paper was reprinted in THE ACCOUNTING REVIEW "because of its historical interest as the earliest authoritative description of the typical American audit program." This was the first of his many contributions to the literature of accounting. His "Income Tax Guide" which dealt with the Act adopted on October 3, 1913 was published in that year and was one of the first books written on federal income taxes. He contributed many articles to the JOURNAL OF ACCOUNTANCY, THE NEW YORK CERTIFIED PUBLIC ACCOUNTANT and other publications on accounting and allied subjects. His contribution to the "Proceedings"—International Congress on Accounting held in New York in 1929, entitled "Consolidated Financial Statements" was later published in book form. He was a co-author of the books "Auditing Principles" published in 1924 and "Wills, Executors and Trustees" published in 1933.

Walter A. Staub was selected by the President and Fellows of Harvard College on recommendation of the Graduate School of Business Administration of Harvard University: ". . .a man recognized as outstanding in accounting, to serve for the academic year 1940-41 as the fourth Dickinson lecturer under the foundation established in acknowledgment of the debt of the accounting profession to Sir Arthur Lowes Dickinson." In August, 1945, a few months before his death, his excellent paper "Significance of the Balance Sheet—What is Book Value?" was written for THE NEW YORK CERTIFIED PUBLIC ACCOUNTANT.

In addition to serving two terms as President of the New York State Society, he was First Vice President from 1930 to 1933 and also served as a Director. He was from 1941 to 1944 Chairman of the Committee on Accounting Procedure of the American Institute of Accountants. In 1935 he was Chairman of the joint committee appointed by the American Institute and the American Society of Certified Public Accountants to work out the plan which eventually resulted in the merger of the two organizations. As a recognized authority in the accounting and tax fields, Mr. Staub was much in demand as a speaker at meetings of various accounting societies, the Controllers Institute, the Practising Law Institute and similar organizations.

Although he gave unsparingly of his time and efforts for the welfare of the accounting profession, he found time for other activities. He served four elective terms on the Millburn, New Jersey, Board of Education from 1924 to 1936, the last several years as President. He was also Chairman of the Finance Committee of the Northern Baptist Convention and President of the Board of Trustees of Overlook Hospital in Summit, New Jersey.

Travel was Mr. Staub's chief form of relaxation. His interest in history led him to make numerous trips to Europe. He also traveled extensively in this country and Canada and to Hawaii. In sports, he enjoyed tennis and maintained a court at his home in Short Hills, New Jersey, where he lived with his wife, five sons and two daughters. Two of his sons are now partners in the firm of Lybrand, Ross Bros. & Montgomery.

Mr. Staub died suddenly on November 4, 1945 while on an overnight trip to his native city of Philadelphia. His passing left a void in his firm and in his profession. Nothing could better describe him nor express more clearly the loss felt upon his death than the following excerpt from a letter of tribute from one of the clients of his firm:

"It would be well nigh impossible for me to adequately express my deep regard for the high qualities of mind and heart with which his personality was endowed—he was indeed a rare character. He possessed in an unusual degree the most delightful faculties one could wish for—the faculty of subjecting a problem to a calm, dispassionate and highly intelligent analysis which gave to his judgment a quality that immediately won the admiration and support of his clients and his friends who detected and invariably appreciated the background of his broad experience and knowledge.

His endearing traits within a sterling character of the strictest personal integrity, provide a memory which will endear him and make that memory beloved by all who knew him."

John A. Lindquist (1892-1961)

By ALBERT V. SMYRK, CPA

History on any subject, whether it be of a nation, an industry, or a profession is primarily the biography of individuals who have devoted their lives for the improvement of their chosen field of endeavor; for history is only a shadow of humanity. And so, some part of the history of accounting is the biography of John A. Lindquist.

John A. Lindquist died on August 26, 1961 at the age of 69, having devoted the last forty years of his life to the profession of accountancy with the accounting firm of Ernst & Ernst.

His start in life was humble. Born in Brooklyn, New York, on August 6, 1892, the son of Hans J. Lindquist and Cecelia Johansson Lindquist, both of Swedish origin, he attended Grammar School, Boys High School and New York preparatory School in Brooklyn, New York. He went to work at the age of 14 as an office boy at the rate of $4.00 per week and he rose to the position of Department Manager. Working in the day time and attending school at night showed his determination to get some of the good things of life that were impossible in his youth.

John received his preliminary and professional education in Accountancy at the New York University School of Commerce, Accounting and Finance from whence he granted cum Laude in 1915. His fraternity was Alpha Kappa Psi. He also served as an examiner for New York University in its Department of Accounting instruction, specializing in Theory of Accounts and Auditing.

He married Ragnhild Westergren on April 25, 1917 and subsequently resigned his position to join the firm of Ernst & Ernst on October 1, 1917 where he began his professional career. He showed the natural ability to become an auditor and accountant and Mr. F. L. Gilbert, now deceased, their resident partner, gave him his opportunity. In time he acquired outstanding technical skill.

During the first twelve years of his employment, the firm was so impressed with his natural ability and judgment that he was advanced rapidly, being admitted to partnership in January 1929.

ALBERT V. SMYRK, CPA, is a member of our Society's History Committee.

In 1936 the New York State Society of Certified Public Accountants admitted him to membership. From 1941 to 1949 he had an unbroken record of service to the Society as a director, chairman and member of various important committees including the following: Natural Business Year, Auditing Procedure, Security and Exchange Commission Accounting, Practice Procedure, Public Relations, War Contracts, and Nominations Committees. He held the office of Director of the Society during the year 1941, 1946, 1947 and 1948.

Mr. Lindquist achieved public recognition in the American Institute of Certified Public Accountants, where he held numerous positions including the chairmanship of the important Accounting Procedures Committee and membership in its Wartime Manpower Committee. He was elected Vice President of the Institute in 1956.

During and after World War I accountancy became an increasingly indispensable profession and the need for standards of performance and ethics were paramount for its growth. There were not many reference books to turn to for guidance, and common sense was a priceless gift for anyone who had it. Mr. Lindquist had it and applied it.

Conferences with other professions strengthened the relationship by dependence of each group for their special skills and qualifications. Thus, cooperation with bankers, lawyers, credit men and other professions was born at a time when bigness and tax laws became complicated. About that time was when John Lindquist made his greatest development. He never boasted of his talents.

He held CPA certificates in the following states: New York, Missouri, North Carolina, Maryland, Virginia, Iowa, Minnesota, Indiana, Illinois, Louisiana, Tennessee, Ohio, Rhode Island, New Mexico, CPA Association of Ontario and registered in the State of Georgia.

In 1950, Lindquist was transferred to the Cleveland office of the firm, to take complete charge of all SEC and technical matters of the firm as a whole.

Prior to his move to the Cleveland office of Ernst & Ernst in 1950 he was trustee for many years of the New Rochelle Hospital in New Rochelle, New York. While in Cleveland he was a member of the Union Club at Cleveland, the Mayfield Country Club and the Mid-Day Club. He retired in October of 1957 when the profession was just sixty years old and he had devoted 40 unselfish years to it.

Men acquire a particular quality by constantly acting in a particular way. John Lindquist was a perfectionist in the presentation of unusual items appearing in financial statements and related notes thereto and in that connection was also highly regarded by the legal profession. Modesty was the only inducement he used when angling for a point; factual matter and order was his first law—a place for everything and everything in its place.

He suffered a cerebral thrombosis in the summer of 1958 and died on August 26, 1961. In his lifetime he had helped many men and never forgot a friend.

[*July, 1963*. Reprinted with permission from *The CPA Journal*, copyright 1963]

Arthur W. Teele (1868-1940)

By LEO T. TAURITZ, CPA

Three years after the American Civil War two boys were born in New England, namely, Arthur Wellington Teele in Watertown, Massachusetts and Rodney S. Dennis at Hartford, Connecticut. Fate destined them to meet some years later in New York City.

Arthur Teele's formal education was obtained at the Watertown High School and the Eastman Business College at Poughkeepsie, New York. He continued his accounting studies while employed as a clerk in a hardware store in his native city.

In 1891, at the age of twenty three, he came to New York City and obtained an accounting staff position with Mr. William Trenholm. Mr. Dennis was a member of the Trenholm staff at that time. Several years later Teele became a partner and the firm name was changed to Trenholm, Teele & Co., with offices at 11 Wall Street, New York City.

Mr. Dennis had applied himself diligently to the tasks assigned to him and, in 1894, at the age of twenty six he also became a partner and the firm name was changed to Trenholm, Teele, and Dennis. However, this partnership was not to last very long, for in 1895 a turn of events caused Mr. Trenholm to leave the firm and open his own office at 10 Wall Street, and the firm of A. W. Teele & Rodney S. Dennis was organized and carried on at 11 Wall Street.

During this period of progress of Teele and Dennis, accountants in this state were seeking professional status and recognition. In 1896, the first C.P.A. law in the United States was enacted in New York State and approved by Governor Levi P. Morton on April 17, 1896. The first examination was held on December 15 and 16, 1896, and 75 certificates were issued in this year. Mr. Teele's certificate bears number 13 and Mr. Dennis' was number 5.

The next step in professional development in this state led the pioneers of those early years to join a professional group for mutual assistance. On January 28, 1897, the New York State Society of Certified Public Accountants was incorporated and the articles of

---

LEO L. TAURITZ, CPA, is a member of our Society's Committee on History. Mr. Tauritz is in practice on his own account in New York City.

incorporation included as charter members the names of Arthur W. Teele and Rodney S. Dennis. The initial group consisted of a handful of men who were determined to carry out the objectives of the Society and as fortune would have it, Arthur Teele was elected to serve as the first Secretary. Funds in hand to conduct the business of the fledgling Society were very meager, thus the first office of this group was located in the quarters of Teele and Dennis until such time as other quarters could be found. The records indicate that the Society was housed rent free and no stipend was paid Arthur Teele as Secretary. He held this office in the years 1897 through 1899.

On April 26, 1898, at a special meeting of our Society, it was voted to establish headquarters in room 1224 of the Johnston Building at 30 Broad Street. This was the year that the firm of Haskins & Sells was established in this building and Mr. Haskins served as the first President of our Society as well as the chairman of the state C.P.A. board. Rodney Dennis also served as a member of the examining board this year.

Mergers of accounting firms are not unique to our time alone. On May 1, 1900 the firm of Teele and Dennis merged with the existing firm of Patterson, Corwin, and Patterson, and the partnership of Patterson, Teele, and Dennis was established at 30 Broad Street. There was a very close relationship between this new firm and Haskins & Sells and for many years a portrait of Mr. Haskins hung on the walls of Patterson, Teele, and Dennis. While these gentlemen were developing their accounting practice they also participated actively in the affairs of our Society, Mr. Dennis served as a Vice President during 1900-1901. Arthur Teele was the senior partner of the firm (A. S. Patterson withdrew on December 24, 1901, and Mr. R. S. Dennis died on March 7, 1904). He served as a member of the special committee on "Department Methods of the Government," in 1907, of the American Association of Public Accountants. His article entitled "Railroad Accounting in relation to the 20th section of the Act to regulate commerce" was published in the December 1908 issue of the *Journal of Accountancy*. He also served on the Board of Examiners of the American Institute of Accountants from 1916 to 1922; as Vice President from 1919 to 1921; as Treasurer 1922 to 1928, and 1939 to 1940. This founding father of our profession and Society charted our paths with zealous devotion to their welfare.

Arthur W. Teele died on January 30, 1940 at the age of 72. All of his efforts have been fittingly characterized in this Editorial in the March 1940 issue of the *Journal of Accountancy*:

> Arthur W. Teele, treasurer of the American Institute of Accountants, died suddenly on January 30, 1940, at his home in New York. He was seventy-two years old. Until a few hours before he died, he had been working at his office with customary vigor. It was characteristic that on the last day of his life he devoted several hours to thought and discussion of the Institute financial affairs. Mr. Teele was one of that small group of men who early in this century threw themselves without reservation into the task of building a profession of accountancy in the United States. He and his fellow workers spared no pains, refused no sacrifice of time, energy or money, in the prosecution of their self-imposed job. The magnitude of their accomplishment is evident today. Mr. Teele had served on almost every important administrative committee of the American Association of Public Accountants and of the Institute. As treasurer, he was a member of the Institute's executive committee for thirteen years. His influence was positive and constructive. He had deep convictions, but no prejudice. If his colleagues argued, he sat apart like a judge. He could find merit in a cause contrary to his own preference.
>
> His integrity was never doubted. Small wonder that he commanded the respect and admiration of every man he met. He was a man's man, and his vitality was inexhaustible. Outside his profession he was as active as within. Everywhere he was a leader. Accountancy gained prestige because he was a part of it. His loyalty was unshakable. He had friends in numbers in which most men count their acquaintances.
>
> Some student of the future, delving into the history of American accountancy, may piece together the record of the career of Arthur Teele. He will be truly inspired if some instinct stirs him to exclaim "There were giants in those days."

George O. May (1875—1961)

By JENNIE M. PALEN, CPA

In November 1891 George Oliver May was sixteen years old. At the English school he was attending he had just made a spectacular tackle in a football game which thrust him into line of captaincy of the team in the following year. Aglow with this rosy prospect, he went home for the Christmas holidays, torn between his eagerness to captain the team and his desire to win a scholarship in mathematics at Cambridge. Unexpected resolution of his problem came when a Christmas visitor whom his family rated highly advised him to go into accountancy, then a new profession and said to be the rising one. Diverted, perhaps, by the appeal of a third course at such a time, George O. May turned to accountancy and to a career in which he distinguished himself on both sides of the Atlantic. By his own admission, that was the first time he had ever heard of accountancy.

The next five years were spent in Exeter in the office of Thomas Andrew, a chartered accountant, as an "articled pupil." He records that his father paid 100 guineas for this training. Though he had been apprenticed to learn broad accounting and auditing work, his experience here was confined almost entirely to the bankruptcy field, in which he acquired an expertness and showed a penetration that won him first place in the chartered accountant examinations, as well as a connection in London with Price Waterhouse & Co. On February 15, 1897, at a salary of £120 a year, he entered the employ of this illustrious accounting firm, for an association which was to last until his death in 1961.

Five months after employing him the firm sent him to its representative in America, Jones, Caesar & Co., at an annual salary of £400 and the prospect of an early partnership. In 1901 Price Waterhouse & Co. founded its own American firm, in 1902 admitted him as a partner, and in 1911 made him senior partner, which he

---

JENNIE M. PALEN, CPA, is a member of our Society and its History Committee. Miss Palen is the author of the distinguished book, "Report Writing for Accountants" (Prentice-Hall) and other works, and is an editor, teacher and a former president of the American Woman's Society of CPAs. Miss Palen is also a widely published poet, whose third collection of poems, "Stranger, Let Me Speak," is scheduled for Fall publication.

remained until his retirement in 1940. After 1940 he served the firm as a consultant. He had relinquished his administrative duties within the firm in 1926 to devote himself to the broader professional problems.

It would be difficult to overstate the value of George O. May's contribution to accounting thought. He was a person of quick intelligence and sound common sense, whose forthright integrity commanded the respect of those on both sides of any discussion. He used these qualities, together with his considerable experience, to the unique benefit of the accounting profession, whose rise to prestige was inextricably woven with his own.

As advisor to the New York Stock Exchange beginning in 1927, he was an early and vigorous spokesman for the stockholder's right to receive periodic audited reports relating to the financial position and operating results of the companies in which he had invested his funds. It was Mr. May who in large part drafted the publication "Audits of Public Accounts," a joint effort of the American Institute of CPAs and the New York Stock Exchange, in which five basic accounting principles, agreed upon by both participants, were enunciated. And it was this collaboration that led to the first authoritative approach to "generally accepted accounting principles" in financial statements and to the now established practice of public reporting of corporate financial data. Mr. May was also the prime mover in persuading the Securities and Exchange Commission, in the early days of its existence, that the accounting profession, not the Federal Government, is the authority for accounting principles.

He brought further credit to his profession through distinguished service in a variety of public posts. In World War I he was an official of the United States Treasury Department and of the War Trade Board. From 1917 to 1932, as consultant to the Treasury Department, he made a notable contribution to governmental and Congressional understanding of the accountant's concept of income in Federal taxation. He served as director of the National Bureau of Economic Research and director of the Council on Foreign Relations. He was chairman of an advisory committee for the Social Science Research Council. At the Graduate School of Business Administration of Harvard University he was the first Dickinson lecturer under a program sponsored by the Dickinson Fund, which Price Waterhouse & Co. established. From these and his many other appointments he emerges as an enduring example of the rising role of the public accountant, public servant and advisor in fields other than his own.

Mr. May was a prolific writer. In addition to more than a hundred published articles, he was the author of "Financial Accounting," published in 1943. With Oswald Knauth he drafted the report of the Study Group on Business Income, which was published in 1952. A collection of his papers under the title "Twenty-five Years of Accounting Responsibility" was compiled by his partners and published in 1936. Another collection from his diaries and papers was published after his death.

His services to the Institute were comprehensive and continuous. He served on the board of examiners, on the committees on Federal legislation, state legislation, development of accounting principles and procedures, cooperation with stock exchanges, terminology, and many others, and in 1944 received the Institute's award for distinguished service to the accounting profession. No one could have deserved it more than the man who so thoroughly earned his unofficial title of Dean of American Accounting. Perhaps his greatest reward was his inclusion amongst the first three members appointed to the Accounting Hall of Fame.

Prior Sinclair (1882-1961)

By HENRY LIEBERMAN, CPA

Robert Prior Sinclair (Pete to his friends) was born in Blackburn, England, on November 6, 1882, son of John and Hanna S. Sinclair. On coming to the U.S. he attended New York University from which he was graduated in 1912 with a Bachelor of Commercial Science Degree.

He worked thereafter as an industrial accountant, became a citizen in 1915, and in the same year married Selina Geib. When World War I broke out, he served as a Captain in the U.S. Army. During his army service he helped with the organization of the accounting department of the Army's Chemical Service.

Following the war he joined the New York Office of Lybrand, Ross Bros. and Montgomery, but spent little of his early years in New York. After an initial engagement in Cuba, he undertook special consultations for the U.S. Shipping Board and was "on loan" to the Board for a year's service as controller.

Upon completion of the U. S. Shipping Board Project, Mr. Sinclair went to Cleveland in 1923 to open a new Lybrand office there, where he remained until 1927. In the announcement of his admission to partnership in 1929, it was noted that he

> . . .amply demonstrated not only his marked ability as an accountant, but also his good judgment and the happy faculty of winning the confidence and cooperation of his co-workers in our organization.

In the years thereafter he remained in the New York office of Lybrand where he served as the Firm's Managing Partner from 1945 until his retirement in 1954.

Prior Sinclair had a distinguished career of service, both to his Firm and his profession. He received his New York CPA Certificate in 1912 and over the years served the New York State Society in many capacities, including the office of President in 1946. [*See Appendix.*]

HENRY LIEBERMAN, CPA, is a member of our Society and of its Committee on History and is a lecturer in Accountancy at the Bernard M. Baruch School of Business and the Public Administration, the City College of the City University.

He also held a CPA Certificate in Ohio and was, of course, active in the American Institute as a member of both the council and the Executive Committee, as well as regular committee work.

The New York State Society of CPAs gave him its Service Award in 1948, and he was also the recipient of awards from New York University. In 1941 the University gave him the Medallion Alumni Award for distinguished service to the University and in 1951 he received the John T. Madden Memorial Award for outstanding achievement in the accounting profession.

Prior Sinclair's contribution to professional literature began early in his career with a pamphlet "System of Accounts for Steamship Managing Agents," and continued over the years with articles on a variety of accounting subjects. His textbook *Budgeting*, published by Ronald Press in 1934, was an authoritative text in its field for a number of years.

Mr. Sinclair was keenly interested in civic and community affairs. During the 1942 gubernatorial election campaign, he headed an accountants' committee for the election of Thomas E. Dewey. He was active in fund raising drives for the New York City Cancer Committee, the United Service Organizations and the United Hospital Campaign Committee, and he was a member of the Union League Club, the Metropolitan Opera Club, the St. George Society, the English Speaking Union, the Pelham Country Club and the New York University Club.

Prior Sinclair died on July 14, 1961 at the age of 78. He was survived by his wife Selina, his son, Robert, three grandchildren, and his sister, Mrs. L. Watson.

APPENDIX

Prior Sinclair's Service to New York State Society of Certified Public Accountants.

As Officer or Director:

1929-1930—Acting Treasurer
1930-1931—Treasurer
1942-1944
and
1947-1948—Director
1944-1945—Second Vice President
1945-1946—First Vice President
1946-1947—President

On Special Committees:

1938-1939—Consideration of a Benevolent Fund
1944-1945—Wartime & Postwar Problems
1945-1946—Public & Civic Affairs
1947-1948—Ex-Officio Advisory Committee

On Technical Committees:

1924-1930—Budgets & Budgetary Control
1930-1931,
1932-1933
and
1935-1937—Chairman of Budgets and Budgetary Control
1931-1933—Member of Bankruptcy Procedure
1933-1934
and 1935—Chairman of Auditors' Liability
1947-1948—Chairman, Awards

On Standing Committees:

1927-1928,
1933-1935—Legislation
1947-1948—Chairman, Legislation
1928-1930—Chairman, Library
1933-1934—Member, Budget and Finance
1947-1948—Chairman, Budget and Finance
1935-1937—Chairman, Ethics
1937-1938—Member, Natural Business Year
1939-1940
and 1941—Chairman, Natural Business Year
1938-1939-
1940-1941-
1942-1943—Member, Furtherance of Objectives of Society
1943-1944—Chairman, Furtherance of Objectives of Society
1939-1944-
1941-1943—Public Relations
1943-1944—Vice Chairman, Public Information
1945-1946—Chairman, Public Information
1947-1948—Member, Public Information
1945-1946-
and 1947—Meetings
1947-1948-
and 1949—Public Information
1947-1948—Cooperation with the Bar
1948-1949—Vice Chairman, Cooperation with the Bar

James F. Hughes (1879-1950)

By EARLE F. WASHBURN, CPA

This is one of a series of articles on New York CPAs who have made outstanding and lasting contributions to both the profession and the New York Society. The articles are prepared under the aegis of the Society's History Committee.

"Jim" Hughes, as he was affectionately known by his many friends, the eighteenth president of our society, had a humble start in life. After completing his public school education, he was employed for some time at clerical work with the Jersey City branch of the Standard Oil Company and with the law firm of McGee, Bedle and Bedle, in Jersey City.

At the age of 18, he decided to secure additional education if he hoped to compete on an equal basis with other men and accordingly entered Philips Exeter Academy at Exeter, New Hampshire. He was graduated there four years later (1901). He was an expert stenographer and so was able to secure a stenographic position with the New Hampshire Supreme Court and put himself through Exeter solely by his own efforts.

After graduating from Exeter, he returned to New York as private secretary to J. H. McClement, C.P.A., of the banking firm of George P. Butler and Brother. He remained with this firm for six years. During this time he became interested in Accountancy and decided to enter public practice for himself. In preparation for this step he enrolled in the Pace Institute (Now Pace College) as its first student. He became known as the "Original Pace Student."

Following completion of the course in Business Administration and Accountancy at Pace he took and passed the examination for the C.P.A. Certificate and formed a partnership with James F. Farrell, C.P.A. also a Pace graduate. The firm was known as Hughes and Farrell. Later Alfred Boyce was admitted and the name became Boyce,

---

EARLE F. WASHBURN, CPA, is a member of our society's History Committee. Mr. Washburn has been a member of the Committee on Publications and Chairman of the Committees on Nonprofit Institution Accounting and Budgets and Budgetary Control. He is presently retired from his position of Controller of New York University.

Hughes and Farrell, with offices at 70 Pine Street, New York City. The firm specialized in Municipal Accounting. He became a member of the Society on November 10, 1911, and of the American Institute of Certified Public Accountants in 1916.

He gave of himself liberally to the Society and his dossier reveals a wide range of service. He was Treasurer from 1918 to 1922; Director from 1922 to 1924 and from 1937 to 1940; and President from 1935 to 1937. He served on many committees, among them Commercial Arbitration, Cooperation with Bankers and Credit Men, and Federal Taxation, the latter from 1924 to 1931. He also served as President of the American Society of C.P.A.'s; The New Jersey State Society of C.P.A.'s; and the Accountants Club of America. He was also at one time a member of the New Jersey State Board of C.P.A. Examiners.

Perhaps the most significant development during his administration was the "decision relating to the future pattern of the executive administration of the society. . .it was urged on the one hand that the society had become a 'Trade Association' the affairs of which should be conducted by an executive vice president, with only nominal functions reposing in the elected officers. On the other hand it was urged that a professional society was not in any sense a trade association and that the control of the professional affairs must rest with the officers and directors elected by the Society from among it's own members. This latter view prevailed and it has become established for all time that *in the public interest*, the control of professional practice, as to competency, and integrity must rest in the hands of the professional body."

Upon election as President, "he promptly began a series of visits to the four up-state chapters (Buffalo, Rochester, Syracuse, and Albany) as the result of which it has come about that Jim Hughes has become throughout the State our most highly esteemed member."

The life of this man should be an inspiration when one considers that he surmounted a great many obstacles before reaching his chosen destination. Many of these have been made easier today for those aspiring to a professional career. True, more knowledge is required, but the pathway to obtaining it is quite a bit smoother than in the past.

ACKNOWLEDGEMENTS:

1. The quoted material is from "The History and Administration of our Society" by Henry A. Horne, CPA, in *The New York Certified Public Accountant*, Fiftieth Anniversary issue (1947).

2. Appreciation is also expressed to Miss Mary Cagney of the Pace College staff for information relating to Mr. Hughes' connection with that institution.

William M. Lybrand (1867-1960)

By HENRY LIEBERMAN, CPA

This is one of a series of articles on New York CPAs who have made outstanding and lasting contributions to both the profession and the New York Society. The articles are prepared under the aegis of the Society's History Committee.

"To see him at work and in counsel is to esteem him for his qualities of mind, purpose and accomplishment; to know him as a man is to love him."

—Walter A. Staub
(October 16, 1937)

William M. Lybrand entered the accounting profession at the age of 20 on December 29, 1887 as a staff accountant for a Philadelphia accountant, John Heins. He soon won the esteem not only of his exacting employer but of three co-workers with whom he was to found the firm that today carries their names: Adam A. Ross, T. Edward Ross and Robert H. Montgomery. Writing of him 50 years later, T. Edward Ross noted, "It was easy to like William at the very start. He possessed then as now a great capacity for making friends, and kindliness, patience and helpfulness have always been characteristic of him."

On January, 8, 1898 the four friends opened an office of their own in Philadelphia as Lybrand, Ross Bros. and Montgomery. The firm today is internationally known.

William Lybrand was very active in the early affairs of the profession. He was the first treasurer of the Pennsylvania Institute of CPAs and he was president of the Institute in the period 1902-1904. During his term as president the Institute established evening courses in accounting, at which he taught the course in Practical Accounting. From these courses the University of Pennsylvania developed its Wharton School of Finance. During this same period he was also active

---

HENRY LIEBERMAN, CPA, is a member of our society and of its Committee on History. Mr. Lieberman is a lecturer in Accounting at the Bernard M. Baruch School of Business and Public Administration, the City College of the City University.

in establishing the nation's first magazine on public accounting, from which today's *Journal of Accountancy* grew in 1905.

Although his initial years were spent in Philadelphia, he moved to New York in 1908 and remained there for the rest of his career. He received his New York CPA certificate in 1914. References in his application for membership in the New York State Society were Elijah Watt Sells, W. F. Weiss, and Edward L. Suffern. He served on many committees of the New York State Society in its early years.

Mr. Lybrand was one of the organizers of the National Association of Cost Accountants in 1919 (now National Association of Accountants) and served as president from 1920 to 1922. In 1947 the partners of Lybrand, Ross Bros. and Montgomery established the Lybrand annual medal award for best manuscripts on accounting submitted to the N.A.A. He was also active in the American Institute for over a quarter of a century, serving on its governing body as well as on a number of major committees, including the historic Committee on Cooperation with the Stock Exchange, whose work aided in post-depression reforms now embodied in the administration of the SEC.

In a long career of professional achievements, William M. Lybrand evidenced a notable ability to disarm criticism and take the sting out of controversy. Carl T. Keller, Lybrand partner in Boston once said:

> I am sure that those of you who have had to deal with William are aware of the following characteristic. Many times in the past I have rushed over to New York, filled with high purpose, burst in upon him with all kinds of enthusiasm, poured out my tale and almost invariably when I finally came up for air I found that we were discussing something quite different, and that my pet had apparently been packed in cotton wool and put in a soundproof vault. There were no evidences of strangulation or other high-handed treatment, but in his quiet and effective way he had slipped around my end. I am afraid that occasionally he was correct.

To all who knew him he was characterized by a dedication to his profession, a genial temperament, and a great human warmth.

Edward Augustus Kracke (1882-1960)

By ARTHUR B. FOYE, CPA

This is one of a series of articles on New York CPAs who have made outstanding and lasting contributions to both the profession and the New York Society. The articles are prepared under the aegis of the Society's Committee on History.

Among the men who have contributed so heavily to progress in our profession one would surely be called the "accountants' accountant." A leading nominee for this role would be Edward Augustus Kracke. Recipient of the outstanding service award of our Society, in 1947, and of the American Institute, in 1948, Mr. Kracke had parallel, vigorous careers in both groups: in our Society he was a director for four years and president in 1948, and at one time or another served on seventeen committees; in the Institute he was on its Council and a member of its Executive Committee from 1943 to 1949, and served as chairman or member of twenty-two committees.

Ed Kracke was educated in the New York schools and in Harvard, where he majored in classical languages—giving him the facility he later needed and used in French and German; and the illumination of his speech with Latin and Greek quotations. He completed the four years study at Harvard in three years, graduating in 1904, cum laude, in the class of Franklin Delano Roosevelt. This basic education he expanded and developed over the years with wide and deep reading in history, economics and literature.

After graduation he tried restlessly fields of banking, finance and real estate, coming finally to a conviction that his field was public accounting. When he was thirty years old, in 1912, he joined Haskins & Sells and rose rapidly through the ranks to become a partner in 1921.

After the first world war, the reconstruction of Europe's industry brought American financiers into active participation and Mr. Kracke was in Europe from 1924 to 1930, rendering important accounting

---

ARTHUR B. FOYE, CPA, is a former president of our Society and of the American Institute of Certified Public Accountants. Mr. Foye is a member of the firm of Haskins & Sells.

service in connection with financing in Germany, France, Italy and Poland and in developing the practice of his firm on that continent. These were years of unremitting work under most difficult conditions and under constant tensions.

He returned from Europe in 1930 and plunged into technical work for his firm, giving attention to some of its most important client engagements and also developing technical procedures for its accounting work. This was a time when the accountants' role in bringing information to investors and lenders unfolded rapidly, given impetus by public demand and by the New York Stock Exchange, the banks, and the newly born Securities and Exchange Commission. It was therefore a time when Mr. Kracke's background, experience, wide vision and keen mind could make great contributions to the profession.

As one of the by-products of his activity he started for his firm in 1933 a statistical survey of accountants' opinions in 500 published reports of 1932. This project was continued by Haskins & Sells until 1946 when it was turned over the AICPA, becoming their "Accounting Trends and Techniques," now in its 18th edition.

Another by-product was his work on inventory valuation. He served as Chairman of the original Inventory Committee of the AICPA, which collaborated with the American Petroleum Institute over the years 1933 to 1936 and reported the "last in, first out" basis as an acceptable method of inventory valuation for certain industries. He continued this interest as a member of the Accounting Procedure Committee of the AICPA. In 1938 and 1939 he served in an advisory capacity to the Treasury Department in the revision of the income tax law in respect of "last in, first out" procedure. When the "first in, last out" method came up in the Canadian courts, Mr. Kracke's able testimony was one of the most important factors in the recognition by the court of the basis.

Mr. Kracke was a guiding spirit in planning the project, sponsored by the Haskins & Sells Foundation, which resulted in 1938 in Sanders, Hatfield and Moore's "A Statement of Accounting Principles." He was a member of the committee in 1934, 1935 and 1936 that revised the Federal Reserve Board Bulletin entitled "Verification of Financial Statements." He was also the draftsman of the Tentative Statement on Auditing Standards, which was published in 1947 and has since become the bible of independent auditors.

Mr. Kracke's preoccupation with professional activities did not give him very much for participation in national activities except through his professional associations. However, his later work for the American Institute of Accountants after the second world war was on committees relating to federal government accounting, and as Chairman of the Committee on Cooperation with the Congressional Appropriations Committees. This led him into close touch with Senator Byrd and Congressman Taber. Always a person of strong and deep convictions he threw himself into this phase of national activity, serving as a member of both Hoover Commissions and as an advisor to the Maritime Commission.

To bring his high technical skills to the fore Mr. Kracke had a number of personal characteristics that made him also a fascinating and great human being. His firmly fixed views of integrity, personal and national, his belief in hard work and his demonstration of it, his conservative, perhaps ultra conservative views, his erudition, his philological competence, his rhetorical fire works, his pixyish sense of humor and his mastery of the art of punning were all a part of him. Pervading all of his life were his warm affection for his friends, his willingness and even eagerness to "go the second mile" for them, and his dedicated devotion to his family, deeply conscious as he was of how much he owed to them for his accomplishments and his happiness.

Frederick W. Wulfing (1894-1960)

By REX F. PALMER, CPA

This is one of a series of articles on New York CPAs who have made outstanding and lasting contributions to both the profession and the New York Society. The articles are prepared under the aegis of the Society's Committee on History.

Accounting's heroes, unlike those of some other professions, are unsung. The age when knighthood, as exemplified by accountants, was in flower never existed. The silver screen and television portrayals of accountants are unfortunately not flattering. But there are nevertheless among accountants, both of the past and of the present, some who, were they better known, would place upon the profession the imprint of chivalry. Such a man was Frederick W. Wulfing.

If accountants were to be represented by a single member from their ranks, he was an individual who could well do so.

From a modest background, with thorough training, diligent work habits, and active support of the highest standards, he rose to be widely known and genuinely admired.

Frederick W. Wulfing was born July 16, 1894, in Maspeth, Long Island, which in those days was the agricultural border of Brooklyn. Though some early accountants had a long line of dour Scots ancestry, the Wulfings were of German extraction.

Mr. Wulfing attended what then was Eastern District High School, and in 1915 received from Columbia University the Bachelor of Science degree. His college sports were wrestling, and track at the 660 yard distance.

Upon graduation he enlisted in the army. He served in the 1916 Mexican border campaign and in World War I, as a sergeant in the 7th U.S. Field Artillery, and thereafter became a Texas Ranger.

With this campaigning behind him, Mr. Wulfing returned to New York. On April 4, 1919, New York State issued to him its Certificate, Number 809, certifying his qualifications as an accountant. In 1920 he

---

REX F. PALMER, CPA, recently was a member of our Society's Committee on History and presently is Chairman of the Committee on Commerce and Industry. Mr. Palmer is Assistant to the Controller of the Great Lakes Carbon Corporation.

was with Park Potter & Co.; next John I. Coe & Co.; then Marvin Scudder & Co. He left the last, as a junior partner, in 1922 to become, until 1929, a principal in Epstein and Wulfing. Then he formed Wulfing and Stillman and in 1937 became a partner in Barrow, Wade, Guthrie & Co. When that firm merged in 1950 with Peat, Marwick, Mitchell & Co., be [*sic*] became a partner in the latter, from which he retired as a limited partner.

Professionally, Mr. Wulfing was a member of the Accountants Club of America, the Insurance Association, the National Association of Accountants, the Association of Stock Exchange Firms—Accounting Division, the Municipal Finance Officers Association, The American Accounting Association, the American Institute of Certified Public Accountants, the State Societies of California, New Jersey, Texas, and New York. The states, in addition to New York, in which Mr. Wulfing held certificates, are: California, Illinois, Michigan, Missouri, New Jersey, New Mexico, Oklahoma, Pennsylvania, Texas, and Virginia.

Service to the communities where he resided was likewise a confirmed habit throughout his life. He served as Trustee of the Incorporated Village of Munsey Park, and as its Mayor, and was President of the Manhasset Board of Education.

The Wulfings enjoyed a happy home life blessed with a daughter and a son. His social connections were numerous and included memberships in many collegiate and other organizations, including: Columbia College Alumni Associates, Beta Alpha Psi (Nu Chapter) Honorary, and Columbia University Club.

Mr. Wulfing's membership in the New York State Society of Certified Public Accountants was continuous. He was a Director of the Society in 1939-40, 1940-41, and 1941-42. He was a member of the State Council on Accounting and was active in the Society's Nassau-Suffolk Chapter. The Committees of the Society on which he served from one to six years were: Budget and Finance, Cooperation with the S.E.C., Legislation, Standard Costs, Court Testimony, S.E.C. Accounting, Governmental Accounting, Membership, Stock Brokerage Accounting, and Professional Conduct.

Impressive as the foregoing may be, it does not fully tell this cheery-mannered, quickly perceptive, and simply honest man's story. The wealth of experience in insurance brokerage and stock brokerage accounting that he accumulated gave his professional recommendations a quiet authoritativeness that was incontrovertible. His interest in the accountant's professional conduct was intense; his sternness with violators was proverbial; and his efforts in the cause of improved professional conduct are worthy of their own story.

Mr. Wulfing died July 7, 1960. His dedication to the profession, and to the Society, and the high example that his life represents were recognized by the Society in its Resolution dated August 2, 1960.

RESOLUTION

WHEREAS, In the death of Frederick W. Wulfing, The New York State Society of Certified Public Accountants has lost a loyal member who has maintained a continuous membership in the Society since 1919; and

WHEREAS, Mr. Wulfing served the Society as a Director and as Chairman of the Committee on Professional Conduct and on many other Society committees; and

WHEREAS, Mr. Wulfing by his dedication to the profession and the Society and by his special activities in connection with the enforcement of our rules of professional conduct has set a high example for all to follow; now, therefore,

BE IT RESOLVED, That the Board of Directors of The New York State Society of Certified Public Accountants hereby records with deepest sorrow the death of its beloved and esteemed member, Frederick W. Wulfing, and its appreciation of his high professional standards and dedicated loyalty in so faithfully serving the Society and his chosen profession.

William Hansell Bell (1883-1960)

By ARTHUR B. FOYE, CPA

This is one of a series of articles on New York CPAs who have made outstanding and lasting contributions to both the profession and the New York Society. The articles are prepared under the aegis of the Society's Committee on History.

The history of the profession of public accountancy in the United States can be divided into three periods. The first was from the beginning of the infiltration into the United States of accountants and accountancy from England and Scotland—the period the commencement of which is hazily in the 1870's and 1880's and which can be said to run until approximately 1910. In this period training for the "profession" was largely practical, essentially the British apprenticeship method without the apprenticeship restrictions. There was relatively little in the way of education in accountancy.

The second period ran from about 1910, roughly, to the end of the second World War.

In this period educational facilities expanded rapidly with many universities creating and developing schools of business and arranging for evening sessions so that ambitious young men who had not the opportunity of full time college work could work during the day and pay their way in the university. It was also a time when audit procedures were being developed and refined, when financial reporting was receiving more and more attention with greater disclosure of financial data, when the wording of reports and certificates was the subject of many articles and much debate. It was also the time when the professional societies were beginning to grow in size and importance.

The third period, from the end of the Second World War to the present time has seen the blossoming of the profession—vastly extended educational facilities, greatly heightened standards of entrance into the profession, new methods and new techniques, growth of the professional organizations and recognition of the value of the profession to the whole economy. Young men interested in the profession are now generally taking full time courses in the universities.

ARTHUR B. FOYE, CPA, is a past president of our Society and of the American Institute of CPAs. Mr. Foye is a member of the firm of Haskins & Sells.

William Hansell Bell was in the middle period and was indeed typical of it. He was born in 1883 in Canada, the son of a clergyman—whose family of six children grew up in the then usual restricted economical existence of a minister's home. They moved to New York State when Bell was a youngster, living in small villages in the Buffalo area. In order to go to high school in Springville, New York, a town which even today has a population of only 3,852, he boarded with a farmer near the town, milking the cows and doing other farm chores for his board.

He graduated from high school in 1900 and for the next six or seven years was in clerical and bookkeeping work in various companies. In one of the latter places, he came in touch with a partner of Haskins & Sells, Charles E. Morris, who was impressed by the young man and urged him to go into public accounting. This resulted in Bell coming to New York in 1907, enrolling as a night student at New York University School of Commerce, Accounts and Finance and seeking, and finally in 1909, receiving a position with Haskins & Sells, with whom he stayed for the rest of his working life. In 1918 he became the fourteenth man taken into partnership in the firm.

Bell graduated from New York University in 1910 with the degree of BCS cum laude and later received the degree of MCS from St. Louis University. He passed his examinations for the New York CPA certificate in 1910, became a member of the New York State Society of CPAs in 1911, of the American Association of Certified Public Accountants in 1912 and at the American Institute of Accountants in 1916.

Always deeply interested in the profession, he served in the New York State Society of CPA's at different times from 1922 to 1946, as director, officer and as chairman or member of twelve Committees and in the American Institute of Accountants on seven different Committees.

He wrote several books on Auditing and Reports and many articles on technical matters. His special field was in the development of technical procedures and in the refinement and improvement of reports, work which brought him to a position of leadership in his firm. His accounting insight was of the highest order; beyond this he was a precisionist, an authority on English usage and a tremendous worker. Today's auditing practices and the form and content of reports are the result of the thinking and the efforts of many of the leaders of the profession, so that no one person can be named as the author, but one of these leaders who gave much to this was William Hansell Bell.

Isidor Sack (1888-1961)

By REUBEN WESTERMAN, CPA

This is one of a series of articles on New York CPAs who have made outstanding and lasting contributions to both the profession and the Society. The articles are prepared under the aegis of the Society's History Committee.

Isidor Sack was born in New York City on February 21, 1888, the eldest son of a large immigrant family. After completing the eighth grade in elementary school he took a job as a bookkeeper and studied accounting on his own. He attended New York University Law School at night, graduating in 1909. He was promptly admitted to the Bar but, by that time, he was doing better financially as an accountant than he could hope to earn as a beginner in the legal field and he therefore did not pursue the practice of law.

He was employed by the State of New York, in the State Comptroller's office, and while there designed a system of uniform accounts for second and third class cities. When he moved to Yonkers 25 years later, he was surprised to find his system still in use by that City.

During World War I he served as a First Lieutenant in the Army Air Corps in Washington. After the armistice he attended the Versailles Peace Conference in an official capacity, to be available to submit data on the size of the U. S. Air Force and air power in connection with disarmament discussions.

After his discharge from the Service he was invited to assist in the establishment of the New York State Income Tax Bureau, as First Assistant Director of that Department. He also organized the New York office of the State Bureau of Motor Vehicles and served as counsel to that Department for several years.

In the middle 1920's he entered the practice of law, specializing in tax matters, in partnership with Herman M. Stein and Nathaniel Ross. This firm was dissolved in the late 1920's.

REUBEN WESTERMAN, CPA, is a member of our Society's History Committee. Mr. Westerman is in practice on his own account in New York City.

Mr. Sack received C.P.A. Certificate #1008 on September 15, 1921 and was admitted to membership in the New York State Society of Certified Public Accountants on January 6, 1922.

He discontinued his law practice in order to associate himself with Lehman Bros., one of the leading investment banking firms of the country, as Assistant Comptroller. He later became Comptroller, and continued in that capacity for a period of over thirty years until he retired in January 1960. He then entered into partnership with one of his brothers, N. Harry Sack, for the practice of law in tax matters exclusively. After a full and active life, devoted to his profession and his fellow men, by untiring service to his local communities, state and country, as well as religious, charitable, civic and educational organizations, he passed away on May 25, 1961 at the age of 73. His wife had predeceased him, but he was survived by two sons.

Isidor Sack was an organizer and leader, serving professional and other organizations in innumerable capacities. He was a Director of The New York State Society of Certified Public Accountants in 1926-28 and again in 1935-36. He was also a chairman and member of many committees of the State Society—standing, special and technical. Some of them were Furtherance of the Society's Objectives, Arbitration, Industry & Commerce, Budget & Finance, Investment of Society Funds, Unincorporated Business Tax, Nominations, Local, State & Federal Taxation, Stock & Brokerage Accounting, Investment Trusts and Petroleum Industry Accounting.

He was chairman of the State Tax Committee for many years, and in that capacity worked actively with State tax officials to cement closer relations with the Society and its members. He was on the Committee which worked with the State Comptroller, including the furnishing of independent technical advice on fiscal matters to the Department of Audit & Control, and in the development of rules and regulations applicable to the New York State Unincorporated Business Tax.

Mr. Sack was also a member of the American Institute of Certified Public Accountants, the National Association of Accountants, a Director of the Accountants Club of America, a member of the Economic Research Round Table, a charter member of the New York University Tax Study Group, and a lecturer at the University's Institute on Federal Taxation. He was co-author of a book on New York Income and Franchise Taxes, and wrote many articles on the subject. A fluent speaker and prolific writer, he lectured to various groups, and wrote numerous articles for professional magazines.

In communial [*sic*] affairs, he served on the Yonkers Community Chest, and was a Special Deputy Commissioner of Public Safety of that City. He was one of the founders of the United Jewish Appeal and was active in a number of Jewish religious and welfare institutions.

General Arthur H. Carter (1884-1965)

By THOMAS G. HIGGINS, CPA

This is one of a series of New York CPAs who have made outstanding and lasting contributions to both the profession and the New York State Society of Certified Public Accountants. The articles are prepared under the aegis of the Society's Committee on History.

The remarkable thing about General Arthur H. Carter, who died on January 3, 1965 at the age of 81, is that he had two distinguished professional careers. Together, these careers spanned a period of forty years—seventeen of them with the United States Army and twenty-three in professional accounting.

General Carter lived an exceptionally full life, and in his day he was one of the best-known CPAs in America. He attained high rank in the Army and high office in our Society and in the American Institute of Certified Public Accountants, and for twenty years he was senior partner of Haskins & Sells.

He was interested in civic affairs and sports, and he loved the out-of-doors. He founded a hospital in Leesburg, Virginia, where he farmed for a few years, and in retirement he became president of the Good Samaritan Hospital near his winter home in Delray Beach, Florida. For relaxation he golfed, fished, and hunted. Mrs. Carter also loved the out-of-doors, and together they spent many a summer fishing in New Brunswick. They were both skilled in horsemanship, the General having been a polo player in his early days with the Army.

Arthur H. Carter was born in Hillsboro, Kansas, on January 6, 1884. He received his early education in Kansas and entered the United States Military Academy at West Point, New York, in 1901. Four years later he graduated as a Second Lieutenant of Field Artillery. After serving in various posts in the United States and the Philippines he resigned in 1915 to enter civilian life.

In 1917 shortly after the United States entered World War I, he reentered the Army as a Major in the Bureau of Ordnance. He was

---

THOMAS G. HIGGINS, CPA, is a member of our Society's Committee on History and a past President of the Society. Mr. Higgins was the managing partner, until his retirement, of Arthur Young & Company.

transferred during the war to the Field Artillery, where he organized and served as Commanding Officer of the Field Artillery Central Officers' Training School in Kentucky. He received an honorable discharge in 1919 as a full Colonel.

It was in 1908, in the Philippines, that an event occurred which, years later, was to have an important effect on his career. In that year he met Marjorie Sells, who was travelling with her father, Elijah Watt Sells, a founding partner of the firm of Haskins & Sells. Two years later, he and Miss Sells were married, and eleven years later, in 1919, he joined the staff of Haskins & Sells. He became a partner in the firm in 1922, after obtaining CPA certificates in New York and Connecticut, and five years later he became the firm's senior partner.

General Carter was active in the affairs of our Society for a long period of years and served as President for a three-year term from 1930 to 1933. He also served the American Institute in a variety of capacities, including that of Vice President.

In the summer of 1940, when President Roosevelt and his Cabinet were convinced that the nation was in imminent danger, Henry L. Stimson was appointed Secretary of War and Robert P. Patterson Assistant Secretary of War. Almost immediately these two men set about the task of surrounding themselves with a team of civilian associates who they believed would combine intelligence, initiative, and loyalty. It was in March 1941 that General Carter was brought on to the staff as Executive Accountant. His duties were to review and recommend improvements in the auditing organization and procedures of the War Department, particularly in connection with cost-plus-fixed-fee contracts. Some two years later, after several promotions, he was appointed Fiscal Director of the Army Services Forces with the rank of Major General and with responsibility for the accounts and all fiscal services of the War Department.

In February 1946, General Carter was relieved from active duty. He returned to Haskins & Sells and some sixteen months later retired from active practice.

Both the Army and the American Institute officially recognized General Carter's services. In World War I the Army awarded him a Distinguished Service Medal for organizing and commanding the Field Artillery Central Officers' Training School; in World War II, an Oak Leaf Cluster was added in lieu of a second medal for further services. Then in 1946 he was presented with a scroll by the American Institute in recognition of his "outstanding service to his country and the accounting profession in the wartime office of Fiscal Director of the Headquarters Army Service Forces."

What were General Carter's strong qualities? In this writer's opinion they were the qualities that one would expect to find in an able, intelligent career Army officer of strong character. He was organization-minded—probably more so than any CPA of his day. He was industrious. He set a high standard for himself and he expected others to meet the same high standard. He was a strict disciplinarian, but he was attractive in conversation and a genial host. No doubt it was his keen sense of organization and the training he received in mathematics at West Point that enabled him to move from an Army career to a career which, within a relatively short period, was to place him at the head of a large and highly respected international firm of certified public accountants.

Saul Levy (1891-1964)

By EARLE F. WASHBURN, CPA

This is one of a series of articles on deceased members of our Society who have made outstanding and lasting contributions to both the profession and the Society. The articles are prepared under the aegis of the Society's History Committee.

Saul Levy, our 24th President (1943-44) was amongst our most distinguished members, both for his devotion to the Society, the profession and to the service of his community. He gave generously of his time and talent to all.

Born in Utica, N. Y., June 25, 1891, he spent his early life in Omaha, Nebraska until 1899 when his family moved to New York City, where he began his career.

He was a devoted family man and responsibility came to him early in life when in 1909 his father died suddenly placing upon him, the eldest child, the burden of guiding its destiny. Meeting this challenge, he decided to continue his education at night and enrolled at New York University where he obtained the BCS degree, magna cum laude, in 1916 and in 1921 he earned the LLB degree, summa cum laude, at the Brooklyn Law School of St. Lawrence University. It was a source of pride to him that his mother, who inspired him to these accomplishments, lived to see them realized, finally passing away at the ripe age of 90.

He became a junior member of our Society December 8, 1916 and, upon receiving his CPA certificate January 9, 1919, was raised to full membership. He later obtained the CPA certificate from the State of New Jersey.

In 1922 he was admitted to the Bar of the State of New York and became a member of the American Bar Association and the New York County Lawyer's Association. Equipped with this professional background, he started a general practice as a Certified Public Accountant in his own office in New York City where he also practiced law, specializing in the field of financial litigation. Among the famous

---

EARLE F. WASHBURN, CPA is Chairman of our Society's History Committee. Mr. Washburn has been a chairman and member of various other committees. He is now retired from his position of Controller of New York University.

cases with which he was associated were those relating to accountant's liability, viz., the *Ultramares* case, the *State Street Trust Co.*, case and the case of *O'Connor*. These became landmarks in this field of litigation. This experience led him to write a book in 1954 entitled *Accountant's Legal Responsibility*, (published by the American Institute of Certified Public Accountants), plus many articles on the subject.

He also represented clients in financial litigation before Federal Administrative Tribunals and Commissions. In performing these services, his name and reputation came to the attention of various government agencies and his talents were often in demand.

He began his public service as a second lieutenant in the Air Force (Production) in 1918-19. During the years 1941-43 he served as an expert consultant in accounting and legal matters to the Fiscal Division, Service of Supply, War Department and in 1946-50 was a special consultant to the Comptroller of the City of New York, serving without compensation. During 1950-53 he was Vice-chairman of the Mayor's Committee on Management Survey, City of New York and Chairman of its Subcommittee on Scope, Plan and Procedure. His role in this development is attested by the following comment in the Preface to the Committee's Report:

> "no member of the Committee has made a greater contribution than vice chairman Saul Levy. Although a busy professional man, he has at great personal sacrifice given unstintingly of his time, energy, and leadership, particularly to the planning of the survey program and to the subsequent determination of important matters of policy."

He also served as a Trustee of the Citizen's Budget Commission, was a member of the Executive Committee of the Citizen's Union and, in 1957-58, of the Committee appointed by the Mayor of New York City to study the proposed sale of the City's three rapid transit powerhouses to the Consolidated Edison Co. It is of interest to note that the Committee recommended a figure of $123 million. The sale was ultimately consummated for $125,840,000. In 1953 he was appointed to the Council on Accountancy by the State Department of Education and served for eight years.

Prior to his election to the Presidency of our Society, he was First Vice-President, Vice President, Director for five years, and chairman and member of many committees, among them Auditor's Liability, Court Testimony, Liability Insurance, Furtherance of Objectives of the Society, Cooperation with the Bar, Budget and Finance, Legislation,

Co-operation with the Comptroller of the State of New York, plus a number of ad hoc committees, such as Wartime Problems. Subsequent to his term of office as President, he served an additional three years as a director, making eight years in this capacity.

In addition to his service to our Society, he was member of the Council of the American Institute of Certified Public Accountants and for a time on it's [*sic*] Executive Committee and a member and chairman of other committees. In recognition of this outstanding contribution to the profession and the civic life of City, State, and nation, he received the annual Distinguished Member's award of our Society in 1947 and that of the American Institute in 1955.

Among his professional associates he was held in high esteem, especially for his moral and ethical standards and had a wide reputation as a speaker in addressing an audience because of his ability to express his thoughts so clearly that there was no guesswork about what the substance of his subject was meant to convey.

On the personal side, his wife, the former Gertrude Romm, was also an inspiration to him and took a keen interest in all his professional, social, and philanthropic activities in the fields of art, music, and education, particularly in the New School of Social Research in New York and the Hebrew University in Israel where she was present at the lecture he gave there just prior to her death in 1961. A son Donald, also shared many of his interests. He was chairman of the Accountant's Division of the American Friends of the Hebrew University and following his death his associates established a program to dedicate a Memorial Library in his honor.

From a humble beginning this man rose to great heights in his profession and his life is an outstanding example of what may be accomplished by those willing to devote themselves to similar objectives. He will long be remembered by those whose good fortune it was to have been associated with him. His final gesture occurred on January 23, 1964, a month and a day before his sudden death, when he delivered a memorable address before the Accountant's Club of America dinner, to the members of the profession he loved so well.

Henry Barker Fernald (1878-1967)

By LEO L. TAURITZ, CPA

This is one of a series of articles about New York CPAs who have made outstanding and lasting contributions to both the profession and the New York State Society of Certified Public Accountants. The articles are prepared under the aegis of the Society's Committee on History.

Henry Barker Fernald was born on January 9, 1878 in McConnelsville, Ohio, a son of Dr. James Champlin and Nettie (Barker) Fernald. He was the third of nine children, seven of whom reached adulthood (but none of which outlived him). Dr. Fernald, whose family had settled in Maine in the early 1600s, was a Baptist minister and held several parishes in different towns in Ohio. Mrs. (Nettie) Fernald's, family, also from New England, had settled in Ohio when that territory was opened up just after the American Revolution. Dr. Fernald moved his family to Plainfield, New Jersey when Henry was in his early teens.

At the age of nineteen we find Henry Fernald enrolled as a student at the College of Arts and Science at New York University. During his years at NYU he participated in sports and won his letters in football and track. On the serious side, he must have devoted himself to his studies because we find that he was elected to the Beta of New York Chapter of Phi Beta Kappa. He graduated in 1901 with a B.A. degree.

Mr. Fernald answered the call of the U. S. government during the summer of 1901 to join the school system of the Philippine Islands, after its seizure in the Spanish-American War. He taught English and other subjects to the Philippinos. After being instrumental in improving the finances of the provincial school department, he was transferred to the Treasury department, working first on the local provincial level and then on the entire Territory.

In 1906 we find Mr. Fernald back in New York and ready to serve the public. His experience in the field of public finance led him to the world of accountancy. He became associated with the firm of Suffern & Son, (Edward L. Suffern was the 7th president of our Society) CPAs, at 165 Broadway, New York City. He received his N. Y. CPA

LEO L. TAURITZ, CPA, is a member of our Society's Committee on History. Mr. Tauritz is in public service on his own account in New York City.

certificate #437 dated November 5, 1909 and was elected to membership in our Society on January 10, 1910. This was followed by membership in our national association on September 19, 1916 and in the National Association of [Cost] Accountants on October 14, 1919.

The firm of Edward L. Suffern was in practice in 1904 and the firm of Loomis, Conant & Company was in practice in 1905. John R. Loomis was the 4th president of our Society. In 1914 Mr. Fernald was a principal organizer of Loomis, Suffern and Fernald. Coming under the influence and guidance of two past presidents it was only natural for him to be inspired to serve our Society. The record tells us that he was a member of 8 special committees from 1918 to 1936; 23 technical committees from 1924 to 1938; and 18 standing committees from 1915 to 1946. He served as a 2nd Vice President from 1917-1919 and 1st Vice President from 1919-1920.

The Accountants Index published by the Institute bears witness to the long list of published articles coming from his pen, beginning with the year 1920, which included such topics as Depreciation, Municipal Accounting, Mine Accounting, Taxes, Accountants' Certificates, Development of Accounting Terminology, Inventories as related to Mining Companies, Preparation of Budgets, Financial System of the State of New Jersey, Income Taxes and Paper Industry Accounting.

He was extremely active in the affairs of his Alma Mater and for this, in March 1932, he was awarded an Alumni Meritorius [*sic*] Service Medal. In 1953 he was awarded an Honorary LLD from NYU. In 1959 the NYU Society for the Libraries presented him with its medal for literary achievement, the Fernald Fund having been responsible for the acquisition of rare books for the University Heights Library.

In 1958 the firm of Loomis, Suffern and Fernald was merged with that of Lybrand, Ross Brothers and Montgomery. Mr. Fernald continued his affiliation with the firm until his death February 8, 1967 in Upper Montclair, New Jersey. He was survived by a son Henry B. Fernald, Jr., A daughter Mrs. Frank L. Allen, Jr., and three grandchildren.

In the Spring 1967 Bulletin of the NYU Society for the Libraries an "In Memoriam" note ends with these words: "He is fondly remembered by the Society as a tall and gaunt figure with a genial disposition and an interest in every person he met."

Those of us who were fortunate enough to come under his influence will long remember Henry Barker Fernald.

Arthur Young (1863-1948)

By THOMAS G. HIGGINS, CPA

This is one of a series of articles on deceased members of our Society who have made outstanding and lasting contributions to both the profession and the Society. The articles are prepared under the aegis of the Society's Committee on History.

As was true of many of those who pioneered in the accounting profession in the United States, the path that led Arthur Young to the practice of accountancy was by no means a direct one. A native Scotsman, it had been his ambition to become an advocate—a lawyer handling only litigation—in his own country, but in his early twenties a hereditary deafness asserted itself. When it became evident to his doctors that his ailment was progressive, they advised him to leave Scotland for a drier climate if he hoped to retain his hearing beyond middle life. Thus, in 1890, he emigrated to the United States at the age of 26, and some four years later, in Chicago, Illinois, established the accounting firm which bears his name today.

EARLY YEARS IN SCOTLAND

Arthur Young was born on December 17, 1863 in Glasgow, Scotland, the third of seven children. His father, Robert Young, who was well known in business circles in Glasgow, was a ship broker and, before that, a ship owner. He was also chairman of the Glasgow Tramway Company up to the time that the City of Glasgow took over the operation of the street railways.

It was in Glasgow that Arthur Young was educated, and he had a distinguished record at both Glasgow Academy and Glasgow University. At the academy he graduated as Dux of the school. At the university he was prizeman in several of the arts classes, and he took his M.A. degree when he was 20. But he did even better in law school, where he took first prize in Scots law and received his LL.B. degree on an honors basis. He also distinguished himself in athletics, and was captain of the university rugby team.

THOMAS G. HIGGINS, CPA, is a member of our Society's Committee on History and a past President of the Society. Mr. Higgins was the senior partner of Arthur Young & Company until his retirement from the firm in 1965.

At the same time that he attended law lectures at the university, Arthur Young served his apprenticeship with an old and well-known law firm in Glasgow. The firm had many trust estates, and looking after the affairs of these estates was a large part of its business. This phase of the business brought Arthur Young into close touch with stock brokers and chartered accountants, and this is where he first became familiar with the work of practicing accountants.

It was shortly before he graduated from law school that Arthur Young became aware of a slight defect in his hearing. After he received his LL.B. degree, his father, following the advice of a London aurist, sent him first to Switzerland and then to Algiers. But while the climate in those parts was better than the moist air of Scotland, it became clear that no climate, however favorable, was likely to halt the progress of his ailment. The doctors talked to him at length, and finally they convinced him of the inadvisability of attempting to follow a career which would involve arguing and fighting law cases in the courts. It was then that Arthur Young decided to emigrate and seek a new career in the United States.

IN THE UNITED STATES

When he arrived in New York early in 1890 Arthur Young, through letters of introduction, became associated with the then well-known international banking firm of Kennedy, Tod & Company. This association did not last long, however; after just a few years the partners, who were quite wealthy, decided to withdraw from business. But while the connection was brief, it proved to be a valuable one for Arthur Young. It was through the Kennedy, Tod partners that he got his start in accounting. They asked him to go to Chicago to supervise the liquidation of a number of their investments there. Shortly afterwards he joined forces with Charles Urquardt Stuart, then controller of a large Boston-owned copper company, and together they opened an office in Chicago under the firm name of Stuart & Young.

In its initial stages the business of Stuart & Young seems to have been a combination of accounting services, investment services, and the work of general agents. In those days there was a great deal of British money in America. Many British investments were in the form of new ventures—some of them highly speculative—and these gave rise to a good deal of accounting work.

During the twelve years to 1906 the firm prospered, but Arthur Young did not find Stuart a compatible partner. At Young's initiative the firm was dissolved in 1906 and the two partners went their separate ways. With his brother Stanley as a partner, Arthur Young then began the firm of Arthur Young & Company, which took over the business of Stuart & Young.

Arthur Young was active professionally and served on many committees of the Illinois Society of Certified Public Accountants and the American Institute of Certified Public Accountants and predecessor organizations. He was president of the Illinois Society in 1912-13. In 1917 he moved his residence from Chicago to New York.

PERSONAL QUALITIES

What were Arthur Young's outstanding qualities? In this writer's opinion they were his business judgment and intelligence, his kindness, his integrity—but above all his energy and enthusiasm for life (this despite the fact that he lost the sight of one eye, through a riding accident, when he was about 52 and became completely deaf in his late sixties).

Some months ago, William Sutherland, who was one of the first partners of Arthur Young & Company, reminisced about the early days of the firm on the occasion of his own ninetieth birthday. Towards the end of the birthday celebration, this writer said to him, "Will, you knew Arthur Young longer and perhaps better than anyone else in the firm knew him. What was your impression of him as a man?" Mr. Sutherland reflected for a few minutes and then replied:

> "Arthur Young, of course was a wonderful person. When I first met him early in 1903 he was not yet forty, and I suppose he must have been one of Chicago's most eligible bachelors—a friendly, handsome, high-spirited man. Just imagine, here was a being gifted far beyond the average—much sought after, striking appearance, equipped with a marvelous mind, cultured, educated—it just seemed that everything was pulling for him. Actually, of course, this was not so. While his deafness in those days was not very noticeable, the time was not too far off when it would be a real problem. And for some reason no hearing aid was to do him any good.
>
> "But if I were to sum up the manner of man that Arthur was, I would say he was a gentleman in the sense that word was used in my early Scottish environment. He was a man who lived by a code; he had principle; he had character. In short he added to life; he embellished it."

The life of Arthur Young is a striking example of how the handicaps, deficiencies, and disappointments which go into the making of any great personal life are the same ingredients from which strong personalities are made. Arthur Young had a long life, and, despite his physical handicaps, a full one. He developed a firm that he was exceptionally proud of. He loved people. He golfed. He entertained. He read widely and he carried on an extensive correspondence, much of it handwritten. He was interested in the affairs of his firm until just a few months before he died at his winter home in Aiken, South Carolina on April 3, 1948 at the age of 84. He is buried in Bethany Cemetery there, on a hillside looking toward the valley.

Samuel D. Leidesdorf (1881-1968)

By ALEXANDER BERGER, CPA

This is one of a series of articles about deceased members of our Society who have made outstanding and lasting contributions to the accounting profession and our Society. The articles are prepared under the aegis of the Society's Committee on History.

Samuel D. Leidesdorf was one of those men who passed through many worlds in his life span. Born in 1881, he died just four days before his 87th birthday on September 21, 1968. At the age of 13, he worked as an errand boy to support himself and his mother (his father had died when he was six years old). Before he died, his accounting firm, S. D. Leidesdorf & Company, had grown to one of the nation's largest. He had also become one of the hardest working men in the United States in philanthropic causes.

In "Sam" Leidesdorf's first job, as errand boy with a malt and hops firm in Brooklyn, he progressed to bookkeeper and, finally, to credit man. As a credit man, he was earning $5,000 a year at the age of 20—a much more handsome salary in those days than is the case today. But he had the courage and vision at that point in his career to look far enough into the future to quit that job, study accounting, and to find employment as a junior accountant at $20 per week. In 1904, when he was granted CPA certificate #283, he was said to be the youngest CPA in New York.

Sam studied accountancy while working as a junior accountant with Alexander Aderer & Co. He was one of the principals of that firm when he left in 1905 to start his own firm.

He started his own practice with no important prior connections. In his own words, "My first professional quarters consisted of desk space in a lawyer's office, with permission to use his room for conferences with clients, and in those days such conferences were not too frequent."

In 1932, Fortune Magazine described Samuel D. Leidesdorf & Co. as a pioneering firm. This was true in several respects. From the

---

ALEXANDER BERGER, CPA, a member of our Society's Committee on History, is Director of International Publications, International Executive Office of Touche, Ross, Bailey & Smart.

beginning, Sam insisted that inventories and accounts receivable were the most important items in an audit and, therefore, had to be checked thoroughly. These practices did not come to be "generally accepted" until 1938. Long before it became mandatory, employees of S. D. Leidesdorf & Co. were not allowed to own stock in a client firm. Probably his most important innovation was the concept that an accountant should be one to whom his clients could bring almost any business problem; that if accounting was the language of business, no one was better qualified to interpret it than a CPA. This willingness to offer clients the benefit of his judgment and experience is commonplace today, but in those days most auditors believed that any questions except those of auditing and accounting were outside their province.

SAMUEL D. LEIDESDORF—THE MAN

Each of us is the product of all of our experience. We function in several environments—professional, social, family—and we have different drives, needs, and qualities. An outstanding quality of Samuel Leidesdorf was his practicality. He grasped problems quickly and offered concrete advice. The reply of George Bernard Shaw when asked which single book he would want if he were shipwrecked on an island ("A book on how to build rafts") would have appealed to Sam. Perhaps it was his practicality that fed his insatiable curiosity about anything that was new or different. He spent hours browsing in hardware stores and was forever sending his friends new gadgets.

His curiosity was not limited to gadgets; it embraced everything that was going on around him. Once, visiting a friend who was having some plumbing work done, he spent several hours watching and talking to the plumber. Later, the plumber asked the owner of the house, "Your friend is a retired plumber, isn't he?"

Samuel Leidesdorf's philanthropic and other communal efforts were almost without parallel. At the time of his death, he was active in twenty-eight charitable, civic, and educational institutions. In none of them was he a mere "name." In all of them he took an active role that demanded much of his time and energy. Those in need of help beat a path to his door and he found time for all of them. It was not uncommon to have an appointment with him and pass a man like Dr. Robert Oppenheimer as you went in and find someone like David Ben-Gurion waiting to see him as you went out.

Dr. George Armstrong, Vice President for Medical Affairs at the New York University Medical Center, commented once, "Sure Mr.

Leidesdorf is Chairman of our board, and he is the Chairman of many boards. Even so, I can always get an appointment with him within an hour and spend as much time as I like."

One of the few dreams he had had that was not realized was his childhood dream of becoming a doctor. Lack of money prevented him from studying medicine, but he was eventually to contribute to medicine perhaps more than he might have as a doctor. One of the buildings at the New York University Medical Center is the Samuel D. Leidesdorf Medical Research Pavillion [*sic*].

Raising money for charities was a specialty of Sam's. He once boasted that, "I'm the best 'schnorrer' in town." Among the many beneficiaries of his fund raising activities were the Red Cross, the Boy Scouts, the United Negro College Fund, the Federation of Jewish Philanthropies, the United Jewish Appeal of Greater New York, and many more.

It is not generally known that the Institute for Advanced Study at Princeton, New Jersey came about largely through his efforts. For many years he had handled the affairs of L. Bamberger and Company in Newark. When the Bamberger family decided to sell their store, he handled the transaction for them. Although originally the Bambergers had wanted to endow a medical school in New Jersey, it became obvious that such an effort would require more money than was available. Sam suggested the alternative of founding an institution for exceptionally gifted scholars and scientists. He was instrumental not only in bringing the Institute for Advanced Study into being, but until his death he was Chairman of the Board of Trustees and Chairman of the Institute. One of the many close relationships that he formed at the Institute was with Albert Einstein, whose financial affairs he managed. One of Sam's stories had to do with an exchange that occurred when he was giving the scientist an account of his stewardship. Mr. Einstein interrupted him with, "Sam, I can't understand this. Is everything all right?" "Yes." "Then let's talk about something else."

Sam's willingness to try something new was illustrated in 1915 when he was engaged by the creditors of a Times Square cafe that was in bankruptcy. To stimulate business, he employed the dancing team of Vernon and Irene Castle and a Parisian dancer named Maurice. Maurice, as it turned out, introduced the fox trot to New York City.

ACCOUNTING PROFESSION ACTIVITIES

The honors and awards given to Samuel Leidesdorf are too long to list. Some were for services, over 50 years, to the accounting profession. He was one of the original members of the State Council of Accountancy and served from 1934 until 1942. He also served on many committees of the State Society of CPAs and of the American Institute of CPAs. One of the more unusual resolutions passed by the Directors of the State Society was the one of August 27, 1925 which expressed gratitude for a loan of $2,500 which helped the State Society during a lean period.

On the occasion of his 75th birthday, Samuel Leidesdorf summed up his life in these words, "I've had a lot of fun, I've done everything I wanted to do in life—well, nearly everything, I did want to become a physician." A man who can say that, and who has helped so many others at the same time, has indeed lived a good and full life.

William R. Donaldson (1893-1967)

By JENNIE M. PALEN, CPA

This is one of a series of articles on deceased members of our Society who have made outstanding and lasting contributions to both the profession and the Society. The articles are prepared under the aegis of the Society's Committee on History.

When William Raymond Donaldson was president of the Society in 1945-46, he mirrored then, as at his death in 1967, the public image that the CPA is constantly exhorted to seek, the image of the all-around, articulate, professional person. It came naturally to him, as the statistics of his education and professional career will show.

It began with education. Having received his law degree from Fordham University in 1916, in the following year he attended New York University's Graduate School of Business Administration. Two years later he was admitted to the Bar and in the same year entered public accounting practice with Philip N. Miller, whom he had known while in France in World War I. Philip Miller had been Comptroller of the American Red Cross Commission to France, and William Donaldson had been with the commission as an assistant to Colonel Grayson M-P Murphy, its chief, and later as Assistant Secretary General with the military rank of captain.

By 1922 he had obtained the CPA certificate and joined the Society. Within a year he became a partner in Philip N. Miller and Company and within six years the firm had become Miller, Donaldson and Company. On January 1, 1934 he took an eighteen-month leave of absence to serve as New York City's Deputy Comptroller. This stint completed, he returned to the firm and remained there until 1945. He left public accounting practice for a time to go into private law practice, then returned to it to become a partner in Crafts, Carr & Donaldson. He was at that time a CPA in New York, Pennsylvania, and Connecticut, as well as a member of the Federal and New York Bars, and had added governmental service to his legal and accounting credits.

JENNIE M. PALEN, CPA, a member of our Society's Committee on History, is the author of *Report Writing for Accountants*.

His first foray in the field of government had been as United States naturalization examiner in 1915-17. However, it was accountancy, not law, that sparked his later entry when, on January 1, 1934, during the first La Guardia administration, he obtained leave from Miller, Donaldson and Company for the purpose of accepting the post of Deputy Comptroller of the City of New York to direct accounting, auditing, and system modernization, following the restrictions laid down by the bankers' agreement and the election of W. Arthur Cunningham, Fusion candidate for comptroller. While in this post he organized and directed an evening course in municipal accounting at The College of the City of New York, especially for employees of the city.

Having previously participated in one of the important studies by the Mayor's Committee on Management Survey, he was selected in 1955 by State Comptroller Levitt as one of the twelve prominent CPAs to serve as an advisory group on matters of government finance, accounts, auditing, and budgets. He later became vice-chairman of the group. He was a long-time member of the Municipal Finance Officers Association of the United States and Canada, as well as president and director of the Suffolk County Taxpayers Association, member of the Long Island Real Estate Board, of the Huntington Township Chamber of Commerce (where he served on the Committee on Township Budget), and of the Long Island Association, serving on its Speakers Bureau and its Committee for Suffolk County Planning. He had become an authority on governmental finance and had made a noteworthy contribution to the field.

Though city-bred, he had a life-long love for the outdoors. It was this, abetted, perhaps, by a Sprague Interest Test that had hinted he would be good at selling real estate, that led him in 1945 to another facet of a many-sided career. To his practice of law and accounting he added that of a licensed real estate broker for Country Life Real Estate in historic Fort Salonga, Long Island.

In this venture he started a model town—a housing development known as *Indian Hills*—acquired 102 acres of rolling woodland and, using colonial architecture, erected a country life center, a country store, a country lodge, and a riding academy: the nucleus of a community that he planned would eventually be self-sustaining to the point where it would "feed, clothe, and entertain some 65 families." Caught up in this project, he wrote numerous articles on real estate, community development, and related tax problems that were published in a number of Long Island newspapers and favorably commented upon in New York City papers.

During all this period he was donating time and energy to a variety of community projects. It was his concern for the welfare of boys living in crowded neighborhoods and for the prevention of juvenile delinquency that first took concrete form. In the pursuit of this, one of the major interests of his life, he functioned for twenty-seven years as a director of the Boys' Club. Navy Yard District of Brooklyn (affiliated with the Boys' Club of America) and for ten years (1937-47) as its president. He also accepted the chairmanship of the Victory Council for the Brooklyn Area of the Boys' Club of America.

He was a trustee of the Kings County Savings Bank, a member of the Downtown Association and of the Knights of Columbus, and a former member of the board of governors of the Crescent Athletic Club of Brooklyn and Huntington, Long Island. In 1946 he was appointed to the board of trustees of St. Francis College and served until his death on its budget and finance committee. In 1948 the college awarded him an honorary degree of Doctor of Laws.

From the time he joined the Society in 1922 he labored continually and forthrightly to promote its interests and those of accountants in general. Member of a vast number of the Society's committees, he was chairman of eleven, among them the Committee on Wartime and Postwar Problems, the Public Information Committee, the Committee on Public and Civic Affairs, the Committee on Furtherance of the Objects of the Society, and the Committee on Municipal Accounting, as well as the Committee on Cooperation with State and Municipal Officers. In addition to his term as president, (1945-1946) he had served as a member of the board, secretary, second vice-president, and first vice-president.

He had been a member of council of the American Institute of CPAs and chairman of the Institute's Committee on Cooperation with Credit Men and had served on similar committees for cooperation with the Stock Exchange and the SEC. He was president for two years of The Accountants Club of America, was president of the New York Chapter of the National Association of Cost Accountants as well as National Director in Charge of Research and Chairman of the Natural Business Year Council.

His articles on accounting subjects appeared in The Journal of Accountancy, NACA Bulletins, and various trade journals. At meetings, at conventions, and on the radio, he was in demand as a speaker on accounting, income taxes, and municipal finance. He was founder and first president of The Catholic Accountants Guild of the Diocese of Brooklyn, which in 1948 gave a testimonial dinner in his honor.

Nor did he neglect the cause of the woman accountant, at that time—in World War II—just on the threshold of her final acceptance into the profession. From the rostrum of the Society where he spoke as president he said that he had employed women accountants on his staff, had found them to be highly satisfactory, and urged his fellow practitioners to employ them and to keep them on in peacetime.

On June 28, 1967, ten days after his seventy-fourth birthday, he died in Huntington Hospital of a heart attack. He left behind an enviable record of service to accountancy and to the community of which he was so indelibly a part.

Henry Abbott Horne (1878-1969)

By JENNIE M. PALEN, *CPA*

This is one of a series of articles of deceased members of our Society who have made outstanding and lasting contributions to both the profession and the Society. The articles are prepared under the aegis of the Society's Committee on History.

With the passing of Henry Horne in December 1969 the accounting profession lost a man of high integrity and a devoted professional.

Henry Abbott Horne was born in Brooklyn on March 28, 1878, the son of a Brooklyn-born father, Henry Bower Horne, and an English mother, Theresa Eleanor Abbott Horne. At twenty-four he married Anna Irwin, also a native of Brooklyn.

His schooling embraced both engineering and accounting studies. His early experience, though varied, slanted steadily toward accounting. From 1895 to 1898 he was an inspector for Gold & Stock Tel. Co. and Stock Quotation Telephone Co.; from 1898 to 1900, assistant cashier at Walsh & Floyd, members of the New York Stock Exchange; from 1900 to 1901, inspector for New York Edison Company; from 1901 to 1910, chief accountant for Bigelow Carpet Co.; from 1910 to 1915, senior accountant, and thereafter to 1932, partner in the CPA firm of Niles & Niles. In 1933 he left for a connection he was to hold for a lifetime—a partnership in Webster, Horne & Elsdon, CPAs.

During this period he served also (1918 to 1919) in World War I as captain in the United States Army Air Service, Bureau of Aircraft Procurement, and from 1919 to 1934 as captain in the United States Army Air Corps Reserve.

He had received his CPA certificate on Dec. 26, 1911, when the profession was still young (his certificate number was 442) and on April 8, 1912 was admitted to the Society, where he was soon recognized as a structural asset. His services to the Society were not only continuous but were so numerous as to defy listing. He became a vice president in 1942, first vice president in 1943 and president in 1944. He served seven terms as director and functioned as chairman or as a member of a great variety of standing, special and technical

---

JENNIE M. PALEN, a member of our Society's *Committee on History*, is the author of *Report Writing for Accountants* and other works.

committees, nearly sixty terms in all—some, of course, concurrent. He was a member of the history committee from 1957 to 1968 and contributed a history of the Society to its Fiftieth Anniversary Bulletin.

Among his committees was that on public utilities accounting, which he chaired for three terms. His many articles and public addresses on this subject bear witness to his proficiency in the field. Between 1936 and 1947 he had a sizable list of articles published in such places as The New York Certified Public Accountant, The Journal of Accountancy and Public Utilities Fortnightly. They dealt with depreciation, intangible assets, rate regulation and other significant accounting and regulatory problems in the public utilities field, as well as with more general subjects relating to public accounting practice.

He was a member of AICPA, NACA, and the Connecticut Society of CPAs. He was chairman of the Institute's committee on public utilities accounting in the 1940s and served also on its accounting procedure and inventories committees. In NACA he was at one time associate director of the Brooklyn chapter and a member of the publications and program committees.

His other memberships included Beta Alpha Psi, Economic Research Round Table, American Arbitration Association, Commerce and Industry Association of New York, American Legion Reserve Officers Association of the United States, Engineering Club (Dayton, Ohio) and Bankers Club, as well as the Accountants Club of America, of which he was a member from the time of its organization and in which he had functioned as governor and as a member of the advisory board.

His hobbies were the healthful outdoor pursuits of walking, swimming and horseback riding.

He was a lifelong member of the Methodist Church and a managing trustee of the Methodist Hospital. One to serve in death as in life, and having no descendants, he bequeathed the bulk of his estate to these two organizations.

This troubled world could use more like Henry Abbott Horne.

Homer St. Clair Pace (1879-1942)--Co-Founder of Pace College

By THOMAS G. HIGGINS, *CPA*

The development of Pace College from a small, privately owned business school, giving courses in accounting and business subjects, to a nationally eminent college with a broad spectrum of such courses, is part of the saga of the accounting profession's rapid rise. One of the founders was Homer St. Claire [*sic*] Pace, a CPA, who devoted much of his life and energy to the advancement of the school. It is fitting therefore that alumni and non-alumni should have some knowledge of this remarkable man; hence this article.

Homer St. Clair Pace, thirteenth president of the New York State Society (1924-1926) and co-founder (with his older brother, Charles, an attorney) of Pace College, was born in Rehoboth, Perry County, Ohio on April 13, 1879 and died after a short illness in New York City on May 22, 1942.

By any standards, Homer Pace was an extraordinarily gifted individual. He was highly intelligent, imaginative, business-minded, and an outstanding administrator. Essentially serious, he began to assume responsibilities at an early age and for the rest of his life was an indefatigable worker for a variety of causes. At 19 he married Mabel Evelyn Vanderhoof and they had three children: Helen, who married George Bowen, Robert Scott; and Charles Richard Pace.

Homer Pace held a variety of positions between 1896 and 1901. For a while he ran a country newspaper with his father. In 1901 he came to New York to take charge of the New York office of the Chicago Great Western Railway Co. and was named Assistant Secretary of that Company. In the following year he became Secretary of the Mason City & Fort Dodge Railroad Co. He resigned as Secretary in January 1907 but remained on the Chicago Great Western payroll until November, 1909.

THOMAS G. HIGGINS, CPA, now retired, was the senior partner of *Arthur Young & Company* for many years. Mr. Higgins has also been a President of the New York State Society of Certified Public Accountants and has been, for years, an active member of its *History Committee*.

It was during his early years in New York that Homer Pace became interested in the practice of accounting. He enrolled as a student at Theodore Koehler's New York School of Accounts and shortly afterwards began to tutor himself and some of his friends to sit for the New York State CPA Examination. He passed the examination in June 1906 and, after acquiring the necessary practical experience, received his certificate in August 1907.

Homer Pace's early experience in New York made two things very clear to him: first, that he liked to teach accounting and, second, that there was a great need for more educational institutions devoted to preparing young men for careers in accounting and business. These perceptions ultimately resulted in the formation of the Pace Institute of Accountancy in the fall of 1906. About that same time, Homer established an accounting practice which later adopted the name of Pace & Pace.

In the early years of Pace Institute there was little accounting literature available, so the Pace brothers found it necessary to provide their own text material. Homer developed a series of lectures on the theory and practice of accounting, and Charles developed another series on commercial law. From time to time their lectures were revised or expanded.

Although Pace Institute demanded a great deal of Homer Pace's energy and imagination, he still found time for a number of other activities. In 1916 he served as Professor of Accounting at the College of Pharmacy, Columbia University, and in 1918-19 he was Acting Deputy Commissioner in the Bureau of Internal Revenue, U.S. Treasury Department, where he reorganized and directed the income tax unit. During the 1920s and 1930s he served on numerous committees of the American Institute of Certified Public Accountants and the New York State Society. He also took an active part in organizing and conducting the International Congress on Accounting held in New York in 1929. It was during Homer Pace's term as President of the New York State Society (1924-1926) that the Directors decided that the Society should be housed in rooms of its own at 110 William Street and when Chapter activities were inaugurated by creating the Buffalo Chapter.

Homer Pace wrote well and spoke well. He loved books and was a great collector of rare editions, and of maps. He was himself the author of several textbooks on accounting and auditing.

During the years 1923 to 1926 Homer Pace became widely known in the profession for his work as Chairman of the AICPA's Committee on Public Affairs. This committee came into being largely as a result of the Institute's adoption of the rule forbidding advertising. Many members felt that, since individual practitioners and firms could no longer advertise, the profession as a whole, through the Institute, should undertake a vigorous campaign to increase public recognition of the value and importance of accounting. Homer Pace played a leading role in this effort and succeeded in convincing the AICPA Council that the Institute should organize a Bureau of Public Affairs, with paid staff. He agreed to head up the committee which would supervise the new Bureau.

Homer Pace had a flair for what we would today call "public relations," and under his leadership the committee tackled the project with enthusiasm and imagination. It obtained good publicity for the profession in newspapers, it arranged for members to make speeches and to participate in public affairs, and through the Bureau it published six carefully prepared bulletins on timely topics which received wide distribution. Yet, although it seemed to be generally acknowledged that the Bureau of Public Affairs was serving a useful purpose, efforts to support the program by membership subscription were unsuccessful and the project was abandoned. While the committee was in existence for only three years, its record was impressive. At the very least it demonstrated what a well-planned public relations program could do to achieve greater recognition for the accounting profession.

During this same period in the early 1920s, it was becoming increasingly evident to Homer Pace and other local practitioners that they were at a growing disadvantage, as the more important financial organizations involved in public security offerings were turning more and more frequently to those large accounting firms that could provide service on a national basis.

Because of this trend local firms felt extremely vulnerable with regard to any client that was expanding. Homer Pace decided that something had to be done about the matter, and he conceived the idea of a close affiliation of a number of long-established local firms. Once he had convinced himself that the idea was sound he began to contact prominent local CPAs around the country—mostly those whom he knew and respected as a result of their Institute activities. This affiliation began to function in 1926, with each participating firm continuing to operate as a separate entity. Although it seemed to work well at first, it soon became apparent that if the affiliation was to be successful some form of central organization would be needed to review reports, prepare manuals, and the like. All of this pointed quite clearly to the need for a formal partnership. That final step was taken, and on January 1, 1928 it was announced publicly that the firm of Pace, Gore & McLaren had been established, with offices in 62 cities in the United States, Canada, and Cuba.

Although Homer Pace must have been extremely busy in the 1920s he still found time to start a project which he had probably been thinking about seriously ever since his early journalistic efforts: namely, the publication of his own monthly accounting magazine to be turned out on his own printing press. Pace tackled this project with his customary zeal. In February 1927 the first issue of *The American Accountant* appeared, and in the following year Homer Pace became the owner of The Plandome Press, Inc., considered to be one of the finest job-printing plants in New York. Some measure of Pace's enthusiasm can be found in the following which is taken from the Editor's Page of the first issue:

> "Thirty years ago, when I was seventeen, I established in Michigan a country newspaper known as the *Pere Marquette Journal*. I bought and borrowed enough equipment, including a Washington hand press, to start with. I wrote the copy, set the type, made up the forms, 'pulled' the press, and handed out or mailed copies of the first issues to my neighbors.
>
> "I remember well my youthful trepidation when the first copy came from the press and was passed upon by my critical fellow townsmen. In submitting *The American Accountant* to the judgment of my co-practitioners and business friends, I find my trepidation is as great (even though my youth be less) as my trepidation was in the earlier venture. . .
>
> "Your appraisal of the result and your suggestions for continuance or modification, will be most heartily appreciated."

Like many other business men, Homer Pace suffered great disappointments during the 1930s. Both the national accounting firm which he developed and his accounting magazine were to become victims of the Depression.

The immediate effect of the market crash of 1929 was to reduce the issuance of new securities to negligible proportions. The demand for accounting services declined sharply and the situation that had brought about the formation of Pace, Gore & McLaren no longer existed. The partnership accordingly was dissolved in 1934, with the participants resuming their original firm names. Speaking recently (in

July 1971) about the firm, one of the partners of Pace, Gore & McLaren said that Homer Pace was one of the ablest organizers he had ever met and that, had it not been for a most unusual combination of adverse business developments, Pace's brilliant idea and executive ability would have resulted in an outstanding landmark in the history of the accounting profession.

The American Accountant did well for a while but got into financial troubles in the early 1930s. It ceased publication with the December 1933 issue.

While the failure of these two projects was undoubtedly disappointing to Homer Pace, he still had his Pace Institute. Although it too had financial problems during the Depression days, it surmounted them and, under Homer Pace's inspired leadership, grew rapidly. By 1938 it had some 3,800 students and a faculty of 110.

During its first three decades Pace Institute did not seek recognition by the State of New York, but towards the end of that period it was decided to apply for a corporate charter. A provisional charter, which was quite broad, was granted in 1935 creating the corporation of Pace Institute and in 1942 the charter was made absolute. In 1947 the charter was amended and the corporation was converted to a non-stock basis under the new name of Pace College. In December of the following year the college became accredited as a degree-granting institution. Homer Pace was President of the corporation from its inception in 1935 to his death in 1942. He was succeeded as President by his son, Robert Scott Pace, who continued as President until 1960, when he became President Emeritus. Charles Pace, the co-founder of Pace Institute, was active in the work of the Institute until his retirement in 1935.

Although Homer Pace had many interests, he never forgot that he was basically an educator. Pace College is his enduring monument, yet he should also be remembered for his many contributions to the organized profession. He clearly holds an important place in the history of the accounting profession and of the New York State Society.

[*June, 1972*. Reprinted with permission from *The CPA Journal*, copyright 1972]

Appendix

[The authors' names appearing in parentheses reflect attribution in the records of the History Committee.]

Committee on History (Harry O. Leete), "Early Development of Accountancy in New York State," *The New York Certified Public Accountant* (March, 1949): 157-162, 176.

Committee on History (Norman E. Webster), "The New York State Society of Certified Public Accountants,: Its Genesis," *The New York Certified Public Accountant* (May, 1949): 327,329.

Committee on History (Orrin R. Judd), "The New York School of Accounts," *The New York Certified Public Accountant* (December, 1949): 755-757.

Committee on History (Norman E. Webster), "Pace Institute," *The New York Certified Public Accountant* (September, 1950): 530-534.

Committee on History (Norman E. Webster), "The Society's First Annual Dinner," *The New York Certified Public Accountant* (March, 1951): 216-217.

Committee on History (Norman E. Webster), "Joseph Hardcastle," *The New York Certified Public Accountant* (September, 1951): 615-618.

Mendes, Henry E., "Frederick George Colley," *The New York Certified Public Accountant* (May, 1952): 300-302, 304.

Committee on History (Norman E. Webster), "Charles Ezra Sprague--Public Accountant," *The New York Certified Public Accountant* (July, 1952): 430-432.

Committee on History (Norman E. Webster), "Robert Lancelot Cuthbert," *The New York Certified Public Accountant* (November, 1952): 689-691.

Committee on History (Norman E. Webster), "The Incorporators of The New York State Society of Certified Public Accountants," *The New York Certified Public Accountant* (March, 1953): 217-221, 232.

Committee on History (Norman E. Webster), "The School of Commerce, Accounts, and Finance of New York University," *The New York Certified Public Accountant* (April, 1953): 260-262.

Committee on History, "More About an Incorporator," *The New York Certified Public Accountant* (May, 1953): 351.

Committee on History (Norman E. Webster), "Society Offices and Secretarial Staff," *The New York Certified Public Accountant* (July, 1954): 454-461.

Committee on History (Norman E. Webster), "Is Accounting History Important?," *The New York Certified Public Accountant* (August, 1954): 511-513, 520.

Committee on History (Jennie M. Palen), "The First Woman C.P.A.," *The New York Certified Public Accountant* (August, 1955): 476-479, 496.

Committee on History (Norman E. Webster), "Robert H. Montgomery, C.P.H," *The New York Certified Public Accountant* (September, 1955): 533-537.

Committee on History (Jennie M. Palen), "Automation--1894," *The New York Certified Public Accountant* (February, 1956): 103.

Committee on History (Howard P. Nicholson), "Public Accountants Practicing in Syracuse, New York, Before 1900," *The New York Certified Public Accountant* (March, 1956): 182-185.

Committee on History (Norman E. Webster), "Early Accounting Firms in New York City," *The New York Certified Public Accountant* (June, 1956): 364-374, 390.

Committee on History (Orrin G. Judd), "Orrin Reynolds Judd," *The New York Certified Public Accountant* (July, 1956): 440-441.

Committee on History (Leo L. Tauritz), "J. Lee Nicholson," *The New York Certified Public Accountant* (September, 1956): 558-559.

Committee on History (Jennie M. Palen), "The City College of New York: A History of Beginnings," *The New York Certified Public Accountant* (November, 1956): 663-670.

Committee on History (Henry A. Horne), "Norman Edward Webster," *The New York Certified Public Accountant* (April, 1957): 266-270.

Washburn, Earle L., "John Thomas Madden," *The New York Certified Public Accountant* (May, 1957): 329-330.

Block, Max, "New York State Tax Forum: In Memoriam-Benjamin Harrow," *The New York Certified Public Accountant* (March, 1958): 211-213.

Committee on History, "Robert H. Montgomery," *The New York Certified Public Accountant* (February, 1959): 114-118.

Lieberman, Henry, "DeWitt Carl Eggleston," *The New York Certified Public Accountant* (March, 1959): 195-196.

Society Release, "Dedication of Haskins Memorial Room," *The New York Certified Public Accountant* (May, 1959) 357-360.

Webster, Norman E. "Early Accounting Coaching Courses," *The New York Certified Public Accountant* (March, 1960): 180-188.

Horowitz, Abraham, "Ferdinand William Lafrentz (1859-1954)," *The New York Certified Public Accountant* (April, 1961): 274-275.

Neary, William J., "Walter A. Staub (1881-1945)," *The New York Certified Public Accountant* (September, 1961): 619-621.

Smyrk, Albert V., "John A. Lindquist (1892-1961)," *The New York Certified Public Accountant* (July, 1963): 493-494.

Tauritz, Leo L., "Arthur W. Teele (1868-1940)," *The New York Certified Public Accountant* (February, 1964): 123-125.

Palen, Jennie M., "George O. May (1875-1961)," *The New York Certified Public Accountant* (August, 1964): 577-578.

Lieberman, Henry., "Prior Sinclair (1882-1961)," *The New York Certified Public Accountant* (December, 1964): 903-904.

Washburn, Earle F.[*sic*], "James F. Hughes (1879-1950)," *The New York Certified Public Accountant* (April, 1965): 276-277.

Lieberman, Henry, "William M. Lybrand (1867-1960)," *The New York Certified Public Accountant* (August, 1965): 601-602.

Foye, Arthur B., "Edward Augustus Kracke (1882-1960)," *The New York Certified Public Accountant* (November, 1965): 832-833.

Palmer, Rex F., "Frederick W. Wulfing (1894-1960)," *The New York Certified Public Accountant* (June, 1966): 451-452.

Foye, Arthur B., "William Hansell Bell (1883-1960)," *The New York Certified Public Accountant* (July, 1966): 534-535.

Westerman, Reuben, "Isidor Sack (1888-1961)," *The New York Certified Public Accountant* (February, 1967): 141-142.

Higgins, Thomas G., "General Arthur H. Carter (1884-1965)," *The New York Certified Public Accountant* (May, 1967): 373-374.

Washburn, Earle L., "Saul Levy (1891-1964)," *The New York Certified Public Accountant* (November, 1967): 856-858.

Tauritz, Leo L., "Henry Barker Fernald (1878-1967)," *The New York Certified Public Accountant* (December, 1967): 944-945.

Higgins, Thomas G., "Arthur Young (1863-1948)," *The New York Certified Public Accountant* (November, 1968): 804-806.

Berger, Alexander, "Samuel D. Leidesdorf (1881-1968)," *The New York Certified Public Accountant* (March, 1969): 198-200.

Palen, Jennie M., "William R. Donaldson (1893-1967)," *The New York Certified Public Accountant* (June, 1969): 451-453.

Palen, Jennie M., "Henry Abbott Horne (1878-1969)," *The New York Certified Public Accountant* (January, 1971): 39, 47.

Higgins, Thomas G., "Homer St. Clair Pace (1879-1942), Co-Founder of Pace College," *The New York Certified Public Accountant* (June, 1972): 475-477.

Index

For Product Safety Concerns and Information please contact our EU representative GPSR@taylorandfrancis.com
Taylor & Francis Verlag GmbH, Kaufingerstraße 24, 80331 München, Germany

www.ingramcontent.com/pod-product-compliance
Ingram Content Group UK Ltd.
Pitfield, Milton Keynes, MK11 3LW, UK
UKHW021833240425
457818UK00006B/184